Go Home and Tell

Bertha Smith

Introduction by Lewis A. Drummond
Timothy and Denise George, Editors

BROADMAN
& HOLMAN
PUBLISHERS

Nashville, Tennessee

4212-58
0-8054-1258-1

Dewey Decimal Classification: 286
Subject Heading: Missions—China \ Missions—Taiwan
Library of Congress Card Catalog Number: 94-6014

Unless otherwise noted all Scripture quotations are from the King James Version.

Interior design by Leslie Joslin
Cover design by Steve Diggs & Friends

Library of Congress Cataloging-in-Publication Data
Smith, Bertha.
    Go home and tell / Timothy George, editor: Denise George, editor.
        p. cm.—(Library of Baptist Clasics; vol. 8)
    Includes bibliographical references and index.
    ISBN 0-8054-1258-1 (hb)
       1.Smith, Bertha. 2. Missions—China 3. Missions—Taiwan. 4.
Missionaries—China—Biography.
    I. George, Timothy. II. George, Denise. III. Title. IV. Series.
BV3427.S6A3   1995
266'.61092—dc20   94-6014
                                   CIP

1 2 3 4 5 6 00 99 98 97 96 95

Contents

General Editors' Introduction

The Baptist movement as we know it today began as a small persecuted sect in pre-Revolutionary England. One critic labeled them as "miscreants begat in rebellion, born in sedition, and nursed in faction." Excluded by law from the English universities, Baptists developed their own structures for pastoral training. They also wrote hymns, preached sermons, published confessions, and defended their beliefs against skeptics, detractors, and rival religious groups of all kinds. From the popular works of John Bunyan and Benjamin Keach to the learned theology of John Gill and Andrew Fuller, Baptists wrote with a passion and with a purpose. In time a large body of Baptist literature was developed, writings that both reflected and contributed to the emerging sense of Baptist identity.

The Southern Baptist Convention was organized in 1845 for the purpose of "eliciting, combining, and directing the energies of the whole denomination in one sacred effort, for the propagation of the Gospel." This was an ambitious undertaking for the 293 "delegates," as they were then called, who gathered in Augusta, Georgia, and embraced this far-reaching vision at the founding meeting of the convention. Through the years the SBC has suffered numerous setbacks and distractions—the Civil War, Reconstruction, the Great Depression, social unrest, denominational strife, and much more. But through it all God has graciously blessed Southern Baptists in ways that future historians will surely record as remarkable. By the end of the twentieth century, Southern Baptists had grown into America's largest Protestant denomination, a fellowship of some fifteen million members in nearly forty thousand congregations supporting more than nine thousand missionaries.

Drawing on this rich heritage, the Library of Baptist Classics presents a series of books reflecting the faith and vision of Southern Baptists over the past 150 years. We are republishing in fresh editions and with new introductions a collection of seminal writings. These works have proven their worth as classics among Southern Baptists in the past and still speak powerfully to Baptists and other evangelical Christians today.

The Library of Baptist Classics includes writings of pastors, theologians, missionary statesmen, and denominational leaders from the past. Some of them are popular, others scholarly in form. They include sermons, doctrinal treatises, missionary biographies, and an anthology of Baptist confessions, covenants, and catechisms. Most of these writings have long been out of print. We present them now in the fervent hope that the Lord will see fit to use them again, as He has in the past, not only to remind us of the great legacy we have received, but also to inspire us to be faithful shapers of the future under the lordship of Jesus Christ.

Timothy George and Denise George,
General Editors

Foreword

STEPHEN F. OLFORD

Miss Bertha Smith—the woman of revival—was unique in every sense of the word. We all know that God never makes duplicates; He only makes originals. But to those of us who knew Miss Bertha there was a striking and stimulating non-uniformity about her. Like the word of the Lord to Jeremiah, it could be said of Bertha Smith, "Before I formed you in the womb I knew you; before you were born I sanctified you; I ordained you a prophet to the nations" (Jer. 1:5, NKJV). She was indeed "formed," "sanctified," and "ordained" to be a prophetic voice to the nations—especially the peoples of China and later the United States of America.

The first time I met her I knew, in my spirit, that Miss Bertha was a woman of God. Her presence and her prayers diffused a divine aroma. Many times we shared the same prayer room and platform. She was on my mailing lists and *never* missed an opportunity to assure me that I would be remembered at the throne of grace for God's blessing on my ministry. If it was not a note, a phone call, or a word of encouragement through a mutual friend, it was Miss Bertha, in person!

My wife, Heather, was equally enamored. "Miss Bertha is a woman after my own heart," she said following a memorable week after the Ben Lippen Conference in Asheville, North Carolina. "She knows and *lives* the victorious Christian life." Heather was so impressed by her walk with God that she shared the chapters from *Go Home and Tell* with her Women's Fellowship at Calvary Baptist Church in New York City, of which I was then pastor. Time and again Heather talked and prayed with Miss Bertha. Having been moved by this godly woman's testimony, she remarked to me, "How the church today needs more Bertha Smiths around!" Here is a saint who belongs to the ages—a warrior of the cross and a missionary extraordinaire.

As I look back upon the years I knew this dear lady, four aspects of her God-honored ministry are etched upon my memory:

Her call to holiness. She never spoke without sounding the note of holiness. Her expositions—from the Book of Leviticus in particular—were awesome! I have seen pastors with heads bowed and tears falling to the ground, crying like Isaiah: "Woe is me, for I am undone!"

Her call to brokenness. This naturally followed on her call to holiness. She saw clearly that "judgment must begin at the house of God." For her, repentance was more than a message for the unsaved: it was for the backslidden Christian as well. She would point out repeatedly that of the seven churches addressed in the opening chapters of the Book of Revelation, five were told to repent.

Her call to prayerfulness. From her days in the Shantung Revival in China, her commitment to a life of prayer was deep and enduring. She would exclaim, "No prayer, no revival!" That is why she established her prayer center at Cowpens, South Carolina. To pray with Bertha Smith was to touch the hem of

God. Her favorite text on revival was 2 Chronicles 7:14: "If My people who are called by My name will humble themselves, and pray and seek my face, and turn from their wicked ways, then I will hear from heaven, and will forgive their sin and heal their land" (NKJV).

Her call to yieldedness. I can still hear her insisting that "there can be no fullness of the Spirit without a life of yieldedness." She was careful to indicate that the verb in Ephesians 5:18 is in the same imperative mood and the present tense. We are commanded to be filled with the Spirit, and we yield to His control initially, and then continually, day by day.

I am delighted that Broadman & Holman is now republishing *Go Home and Tell*, along with selections from *How the Spirit Filled My Life*. My earnest prayer is that God will use these classics, by His Holy Spirit, to instruct and inspire a new generation to shun the mediocrity of our decadent times and to join the aristocracy of heaven's honored servants like Miss Bertha Smith.

Introduction

LEWIS A. DRUMMOND

Few parents realize that those destined for greatness could be bundled up in the tiny body of their newborn child. Certainly John and Frances Smith never imagined that on November 16, 1888, their fifth child, whom they named Olive Bertha, would be such a personality. But destiny was written into the fabric of her future.

A farm a few miles outside Cowpens, South Carolina, became little Bertha's early home—her first name "Olive" was soon forgotten. When Bertha was seven, John Smith moved his growing family into town. He built a beautiful Southern-style home that can still be seen today. Bertha spent many happy hours there in a warm family setting. It was a disciplined family that Bertha grew up in, and that in turn fostered a self-discipline which held her in good stead for the one hundred years she lived. She needed to be a strong disciplinarian—for herself and others—because God had a plan for her life that demanded such.

Bertha proved to be a precocious child when she entered school in Cowpens. She never failed to make the honor roll, and she loved it. Pride had a good grip on her. The teachers boasted of her accomplishments, and Bertha herself said she "knew no better than to believe it." One day that pride would be submitted to the lordship of Jesus Christ and she became a humble servant of her Lord. But in the meantime, she reveled in leading others and excelling in virtually everything.

The school in little Cowpens in the 1890s was very different from today's classrooms. Students were disciplined and any breach of etiquette would not be tolerated for one minute. Bertha fitted in well.

The school itself was a simple, two-story wooden building, with few amenities. Bertha related that, "A large iron stove stood in the center of the big room, which kept us either too hot or too cold." The pupils sat two at a desk and gave strict attention to the teacher. When reciting their lessons, the students had to recite on a long wooden bench that stood in front of the class. Moreover, they had worship each day in the school and even memorized Scripture.

Bertha Smith's spiritual pilgrimage seemed much like the journey of Bunyan's chief character in *Pilgrim's Progress*. It did not prove an easy journey to the cross of Pilgrim—or for Bertha. She fell under conviction of her sin and need of Christ's salvation quite young. She attended the First Baptist Church in Cowpens and heard faithful preaching and teaching of the gospel. This brought about the early stirring of the Spirit in her heart and the struggle began that lasted some years.

When Bertha was ten, an evangelistic week was held in her church. They called it a "revival meeting." Bertha would learn the real meaning of "revival" later in China. Actually, she became a "Woman of Revival," as shall be seen. But in the evangelistic setting of the local Baptist church, God spoke to Bertha's heart. But she should be allowed to tell her own story. She wrote:

I was ten years old when, one hot July night as I sat beside the second window from the front, the Word of the Lord went to my heart! For the first time I saw myself, at least a little glimpse of what I looked like, in the eyes of Holy God. While people called me a good girl, I would not do in His sight, who saw all the pride of my heart—the selfishness and the wanting to be first in everything, just to be praised by teachers. I wanted to make a hundred on all of my examinations, but I did not want anyone else to make a hundred! I had to excel! What an awful human being, a chip off the old block, Adam, after the devil entered into him!

Praise the Lord that we had a man of God for a pastor who knew that every human being was just like that, and he knew the remedy: Jesus Christ had come and died and taken in Himself the sin of the human family; and that was what he proclaimed.

I wanted to go to the altar that first night, but on the evening before, a girl my age had gone and people said that she was too small, that she did not know what she was doing. Therefore, I did not dare go, but there was no peace of heart for me during the remainder of that meeting, or any other time.

The next year when the revival meeting began, I publicly announced myself a lost sinner by going to the altar and telling the Lord about my sins. In spite of the fact that I had been silently confessing for a year, that was my first chance to let other people know that I was conscious of my being one of the Lost.

No one was trained to do personal work at the altar. Only the pastor was at the altar to help people, and there were always so many older ones there, who took first place, that he never got to me. I had to go on another year with my burden of sin, shedding many a tear in secret. Over and over again I told the Lord about my sins and pled for His cleansing.

About the third year, I was at the altar next to a woman whom the pastor came to help. It seemed to me that he talked with her a long time. He just stuck his head over toward me and said, "Just trust the Lord and He will save you." He was right, but I did not know what he meant by trusting the Lord. So that meeting came to an end with the cry of my heart being, "the summer is ended and I am not saved" (see Jer. 8:20).

When I went fifteen miles in the country to my grandmother's in the summer and attended their Big Meeting, I would just have to go to the altar. Occasionally we went to other nearby country churches for their summer meetings, and I could not but make my distress known. I went forward so much at my home church that I was afraid people would think that I was just going for the fun of it. I could have assured them that it certainly was not fun. Sometimes I would almost hold to the bench to keep from going forward but then I went home feeling worse then than when I went; and when I did go, it did no good! Oh, the wretched girl that I was!

After our pastor had been with us for fifteen years, he resigned and pastored another church in the community. When his revival meeting came, we went. I was among those at the altar wanting to be saved from hell. I was about fourteen by that time, and I suppose the pastor felt that I was old enough to have some attention. He said, "Bertha, if you will just trust the Lord, He will save you. Are you trusting Him?"

I replied, "Yes, I am trusting the Lord."

(Now, what about one human being telling another that he is saved when the advisor cannot see whether or not a miracle has taken place inside?) He went back to the pulpit and asked anyone who had trusted the Lord at that service to stand. I stood, but I went home just as much in the dark as ever. I knew a good bit about the Lord, but He was away out yonder and I was here, under the burden of what I was in the sight of God, with no connection between us.

Two more summers passed, with a pastor who did no personal work. Then one last Sunday morning, after I had gone regularly to the altar as usual, the pastor asked if any at the front were ready to come to Jesus Christ and take Him as Savior. For the first time, I saw that we come to the cross of Christ to be saved. Formerly I had not differentiated between God the Father and God the Son, and I did not know what was meant by "trusting God." Even though my advice had been right, all of the Godhead was God to me. I had been all those years trying to approach God the Father directly, no doubt even calling him "Father," when He is only the Father of those who believe His Son (Gal. 3:26). I learned that what the preachers meant by trusting God to save meant to trust God the Son, who settled my sin and my sinful self when He took my sins and me in His own body on the tree.

I was on the front seat, having gone forward at the first verse. I knew that I would go; there was no use to wait. It was but a step to where the pastor stood. I took it, gave him my hand to signify that I trusted in Christ's death to save me. By the time I took the second step, which was back to my seat, my years of burden of sin had rolled away, and the joy of the Lord filled my soul.

I think sometimes if the Lord could ever save anyone the wrong way, He would have saved me! He must really have been sorry for me. I praise Him that He never let go, but made that conviction stronger and stronger until someone said enough about Christ's death, or Christ being the Savior, for me to lay hold on what He had done for me. There is no direct road from the sinful heart to God the Father. I tried to make one, but it did not work! My sin was settled at the cross, and through Christ's death I at last came, which is the only way that anyone gets to Him.

I went home so thrilled, and so sorry for everyone else who was not in tune with the Lord, that I did not want any of that good Sunday dinner. My parents and two older sisters and both older brothers were church members and one brother and sister younger were old enough to be saved, so I just had to go to my place of prayer by the trunk in the walk-in closet in my room and plead with God for the family and for friends and neighbors.

After Bertha's conversion, another revival meeting was held in Cowpens. Three traveling Methodist ministers, all brothers, conducted the services. There Bertha discovered the secret of the Spirit-filled life and the absolute surrender to Christ such a life requires. The Bible became a new book as her prayer life and witnessing took on a new glow. Her pilgrimage deepened as she walked through her teenage years with the Lord Jesus Christ.

Bertha completed her high school days and went off to Linwood College near Gastonia, North Carolina. After one year at Linwood, she transferred to Winthrop College in Rock Hill, South Carolina. God began an even deeper work in her heart during Winthrop days. She met a group of students who were members of the Student Volunteer Band. These consecrated young people had dedicated their lives to the mission field. They suggested Bertha join their organization. She had begun to feel perhaps God wanted her to be a missionary, but she was not quite sure. Yet, to join the Band meant she must sign a pledge to become a foreign missionary. This brought about a crisis in her life: did God want her on the foreign field or did He not? She prayed and prayed. Then on Sunday afternoon, January 9, 1910, the climax came. It was a struggle, but it became clear—God did have His hand on her to become a missionary. A rich assurance came over her: God's will was found. She joined the Band and set her vision on the foreign mission field. Bertha thought God would most likely send her to Africa. But she simply trusted the Lord to guide her. He did.

Now with the vision clear, college life took on a new tone for Bertha. She read all she could on missions. Her burden for a lost world deepened. While home on vacation from college one summer, she organized a Young Woman's Auxiliary and Royal Ambassador chapter in Cowpens. These were organizations for young people to study about and pray for missions. Her service to Christ became her delight.

After graduation from Winthrop (1913) and one year of public school teaching in Blackburn, South Carolina, Bertha traveled to Louisville, Kentucky, to attend the Woman's Missionary Union Training School, an auxiliary of the Southern Baptist Theological Seminary. College and seminary training were mandatory for missionary appointment by the Southern Baptist Foreign Mission Board. That was the appointment Bertha sought, so off to seminary she went.

Bertha spent two delightful years in Louisville and soon graduated. Now she felt ready to be appointed to her field. The field? Not Africa as she had anticipated. The great need of the hour centered in China. Thus she focused her spiritual eyes on the Far East.

Her tentative appointment came in 1916, but could not be finalized for one year because of the conditions brought about by World War I. So she spent another year teaching, this time in Spartanburg, South Carolina. Then on July 3, 1917, Bertha received her formal appointment to China and was on her way. The future looked very bright.

Bertha arrived in Shanghai and embarked from the steamer, *The Little Empress of Japan*. She soon found herself on the way to Peking (now Beijing) for language school. As always, she excelled. She became proficient in Chinese Mandarin and studied it for many years throughout her missionary service. Actually, she could speak it with almost no accent. The Chinese marveled at her adeptness in the language.

After one year of study in Peking, Miss Bertha, as all affectionately called her, went to her first field assignment in Laichowfu in Shantung Province. Not only did she continue to improve in the language, but her fellowship with Christ matured as well. She was well on the path of becoming a very able missionary. She took charge of the girls boarding school, serving in that capacity for fourteen years.

Of course, there were cultural adjustments to make; China is a long way from Cowpens. But the self-discipline Bertha learned as a child held her in good stead, and that, along with her walk with the Lord, helped her become a very happy missionary. Moreover, God continued to deepen Bertha's spiritual experience through summer missionary conferences. She began to learn the secret of real Christian victory through identification with Christ in His death and resurrection (Gal. 2:20). She sensed God doing something most significant in her life.

The truth that Bertha came to realize and experience in the context of the summer conferences is commonly called the "Keswick" message. It derives its name from spiritual life conferences held in Keswick, England, a town in Britain's lake district. The message grew out of the so-called "Higher Life" conferences. The essential biblical message of the movement centered on:

- The serious problem of sin in the believer's life and the subsequent rupture of a dynamic fellowship with Christ (1 John 1:8, 10).

- The necessity of brokenness over sin and the honest confession and restitution required (1 John 1:9; Matt. 5:23–26).

- The centrality of absolute surrender and obedience to Christ by believers (Rom. 12:1–2).

- The seeking of the Holy Spirit's fullness (Eph. 5:18).

- The "identification" believers share with Christ in His death and resurrection as the basis of victory over temptation (Rom. 6:1–12; Gal. 2:20).

- Commitment to evangelism and missions (Matt. 28:18–20; Acts 1:8).

This basic message of the Keswick, or "deeper-life" movement as it is sometimes called, became the biblical truth basis of the Shantung revival—as it has been in all true great awakenings. And this is primarily what set the stage for the awakening that finally reached all of China.

Despite Bertha's spiritual development, she felt very uneasy about a disturbing problem among the Chinese believers. The native churches languished in a serious spiritual slump. Apathy and unconcern characterized most of the Chinese Christians. Few people were being saved and it seemed that many of those who did make a profession of faith and join the church came to be known as mere "rice-bowl" Christians. That is to say, they joined the congregations to get a job or a handout from the missionaries. What to do?

Right at that juncture, serious political unrest swept through Shantung Province. In March of 1927, the American consulate instructed all the missionaries to go to the port city of Chefoo until the political situation could be resolved. So some two dozen Baptist missionaries congregated in a small mission compound—with three small buildings—in Chefoo. They decided they should pray; with that many people crammed together, they had better pray. So they gathered each morning for a time of intercession.

At first their prayers were directed to the Chinese believers they left behind. But then their own needs and burdens began to surface, and the prayers shifted primarily on themselves.

Right at that stage Miss Marie Monsen, a Norwegian Lutheran missionary, came and did a series of Bible studies for the Baptist missionaries. God spoke deeply and profoundly to all their hearts through the great woman of God. Marie told of all God does in reviving His people. The first glimmerings of real revival were seen.

Charles and Ola Culpepper, fellow Baptist missionaries, requested that the group pray for Ola's eyes. She suffered from optic-neuritis, a painful deterioration of the optic nerves. To pray for a physical healing in those days seemed a bit strange for Baptists. But they decided to do so, nonetheless. And what happened can only be described as the birth of the great Shantung revival. But let Dr. Culpepper tell the story himself:

> As Miss Monsen gave her testimony, Ola began to be impressed with the fact that she should go and talk to her about the eye damage. We made an appointment and went to her apartment. As she met us at the door, Miss Monsen's first question was, "Brother Culpepper, have you been filled with the Holy Spirit?" I stammered out something less than a definite reply. Then, recognizing my uncertainty, she carefully related a personal experience fifteen years earlier when she had prayed for and received the promise of the Holy Spirit as recorded in Galatians 3:14. After visiting with her for two hours, we urged her to come to our home to pray for Ola's eyes.
>
> That night we were deeply troubled. Prayer for healing seemed unorthodox for Baptist people. But in private we read James 5:14–16 and were greatly encouraged. The words "confess your faults" particularly pierced my heart. A consuming realization that our hearts must be completely open to God pervaded all our senses. I began to feel the Lord was going to undertake a great thing for us.
>
> The next morning about twenty people came to our home for prayer. We felt an electric excitement, a feeling that God was preparing us for something we had never known before. After praying for several hours, we all seemed in a complete spirit of communion. Suddenly Ola took off her glasses and laid them on the mantle. Following the instructions in the Book of James, I anointed her with oil. Then we all knelt and continued praying. It was as though God had walked into the room. Everyone prayed aloud. We felt that Heaven came down and Glory filled our souls.
>
> As we prayed, the male Chinese cooks from both missionary residences in Chefoo walked into the room. Their hatred for each other was common knowledge. But, as the power of God's Holy Spirit worked, they went to each other, confessed their hatred, sought forgiveness, and accepted Christ as personal Savior.

In the midst of our joy for the cooks' salvation, we had completely forgotten Ola's eyes. Then someone remembered and asked her, "What about your eyes?" She replied, "They feel all right and the pain is gone."

It never returned. This was the most wonderful experience in our lives. We had never known such spiritual joy. The events surrounding those days in Chefoo were the prelude to the great Shantung Revival.

Not only was Mrs. Culpepper healed, Bertha Smith took a giant step forward in her faith. She related:

I had gone into that room, so far as I knew, absolutely right with the Lord. I would not have dared to go otherwise. But when I stretched my hand out to Mrs. Culpepper's head, I had to bring it back. There stood facing me a missionary with whom there had been a little trouble. In her early years she had been head of a girls' school, but for several years she had been teaching illiterate women to read.

I had been asked to serve as principal in our boys' school in Chefoo while the missionary principal was on furlough. I had majored in education, and by that time had had ten years' experience in teaching and thought that I was "the last word" in education! I had recommended Miss Hartwell to lead daily worship in that school. After a few weeks, I asked another missionary to tell her that methods for teaching old women were not appropriate for high school boys. She was hurt, of course.

But what about my proud self? I did not have a particle of sympathy for her. Right there before everyone, I had to say, "Miss Hartwell, I did not have the proper attitude toward you about that school affair. I beg you to forgive me!" My hand then joined the others and we prayed. Had I refused to confess that sin, and joined in the prayer with it covered, I believe that I would have hindered the prayer of the others, and the eye could not have been healed.

Because all were right with God and of one heart, heaven came down! We did not have to wait to see whether or not Mrs. Culpepper's eye was healed! We knew in our hearts that she would never have another attack. The Lord had heard the prayers of such human frailty and had performed a miracle in healing one whom we so loved! She did not put her glasses back on. While the sight was not restored completely in the weak eye, both were strengthened and not once has she had any more pain, though using her eyes steadily for reading and needlework.

Walking around the room rejoicing and praising the Lord, we were all on a mountaintop of ecstasy. Then I had to be the joy-killer. There came over me such a sense of our inconsistency, that I had to speak of it.

"What kind of missionaries are we?" I asked. "We have gone through a week of heart-searching, humbling ourselves before each other and before the Lord, in order that we might be altogether right with Him, so that He could hear our prayers and heal the physical eye of one of our own number. Yet we have never gone to this much self-negation for preparation to pray for the opening of the spiritual eyes of the Chinese to whom we have been sent." Our mountaintop of ecstasy suddenly became a valley of humiliation. We all went to our knees in contrite confession for having been so careless as to have gone along supposing that we were right with the Lord, while holding all kinds of attitudes which could have kept the Lord's living water from flowing through us to the Chinese."

That became the beginning of the awakening—and what an awakening it proved to be.

When the missionaries were able to return to their responsibilities, they returned different servants of Christ than what they were when they left their respective fields. They began to share what God had taught them—not just about physical healings, that was a very minor part of the awakening—but about a walk with Christ in confession and cleansing of sin, of being filled with the Spirit, of absolute surrender to Christ's Lordship, and of witnessing to the gospel in behalf of the unbelievers. And the new spirit of commitment spread like wildfire. The churches came alive, the seminary exploded with growth (from four to one hundred fifty students) and multitudes were saved, including many "rice-bowl" Christians. The churches overflowed with new converts. What days they were.

Then the revival spread all over Shantung Province; finally, all over China. That is why Miss Bertha can rightly be called a "Woman of Revival." China was blessed beyond measure, and Bertha Smith had no small part in it all. Through the years of Bertha's missionary service, she touched thousands of Chinese.

Multitudes came to faith in Christ and many believers were deepened and matured in the Lord through her ministry. She became in herself a saga of missionary effectiveness.

Many of Bertha's experiences during the revival read almost like a page out of the book of Acts. First, the Christians themselves were profoundly and radically transformed. The Spirit of God touched many lives. One of those was the Chinese cook of the Larsons, Baptist missionaries. The cook had formerly been an apparently warm-hearted church member, actually conducting Bible classes for the other Chinese servants. But during the meeting at Bertha's station in Laichowfu, he became deeply convicted of his own personal sins. He could find no rest or peace. One morning at six o'clock he came to Miss Bertha. The burden of his sins robbed him of sleep; he had not been to bed the entire night. He first sought Miss Bertha's forgiveness for having said untrue and unkind things about her. Miss Bertha said he should go to others and tell them that the things he had said about her were not true. He did so. Then he went to the Larsons and confessed he had stolen money by buying food for them on the market. He had been pocketing the difference between the market price quoted to the Larsons and the price he had actually paid. He offered to work for two months without wages, believing that would put the matter square. The Larsons let him work without wages; they knew the Holy Spirit was doing a work in him and he would have no peace otherwise. Miss Bertha said when she saw the cook for the first time after his reviving experience, "his face looked like that of an angel."

In the Chinese churches in Bertha's days, a dividing screen separating the men from the women was put in place when the church gathered for worship. Miss Bertha confessed that she was often guilty of peeping over the screen to see how many men were in church—the little technique she used to be able to say what she felt would be relevant for the folk. This is how she saw the face of the cook "that looked like an angel." At a prayer meeting Miss Marie Monsen, who was speaking at the time, asked someone thoroughly right with God to pray. The cook immediately arose and began his prayer: "Lord, I thank You that I am no longer I."

After the meeting Misses Bertha and Marie Monsen traveled together to Laiyang, the hometown of the revived cook. Traveling with the ladies were several other missionaries and the cook. The missionary group went by car to Laiyang. However, there was no room in the car for the cook, so he rode his bicycle and arrived the next day. In a prayer meeting that night, Miss Monsen once again asked for any brother who was right with God to lead in prayer. The cook rose and prayed. As Bertha expressed it, such a volume of praise to the Lord poured forth that his old friends around him wanted to know how such a change had come over him. The cook's new commitment became typical of what God did in multiplied ways as the revival spread. In a true awakening the Holy Spirit profoundly probes God's own people and transforms them.

Moreover, one could hardly count the number saved in the revival. Even some preachers came to saving faith in Christ during the awakening. Bertha tells of a Mr. Chow, a Chinese preacher. Mr. Chow, an evangelist in the area, became uneasy about his own relationship with the Lord. After every service he would seek out Miss Bertha. He wanted some evidence that he had truly been born again. At last Miss Bertha asked, "Mr. Chow, what are you trusting in for salvation?" He straightened himself up and immediately replied, "You need not tell me that after I have walked for twenty-five years over this country telling people about the Savior, the Lord is going to turn me away from heaven's gate!" Miss Bertha immediately replied, "If that is what you are trusting in, you most certainly will be turned away!" Bertha never hesitated in frankly telling the bare truth. The evangelist came to Christ alone for salvation!

And there were actual, verified physical healings as well. Real revival produces incredible experiences.

So the awakening spread and deepened. Thousands found Christ as Savior through a revived church as the movement engulfed the land. But that is what revival is all about. Bertha really did become a "Woman of Revival."

In 1931, four years into the awakening, Miss Bertha sailed back to America for a much-needed furlough. She almost filled the role of a "workaholic," as her dear friend and fellow missionary, Martha Franks, called her. She really did need rest. Yet Bertha worked hard even at home. Her furlough was soon up and she prepared to return to the field. However, the Great Depression had engulfed America and the Baptist Foreign Mission Board could not send her back. Funds simply were not available. What a disappointment! Yet Bertha became convinced God wanted her back in China and she committed herself so to do. What a dilemma! What could the answer be?

Bertha's decision to return to China obviously raised some very significant questions: How would she be able to go? Where could the funds be found? How would she be sustained when back in China? Once again God spoke to her in a fresh way. Although she had read the Book of Isaiah many times, these words suddenly stood out and challenged her: "I will go before you and will level the mountains; I will break down gates of bronze and cut through bars of iron. I will give you the treasures of darkness, riches stored in secret places, so that you may know that I am the Lord, the God of Israel, who summons you by name" (Isa. 45:2–3, NIV). Bertha's heart overflowed with joy when she read that promise. "Thank you, Lord!" she exclaimed, "the 'how' is now the Lord's concern. The riches are His secret. Since He knows, that is sufficient."

Bertha was now ready to step out on simple faith. She had God's promise. This step, however, would mean being willing to give up the privilege of working directly under the Southern Baptist Foreign Mission Board. It would also probably mean not serving with the missionaries whom she loved so well. Bertha was not disillusioned with Southern Baptists. On the contrary, she was convinced that the methodology and policy of the FMB constituted the best approach to missions in China. But she felt she must respect the Holy Spirit, follow His leadership, and return to China. She had friends who had gone out by faith. She appreciated all they were contributing to the cause of Christ in China. Now she would step out on the same principle.

Bertha continued corresponding with the secretary of the Southern Baptist Foreign Mission Board. She suggested returning to China and working under the same relationship to the FMB, but with some definite stipulations. First, she would work on the same field in Shantung and serve with the missionaries that she knew and loved so well. Further, she would be affiliated with the Chinese Baptist Convention as formerly, but she would not receive funds from the FMB for any purpose whatsoever. She also made it clear to T. B. Ray, the secretary of the Foreign Mission Board at that time, that she would make no appeals to any churches in America for funds. This would have flown in the face of the Southern Baptist's "Cooperative Program," a financial program wherein churches gave a certain amount of their weekly offerings to Southern Baptist causes worldwide. It was therefore forbidden for any who were appointed by any of the Southern Baptist agencies to solicit funds from churches directly. Miss Bertha gladly submitted herself to the restrictions. She told Dr. Ray that if she could never be supported by the FMB again, she would in no way hold the Board responsible. As the correspondence was sent off, she prayed to the Lord earnestly and fervently seeking that God would give the Foreign Mission Board an agreeable mind to her conditions upon her return. God answered that prayer. Dr. Ray's heart was touched and he agreed to every stipulation.

So Miss Bertha sailed back to China for many more fruitful years of service. And God met every need, honoring her faith. Later, funds did become available and the mission board supported her once more.

As the work progressed through the years, ominous storm clouds began to gather over the vast land of China, conjured up by the Japanese. Then the hurricane blew in. In 1936 and 1937 Japan invaded China. In the latter part of July 1937, the American government asked Bertha to go to the coast for safety; but she stayed in Tsingtau, her station at the time. She would trust God and keep up the work. But the inevitable loomed on the horizon—invasion and, finally, internment. During the difficult days of Japanese occupation, the work did go well, regardless of the restrictions. It was amazing how much was actually accomplished. Bertha continued her teaching, especially her Bible lessons. A typical outline in these days reads as follows:

The Healing of the Demon Possessed Boy in Mark 9:14ff

vs. 14–17: The nine apostles left behind (Peter, James, and John were on the Mt. of Transfiguration) were in defeat

vs. 17: The devil was rejoicing; the nine disciples were unbelieving

vs. 19: Jesus was patient

vs. 20: Devil was at his worse before Jesus—showed his (diabolical) power

vs. 21–22: Jesus questioned the father (of the boy)

vs. 23: If you *can* believe—the boy could not believe. The father had to believe for the boy! The father identified himself with the suffering boy

vs. 24: The father's prayer—help me believe

vs. 25: Jesus rebuked the devil

vs. 26–27: The devil does not give up easily. He never does! Not with *you*! (But he) had to come out—did (his) worse.

vs. 28: Disciples asked, "Why?" Answer: "Go to the place of prayer!"

Nothing could daunt her spirit of sharing God's truth.

But the inevitable did come: internment. On December 8, 1941, the Japanese came into the mission school and ordered Miss Bertha and the teachers to the missionaries' residence grounds. After twenty-five years on the field, Miss Bertha was interred in her home. But she claimed the promise of 1 Samuel 14:45, "There shall not one hair of his head fall to the ground." God kept His Word; Bertha fared quite well during her confinement. Restricted to her home and yard, she could spend much more time in prayer, continue to study the Bible—and the Chinese language—and practice the piano. She loved music.

Then came relief. Bertha was repatriated. That appeared almost like a miracle in itself. She sailed home on the *Grypsholm*. On August 27, 1942, she sailed into New York harbor and thrilled to see the Statue of Liberty. Bertha returned to Cowpens and was reunited with her eighty-two-year-old mother. What a reunion it was!

After the Allied victory in 1945, Miss Bertha sailed back to China. She had left all her household supplies stored in Shanghai, including her cherished piano, so she had all she needed to carry on her ministry. But then even more ominous clouds began to gather. The Communists were on the march. Before long, Bertha's station was surrounded by Communist troops. The end drew near.

The Baptist missionaries were at the mercy of the atheists. They found refuge in a Roman Catholic mission as the Communist hoards bombarded the city. But God protected His precious servants. Bertha was huddled down in a room in the Catholic mission when the soldiers actually invaded the compound. Let her tell the story. It is fascinating:

> At that moment one of the communists came to the end of the hall and threw a hand grenade that exploded on the cement floor just before our open door, about three feet from me. I sang under the bed!
>
> > The soul that on Jesus had leaned for repose
> > I will not, I will not desert to His foes;
> > That soul, though all hell should endeavor to shake,
> > I'll never, no, never, no, never forsake!
>
> It seemed that all hell *was* endeavoring to shake and succeeding fairly well, but our God was there, keeping our hearts in peace.
>
> After a while one of those grenades hit the brick pillar between the two windows in our room. The column was shattered, and bits of brick and cement flew over the room. Ceiling and walls were speckled except for one place. When Alex moved, an outline of his head and shoulders showed where he had been leaning. Not one of us had been touched! Miracle!"

Still, the Communists won, and China fell. Chiang Kai-shek and the nationalist army retreated to Formosa to set up a free Chinese state and government.

Of course, expulsion for the missionaries was inevitable. The edict soon came forth: Bertha had to leave her beloved China.

Where to go? Home? Another field? Perhaps Africa? God again opened a wide door. Miss Bertha was sent by Dr. Baker James Cauthen, Southern Baptist Secretary for the Orient, to Formosa. She would still be with her beloved Chinese people. A new saga opened for Bertha.

No Southern Baptist work existed in Formosa (now Taiwan). Miss Bertha, Woman of Revival, would be the ground-breaker and carry the revival spirit to the new nation of free China. Through much prayer and commitment, trusting the promise of God to supply all her needs (Phil. 4:19), overcoming all barriers, off she went.

The early days in the new island nation were far from easy. Lodging, food, and getting a start for the work proved most difficult. But God had promised to supply all things necessary and He did. Bertha finally secured a house and began worship services on Sunday in her own home. She made friends with American diplomats who were Christians and the work went forward.

In an unbelievably short time, a church emerged—then another and another. People were being saved as new churches were constituted. So many came to Christ in Bertha's own home that as they knelt by her couch, shedding tears of repentance, the sofa was literally ruined. Bertha said the tears made the upholstery into a "beautifully brocaded" piece of cloth. Such was God's work. The stories emerging out of those days are glorious, as the reader will see. The work became well established and a strong Baptist witness remains in Taiwan to this day—thanks to this pioneer missionary of revival.

But now the end of Miss Bertha's Chinese ministry drew near: she approached the age of seventy. The Southern Baptist Foreign Mission Board required all missionaries to retire at age seventy—no exceptions. And that "no exceptions" clause meant Bertha. What a wrench in her heart. She said,

> Becoming of age! What pain! I never dreamed that anything in this life could ever hurt like giving up work with the Chinese and returning home. I was still doing about fifteen hours of work a day, and I never became too tired to get up rested the next morning.

Foreign missionaries are automatically retired by our mission board on the first day of the month following the month in which comes the seventieth birthday. My birthday is in November, and that year November 30 came on Sunday, my last day to work as a regular missionary.

I felt that I was just then qualified from experience for missionary work. The forty-one and a half years had been very short, interesting indeed, at times thrilling, and always rewarding. Every trial along the way had been forgotten as soon as the next person was saved.

Yet, Bertha knew the will of God was being accomplished, so she surrendered to the inevitable and prepared to go home. She bid a tearful farewell to her beloved Chinese friends. The end had come. But had it? Hardly! A new day and ministry was just dawning. She had a commission from Christ to "Go Home and Tell." She had to share with America all God had done in the great Shantung revival. And tell it she did!

Bertha had received a small inheritance just before retiring from the Board. She took those funds and on her way home flew around the world visiting Baptist mission fields. Wherever she landed, a mini-revival descended. It was incredible.

Back in Cowpens, she returned to the lovely old home her father had built, and there she lived with her sister Jenny. Invitations flooded in to speak and share the principles of revival. She traveled far and wide across America, and went to foreign countries to share. For almost thirty incredible years, she carried on an exhausting ministry telling the story and seeking revival in America. She founded the Peniel Prayer Center, where Bible conferences are still regularly held. Her ministry in America all but rivaled her forty-one years among the Chinese. She served right up to the end. But the end had to come. The trumpet sounded, the summons came, and Bertha put her foot in the Jordan River and entered glory.

Bertha had wanted to live to be one hundred years old; but she went home to her Lord on June 12, 1988, just five months before her one hundredth birthday. Disappointment? Not really. The Chinese count one's age not by birth, but by the year of conception. So Chinese style, Bertha made one hundred. And that would have pleased her well.

Sources

Culpepper, C. L. *The Shantung Revival*. Dallas: Crescendo Publications, 1971, 13–14.

Smith, Bertha. *Go Home and Tell*. Nashville: Broadman Press, 1965, 15–17.

———. *How the Spirit Filled My Life*. Nashville: Broadman Press, 1973, 15–17.

———. Personal Papers. Peniel Prayer Center, Cowens, South Carolina.

PART I

Go Home and Tell

CHAPTER ONE

In the Lord's School

Eight years after volunteering for foreign mission work, I was appointed to work in China by the Foreign Mission Board of the Southern Baptist Convention, July 3, 1917. I arrived in Shanghai, September 4.

Although my four years in college, two of teaching, and two in seminary were preparation for the work, I found that the most important lessons had to be learned after reaching the field.

Loneliness

Lo, I am with you alway (Matt. 28:20).

The first year was spent in Peking, studying the language with other young people in the College of Chinese Studies, where all was new and interesting. I then went to live in Laichowfu, Shantung, which was four days' travel from the port of Chefoo by mule litter—speed limit three miles per hour! And I assure you that it was never broken!

I made the eighth missionary there. The youngest of the others was forty years old. I was still in my twenties and then did not know any better than to think that she was an old woman.

I continued language study with a private teacher five hours a day, and in addition taught a few English classes in the two mission high schools. At five o'clock I needed recreation. Those seven missionaries got their exercise walking to visit inquirers, or Christians who were sick either in body or soul. They were so given to their work that other missionaries called them "the devotees."

Being assured that it would be safe to walk alone in the fields from five o'clock to six each day, if I kept in sight of our mission building, I started out walking the paths that surrounded the tiny farms. I was just lonesome and homesick enough to die. Needless to say, I lost my joy in the Lord and became sorry for myself (a poor subject for any woman to get on her mind).

One day I came to myself and talked to the Lord like this:

> I did not come to China of my own accord. In Your Word You say that when we go to tell people about You, You go with us, even unto the end of the age. Now the end of the age has not come, so this promise includes today, right now!

And when I began to praise Him for His presence, He was there.

Language was studied with a new zest. Drilling on the pronunciation of English words was no longer a burden, for my Lord was in the room with me, enabling me and helping the Chinese students. And what a joy to have an hour alone with my Lord in the fields where I talked aloud with Him, even though some Chinese occasionally walked up behind me and probably thought that I was out of my mind. I not only talked with the Lord, I wanted Him to talk with me; so I carried my New Testament and memorized many choice verses, stopping long enough to read one and then to repeat it over and over to the Lord as I walked.

Fortunately, as a child I had done a great deal of memory work in both Sunday school and public school. In those days, most public schools had morning worship, and Scripture passages were assigned for memory work. Later, when I was a freshman in Winthrop College, I memorized 615 Bible verses. Miss Helen Miller Gould made this assignment, for which she gave a nice leather-bound Bible. Now, all these passages came to life as I repeated them to the Lord day after day in my walks.

Sometimes I took a hymnbook and learned hymns in the same way, changing the third personal pronouns to the second, so that instead of singing *about* the Lord, I sang *to* Him. Through the years I have never had another lonely moment on land, sea, or in the air, neither have I ever had quite enough time to be alone with the Lord.

My Covenant

As soon as Zion travailed, she brought forth her children
(Isa. 66:8).

One of my first China heartaches was in seeing a land where there was no observance of the Lord's Day. I could not get accustomed to all the shops being open and people going on with their field work. When the missionaries did not buy from the street vendors, they would ask, "Is it Sunday?"

Even worse were the sights on the big market and temple days. The crowds came from every direction, bringing their wares for sale. The grandmothers and children came along to go to the temple to worship. The offering of a bolt of flowered paper or silk, according to the financial status of the family, was first burned in the big pot in the courtyard. Then the worshipers walked up steep rickety stairs and bumped their foreheads on the floor before a dumb idol.

High school students stood in the courtyard and laughed at what they called the superstition of their own mothers and grandmothers who still believed in gods. In the city government high school, 398 of the 400 students were members of what they called "The No-God Society." Of the twenty teachers, all but two were members of that same society. They were just as lost as were the ardent idol-worshiping grandmothers, the mercenary men, and the wives and sisters at home. All were "as sheep without a shepherd." My heart was made sick over them, as I knew that their only hope was in coming to know my living Lord.

I had been convinced that it was not the Lord's will for me to marry. Up until my second year in China, I had thought that I would be content to live single. How little did I realize what I was saying when I sang so sincerely, "I Surrender All." The Lord gave me a mother heart, the depth of which I had not fathomed, until I saw the difference in the life of a single woman and those who were living with the one whom they had chosen for a partner, and their own precious children. The married missionaries were in the will of the Lord; why could not such a life be the Lord's will for me? But these questions were answered for me in a very real and transforming experience with the Lord.

I had been in China less than two years when my father passed away in the influenza epidemic of 1918. It was necessary for me to go to Chefoo, to the nearest U.S. consulate to sign legal papers. This meant eight days of travel there and back. I passed through one mission station going, and another returning, and stayed in the home of missionaries while in Chefoo. By the time I had started on the last stage of the journey back to Laichowfu, I had seen seven happy families with their children.

The mule litter by which I traveled was a frame of two long poles forming shafts for the mule in front and the one in the back. Ropes were laced across the middle section between the two mules. Over the ropes was a bow frame covered with a straw mat. The passenger always provided a thick quilt-like cover to fit over the mat to protect from heat in summer and cold in winter. Pillows were used, and a mattress made for the purpose was put on top of the suitcases. Sitting and lying were equally miserable.

Since mules could not be drilled in keeping step, one mule would jerk the passenger in one direction and before she got there the movement of the other mule would pull her back. At the same time, she was being shaken up and down and crosswise until she felt like the contents of a whirling washing machine.

After leaving the last mission home before reaching my station, I traveled for two days along a lonely road. Realizing what I was going back to, and that this was for life, I wept most of the first day. By the next day I knew that something had to be done.

For safety I always walked ahead of the driver of the mule litter. Local bandits sometimes needed the clothes of the traveler! For a while I walked very fast, getting far enough ahead to stop and talk out loud. On that solitary road that ran along by the mountain range between Laiyang and Laichowfu, I stood. Calling upon a nearby peak to be my witness, I made a covenant with the Lord:

> Lord, I want to enter into an agreement with You today. You called me to China and You gave me grace to follow in coming. I am here to win souls for You. The only thing that will take the place of my own children will be spiritual children. If You will take from my heart this pain, I will be willing to go through with just as much inconvenience, self-denial, and pain to see children born into the family of God, as is necessary for a mother to endure for children to be born in the flesh!

In desperation I was calling upon the mighty God for help in facing the difficulties and accepting the compensations of His service, and I was not disappointed.

From that moment forward there were no more tears, for the Lord met my every heart need. I became content with my lot and began to study the Bible and books on soul-winning with a new interest. Prayer became more definite for individuals, and every opportunity to speak for the Lord was seized. The transaction has lasted until this day, and many, many times I have praised the Lord for the privilege of being a single woman with the other person's soul-need having first place in my heart.

Paul spoke of travailing in pain for the Galatians whom he had won to the Lord (4:19), and Isaiah stated that as soon as Zion travailed, sons and daughters were brought forth. When I have a heartache for a person, which can be likened to the Holy Spirit praying through me with groanings which cannot be expressed in human language, that person is soon saved. Would that I had experienced more of that kind of heart agony!

Christ, My Victory

Thanks be unto God, which always causeth us to triumph in Christ (2 Cor. 2:14).

Before going to China I had put myself, once and for all, into God's hands, to be or to do whatever He should choose (Rom. 12:1). This decision made the way for the Holy Spirit to fill me, and when He did, Christ was enthroned in my heart and life. This infilling was a transforming experience and led me to the mission field.

In the summer of 1919, Dr. R. A. Torrey came to China to lead conferences at summer resorts. For ten days at Peitaiho I heard him speak twice a day on the work of the Holy Spirit in the life of the Christian. What a blessing! Still, not knowing how to walk in the Spirit, I was often filled today and empty tomorrow.

The next summer, Dr. Charles G. Trumbull, editor of the *Sunday School Times*, was the conference speaker, assisted by Miss Ruth Paxson, author of *Life on the Highest Plane*. Through these friends, I came into the glorious Bible truth that Christ lives in me. Joyous release! No longer did I have to strive for victory over self, the world, and the devil, but just to act on the fact that Christ was my victory and, to quote Dr. Trumbull, "Let go and let God."

When I went to Dr. Trumbull for a personal talk on how to let Christ be my victory, he called attention to the word *is* in the Bible. God, to Moses, was the ever-present God. "I am" was His name. "The Lord is the strength of my life" (Ps. 27:1). "There is therefore now no condemnation to them which are in Christ Jesus" (Rom. 8:1). "The Lord is my light and my salvation" (Ps. 27:1).

These Scripture passages so took hold of me that I realized I had been like the beggar outside the Beautiful Gate of the Temple. It was a good place for the man to beg, but he was still helpless. After Peter took his hand, and the Lord healed him, he ran, jumped, and even rushed into the Temple praising God (Acts 3).

When I saw the glorious truth that the Lord *was* at that very moment my victory over every sin, over every disposition, and over every circumstance, I was filled with thanksgiving. When I had praised the Lord, Dr. Trumbull wrote in his notebook by my name the words, "A five-thousand-dollar gift!" But that did not half express it. I so walked on air that it was a year before I was convicted of an old sin, and how brokenhearted I was then!

Sometime afterwards I made a special study of 2 Corinthians 9:8. For two weeks I used the one verse at a Christians' Bible class, taking one word each day.

God: The living, all-knowing, all-loving, ever-present One deserved my constant adoration and worship.

Is: God here and now *is* all that He ever has been!

Able: He is the all-powerful One who spoke the universe into existence. Certainly He is *able* to do for me all that I can ever need.

To make: God, having created all from nothing, can make that which does not exist in order to supply my need. He "calleth those things which be not as though they were" (Rom. 4:17). He will make all things work together for my good (Rom. 8:28).

All grace: That which is the favor of God; I cannot by any effort merit it. It being God's free gift, I can only accept it. God gives not just enough grace for one specific need, but *all* grace, every kind of loving favor sufficient for every situation.

Abound: There would not be just enough strength, wisdom, and patience to get by, but abundance which could never give out.

Toward you: To whom? "God is able to make all grace abound *toward you*," which means *me*! Regardless of any lack I may have in natural ability and gifts, that grace abounds toward me. I can take it according to my need.

To every good work: Why is such abundant grace given to me? Is it that I sometimes may do a little service for Him? It is that I may *always* serve Him! How? Am I just to serve in my own human weakness? No! I, "always having all sufficiency in all *things*, may abound to every good work."

What a sentence! You may be sure that by the time that I had worked on this verse for two weeks, it had come alive for me. Such a victorious, abundant life would only be the normal life for one in whom Christ Himself was actually living His own life. Shame on me that at times afterwards I forgot that magnificent truth!

However, when I recalled and acted upon it, the Lord was there meeting every need. Dr. Trumbull taught us to sing, not "I Need Thee Every Hour," but "I Have Thee Every Hour." Oh, "I have Thee," and what a difference!

One Presbyterian minister at the conference said in his testimony, "I'll have to change my whole praying vocabulary." Yes, he would be thanking the Lord for all that He already was to him, instead of begging Him to become this or that.

Truly, life for many of us was to be on a higher plane. Later, when I had to go through bombings and shellings and be responsible for standing firmly before the Japanese soldiers, what the Chinese friends called courage was not just courage. It was Christ Himself living His life in me, meeting every need in His abounding way.

This precious truth, that Christ lives His life in us, became especially valuable through the years when it was necessary for me to rebuke sin. Because Christ was living in me and being permitted to express Himself through me, I could reprove without a thought of what the consequences might be toward me personally.

Nerves

When he giveth quietness, who then can make trouble?
(Job 34:29).

Winds often blew over the treeless plains of Shantung at such a gale that I wondered if the house could take it. In addition to the winds, there were the dust storms. At midday the sky would turn yellow, and all city shops would close. Everyone would rush home and close the doors; but even then, the fine silt would creep in at every crack and keyhole.

When I awoke in the mornings, the only white place on the bed would be that portion of the pillow protected by my head. These dust storms usually lasted for three days, and only the sustaining presence of the Lord enabled me to endure them.

One evening the wind was raging at bedtime. My Old Testament reading was in Psalm 127, and a statement jumped up from the page into my heart, "He giveth His beloved sleep" (v. 2). I said, "Thank You, Lord. I am Your beloved because You see me in Your beloved Son, so I take sleep from You." In a moment I was sound asleep until morning, even though the wind raged on through the night. From this experience I learned to take peace from the Lord during the varied storms that arose in the work.

The saintly missionary, Blanche Rose Walker, who lived in a little Chinese house alone, was having thirteen guests for meals during a convention. In writing to me about it, she added, "The Lord is holding on to my nerves." I said, "Surely, Lord, You are the One to hold on to a woman's nerves, for she can't hold them herself." I turned mine over to Him and He has held them ever since.

Satisfied

While I live will I praise the Lord (Ps. 146:2).

After completing my first two years of language study, I took charge of the girls' boarding school. I was able to teach some Bible in Chinese, in addition to my English classes. However, when I observed one of my teachers in the trigonometry class, I scarcely would have known if he had held the book upside down. But further work on the language was continued with a teacher three hours a day for the next five years, until furlough time.

The missionary's term of service in China was seven years for the first term, and nine afterwards. So many people went to heaven, instead of back home to America, before the nine years were up that the term was cut to seven years. My second seven years, I studied two hours a day with a teacher; and my third seven, I had a teacher come twice a week for two hours at a sitting.

While in charge of the school, I felt I was doing the greatest work in the world. Girls came in from country villages over five counties. Some came from Christian homes, others came from non-Christian homes where some man of the family clan had been "outside" to a port and returned wanting the girls of the family educated. Often a student became the first Christian in her village, and her home became a place for a Bible woman or missionary to gather in the neighbors and tell them about the Savior. Some of the girls became teachers or nurses, and a few of them full-time church workers. But most of them became Christian homemakers.

The greatest privilege of my first ten years was that of living with the saintly Miss Alice Huey, of Alabama. Dr. Jeannette Beall would say, teasingly, "Huey is of the heavens, heavenly; Bertha is of the earth, earthy." The mission built a house for us beside the school, and I was able, with personal money from home, to buy enough land for us to have a yard in grass, a vegetable garden, and plenty of flowers.

A gardener who loved every leaf that grew was secured for three or four dollars a month. After eating from that wage, he bought a little land each year. Although he was present for our household worship at six each morning and heard the Word in his own language, it took an object lesson to stop him from working on Sunday.

One Sunday upon returning from an afternoon Sunday school, I found the yard with rows of seedlings freshly set out. When I went out the next morning and pulled up every one and asked him to reset them, he was cured.

A pair of scissors was kept by the front door, and when we escorted guests to the outside gate, a bunch of flowers was cut for them. Non-Christians often came just to see the flowers, and no doubt the flowers made a good impression for the Lord.

Sometimes as I thrilled over the beauty of the flowers and rejoiced because of conviction for sin in the heart of a new girl, or the growth in grace of those who loved the study of the Word, the Holy Spirit would whisper to my heart, "Would you be willing to leave your home here and the school which you so love, and go to the new work in the western part of the province?" I always answered, "Yes, Lord, if that is what You want!"

CHAPTER TWO

A New Thing

When I reached North China, I found missionaries grieved over the lack of spiritual fervor on the part of most church members. In every mission station, leaders were praying for an awakening. As the years went by, the missionaries began to fear that many of the church members had accepted Christianity in their minds without having been born of the Spirit.

Longing for Revival

If I regard iniquity in my heart, the LORD *will not hear me* (Ps. 66:18).

After Dr. Trumbull's Victorious Life Conference in 1920, when some of the members of my station were blessed, missionaries and

Chinese leaders set aside the first day of each month, regardless of the day of the week, as prayer day for revival. Some stayed at the church from nine to twelve o'clock and from two to five just to pray. Others went whenever they could. A different leader directed the praying each hour.

This schedule was followed for several years, and though we saw more blessings upon the work, we did not see the revival for which we had longed and prayed. In March, 1927, when the southern revolutionary army burned Nanking, the American consul in Chefoo telegraphed missionaries: "Proceed to the coast at once." Those on the south side of the peninsula and in the western part of the province went to Tsingtau, while those on the north side went to Chefoo.

Twenty-seven missionaries, both singles and couples with children, plus their dogs, packed into two mission residences in Chefoo. Humanly speaking it would have been a difficult time indeed, but we had the Lord!

The "Red" influence in the army at that time led the soldiers to ridicule churches and persecute Christians. In a city in Hunan in a street parade, an old beggar man in rags was labeled "God the Father," a donkey was labeled "Jesus," and an ox, the "Holy Spirit."

Longing for our missionaries in Shantung to stand true if persecution should reach them, we in Chefoo began to meet for an hour every morning after breakfast to pray for them. Soon we were praying until midday, but no one remembered to pray for the Chinese Christians. All were beseeching the Lord to show *us* what He had in mind to teach *us* by permitting us to be torn from the work which we loved more than our own lives, and to be packed up in the port city.

As the days passed, we asked Jane Lide to give some Bible messages on a subject, "Christ, Our Life," which had recently become very precious to her. The Holy Spirit used the Word, as she presented it, to give each of us a clearer look at ourselves and at the all-sufficient Christ who was wanting to live His life in us all the time!

While we were weak, He wanted to be strength in us.

While we were stupid, He wanted to be wisdom in us.

While we were sinful, He wanted to be holiness in us.

While we were easily aroused and intolerant, He wanted to be patience in us.

While we were proud of the talents which He had given us—the education which He had made possible, of the experiences through the years which He had guarded, and even of "our work" which we had been able to accomplish for Him—He wanted us to die to self and let Him be our humility. If in any respect we were unwilling to go all the way with the Lord, He Himself would be willingness in us.

Needless to say, as we dug into the Word along these lines, we were convicted of sin, enriched in our lives, and stirred with a deepened desire for revival in the Chinese churches.

Missionaries from several North China provinces were refugeeing in Chefoo at that time. Among them was Miss Marie Monsen, an Evangelical Lutheran from Norway. We heard how she had been used of the Lord for twenty-five years in Bible teaching and evangelistic work and in seeing the sick healed. Consequently, we invited her to meet with us in our prayer meetings.

While she did not ordinarily mention the healings, upon request she shared with us some of the experiences of seeing the sick healed by the Lord.

One of our number, Mrs. Charles Culpepper, Sr., had suffered much from optical neuritis, which had left only partial vision in the eye affected. A few months before we were called to Chefoo, the good eye began to cause trouble. The mission doctor in Laichowfu advised her to go to Peking for treatment.

The Culpepper family went to Union Medical College Hospital. Due to the philanthropy of John D. Rockefeller, Jr., the world's best specialists were to be found there. The eye specialist at that time was from Vienna, Austria. He changed her glasses but gave no encouragement about an improvement in the general condition of her eyes.

During those days in Chefoo when we often had fellowship with Miss Monsen and heard her tell how God had marvelously healed all sorts of diseases, Mrs. Culpepper started having eye trouble again. There was still no eye specialist nearer than Peking, which was over two hundred miles away. She did not believe he could do much for her, even if she could receive his care. She truly felt discouraged.

One evening the thought came to her to ask Miss Monsen and the prayer group to pray that the Lord would heal her. It was a very difficult thing to bring herself to do, for she still had the prejudice which had been in her mind for years concerning faith healing. But, reassured by her husband, they went together to speak to Miss Monsen about it.

By that time some of the refugeeing missionaries had returned to the United States, leaving eighteen of us. Some of them said that miracles of bodily healing were granted to first-century Christians as a proof that Jesus had risen from the dead. Now that the New Testament was completed, God expects people to believe the written record. Others said, "My God shall supply every need of yours." Certainly this was a definite need with no human remedy.

Since praying for the sick to be divinely healed had never been in her way of belief or practice, Mrs. Culpepper had never studied the Bible from this viewpoint. It was really the work of the Spirit during those days that brought her life before her like a movie. She began to see her real self as God saw her. Only the power of the Holy Spirit could have given her strength to talk very frankly with her husband, confessing sins against him and others. Even greater courage was given her to say to the whole group that she was most unworthy to be one of their number.

She was not the only one who was getting altogether right with God during that week. All of us who expected to pray for the eye were doing deep heart-searching. We were calling upon the Holy Spirit, who is Light, to shine into the deep recesses of our beings, to reveal anything that He was ready to prune out at that stage of our Christian development.

When the day agreed on arrived, twelve were present in the prayer meeting. Dr. Culpepper read from the fifth chapter of James. He did not try to explain it; he was not leaving out anything of which the Bible spoke. He then put some olive oil on Mrs. Culpepper's head and asked all to come up and lay their hands on her head and pray.

I had gone into that room, so far as I knew, absolutely right with the Lord. I would not have dared to go otherwise. But when I stretched my hand out to Mrs. Culpepper's head, I had to bring it back. There stood facing me a missionary with whom there had been a little trouble. In her early years she had been head of a girls' school, but for several years she had been teaching illiterate women to read.

I had been asked to serve as principal in our boys' school in Chefoo while the missionary principal was on furlough. I had majored in education, and by that time had had ten years' experience in teaching and thought that I was 'the last word' in education! I had recommended Miss Hartwell to lead daily worship in that school. After a few weeks, I asked another missionary to tell her that methods for teaching old women were not appropriate for high school boys. She was hurt, of course.

But what about my proud self? I did not have a particle of sympathy for her. Right there before everyone, I had to say, "Miss Hartwell, I did not have the proper attitude toward you about that school affair. I beg you to forgive me!" My hand then joined the others and we prayed. Had I refused to confess that sin, and joined in the prayer with it covered, I believe that I would have hindered the prayer of the others, and the eye could not have been healed.

Because all were right with God and of one heart, heaven came down! We did not have to wait to see whether or not Mrs. Culpepper's eye was healed! We knew in our hearts that she would never have another attack. The Lord had heard the prayers of such human frailty and had performed a miracle in healing one whom we so loved! She did not put her glasses back on. While the sight was not restored completely in the weak eye, both were strengthened and not once has she had any more pain, though using her eyes steadily for reading and needlework.

Walking around the room rejoicing and praising the Lord, we were all on a mountaintop of ecstasy. Then I had to be the joy-killer.

There came over me such a sense of our inconsistency, that I had to speak of it.

"What kind of missionaries are we?" I asked. "We have gone through a week of heart-searching, humbling ourselves before each other and before the Lord, in order that we might be altogether right with Him, so that He could hear our prayers and heal the physical eye of one of our own number. Yet we have never gone to this much self-negation for preparation to pray for the opening of the spiritual eyes of the Chinese to whom we have been sent." Our mountaintop of ecstasy suddenly became a valley of humiliation. We all went to our knees in contrite confession for having been so careless as to have gone along supposing that we were right with the Lord, while holding all kinds of attitudes which could have kept the Lord's living water from flowing through us to the Chinese.

Within a few weeks we were able to return to our various posts of work. Everyone went back teaching and preaching the tragedy of sin in the life and heart of a Christian. First our preachers and Bible women were convicted of sin, and then the teachers in our mission schools and other church leaders began to see themselves.

One evening as I went into the schoolyard, one of the Chinese teachers asked to see me. When we went into my office and I started to light the lamp, she said, "Please do not make a light. I cannot look into your face and make this confession!" Sitting there in the dark, she suggested that she bring her high school diploma back to me because she had cheated on one of her examinations. Knowing that the Lord was dealing with her, I had to tell her to bring the diploma back. I would not be willing for her to keep it under those conditions with my name on it.

I kept the diploma with my precious things until the Japanese occupied my house and relieved me of all my valuables and invaluables.

Later, that teacher, who had gotten right with the Lord at such a price, was able to hear the call of the Lord to other work. She resigned from the school, attended our North China seminary for three years, and became one of our most effective Bible teachers.

The pastor of our city church remarked that he had been like a fireplace with wood all laid but no match struck. When he got all known sin out of his heart and let the Lord reveal to him the unknown, the fire blazed.

Some of the missionaries who were refugeeing in Tsingtau came in contact with one who was preaching on the "Fullness of the Holy Spirit." Pearl Caldwell began in earnest heart-searching and deep humility to seek all that the Lord had for her, and was literally filled to overflowing. When she returned to Pingtu she began majoring in her teaching on the *power of the Holy Spirit* as shown in the Acts of the Apostles, and soon the preachers on the Pingtu field began to hunger for what they saw in her.

Miss Marie Monsen

Let every thing that hath breath praise the LORD
(Ps. 150:6).

After the healing of Mrs. Culpepper's eyes, the missionaries of Hwanghsien recommended Miss Monsen to their city church for a two-week meeting. The Chinese church invited her for the following spring, without knowing anything of her message or of her methods. They did not want to miss anything which the missionaries thought would be a blessing.

When Miss Monsen was packing to go from Tientsin over to the port of Hwanghsien, the Holy Spirit kept suggesting to her that she should buy some apples. The voyage over was only one night, but since the voice was insistent, she bought a basket of apples, thinking that someone might be sick and need them. She also took a box of chocolates, which someone had sent to her for Christmas.

Her steamer was taken over by twenty pirates, and for days she had an apple a day and a few chocolates. By the time the chocolates were eaten, food came from another source: the second mate, who had a box of eggs hidden in Miss Monsen's compartment, began sharing these with her. At two o'clock in the morning, he would slip four of the eggs down to the galley, boil two for himself and two for her, then sneak them back to her while the pirates were asleep.

When Miss Monsen returned thanks, she asked the Lord to make the eggs take the place of meat, bread, vegetables, and every vitamin that she needed. She would not eat the food served to her by the pirates since it all was stolen loot.

She not only had food to eat, but Miss Monsen virtually became the captain of the ship. Of the two hundred passengers and thirty-five crew members she was the only one who was not put into the hold. Her small compartment had only a wooden shelf for a bed. She had taken no bedding, but as she sat on her "shelf" and quoted the promises of God, it became her "throne." She gave orders to the pirate chief to give air to the passengers below, to keep the deck washed clean, and to be responsible for seeing that the dozen women passengers were not molested.

Time and time again the pirates planned to take her off the steamer and hold her for ransom. She calmly quoted the Lord's promises and trusted Him not to let her be taken off.

Through the entire province of Shantung her testimony spread as to how the Lord kept her heart and mind in peace, provided the necessary food, and saved her from harm at the hands of the wicked opium fiends. As a result, all of the churches of the province wanted her to come for meetings.

During the first years of her missionary career, Miss Monsen's main work was that of teaching the Bible to church members. After fourteen years of this work, she reached the conclusion that most of the members had been convinced of the truth in their minds, without having been born of the Spirit. She would quietly say, "Dead people cannot eat!"

Believing that "the love of Calvary could not be appreciated until the people had heard the thunder of Sinai," it became her custom, at one service a day, to hold up God's holy standard for man. At the other daily service, she dealt with specific sins. The time between the two services she spent in prayer for the Holy Spirit to use the Word to bring conviction for sin to the hearts of her hearers.

Standing by the church door at the close of the services, she would take the hand of each one and look straight into his eye and ask, "Have you been born of the Spirit?" If he answered in the affirmative, the next question would be, "What evidence do you have of the new birth?" When the evidence was not clear, her next statement would be, "I'm uneasy about you. Ask the Lord to show you your position before Him."

We missionaries never gave comfort to anyone who became uneasy. We urged him to go make confession, and restitution where necessary, and keep praying for the Holy Spirit to continue to reveal sin.

In those days we never invited people to go forward confessing Christ as their Savior. All of them would have gone to keep the speaker from "losing face." We dealt with them individually until they were clearly saved. Then they were assigned a class to study the meaning of church membership. Each one had an opportunity to give his testimony to the church group before being received for baptism.

It was a moving experience to see people come to us who could neither eat nor sleep nor hold their heads up because of the burden of sin. Release came when they had put their sin on Christ and made peace with everyone to whom confession was due. When Christ had been enthroned in the heart, abounding joy came.

After the meeting in Laichowfu, I went with Miss Monsen and others to Laiyang, where we had no missionaries at that time. We took the Larsons' cook to cook for the party. He had formerly been a warmhearted church member and of his own accord had conducted a Bible class for other servants.

During the meeting at Laichowfu he had become so convicted that he had no peace for days. One morning at six o'clock he appeared at my door. He had not gone to bed all night, so burdened had he been over his sins. He begged me to forgive him for having used his unclean lips to say things about me that were not true. I suggested to him that the people to whom he had said them perhaps didn't know that they were not true, so it might be well for him to go to them and make confession.

With the tears streaming, he told me what a hypocrite he had been, how blind to the sin of his own heart and life! He went to the Larsons, confessing that he had made money buying food for them on the market. He had been pocketing the difference between the market price quoted to the Larsons and the price he had actually paid. He did not know exactly how much he had stolen in that way, but offered to work two months without wages, believing that that would cover it. They agreed, since they knew the Lord was dealing with him.

The next time I saw him, after he left my home, he was in a church service. As I walked down the aisle, I was often guilty of peeping over the screen that separated the men from the women. Before taking my seat, I wanted to know how many men we had at church. This time I could see only half of that cook's face, and lo! it looked like that of an angel!

When Miss Monsen asked someone who was altogether right with God to lead in prayer, that cook arose and started off by saying, "Lord, I thank You that I am no longer I."

The missionaries went by car to Laiyang, the home town of this cook. There was not room in the car for him so he rode his bicycle and arrived the next day. The first meeting of the series was nearly over when he arrived. When Miss Monsen again asked for a brother who was right with God to lead in prayer, the cook arose and sent up such a volume of praise to the Lord that his old friends gathered around him after the service wanting to know how such a change had come over him. It was that way after each meeting. I would go on home and start the meal on that coal cookstove, knowing that the cook was worth more to those people than I could be.

Mr. Chow, an evangelist on that field, became uneasy about his own relationship to the Lord. After every service he would come to me, wanting some evidence that he was a saved man. I wanted him to produce the evidence. The last day I asked, "Mr. Chow, what are you trusting in for salvation?" Straightening himself up, he replied, "You need not tell me that after I have walked for twenty-five years over this country telling people about the Savior, the Lord is going to turn me away from heaven's gate!" My reply was, "If that is what you are trusting in, you most certainly will be turned away!"

Miss Monsen had the custom of awaking at 2:00 A.M. to pray for the churches where she had led meetings, presenting to the Lord those who had been blessed and others who had heard the message. As she expressed it, she prayed "that those who had had the sword thrust into their hearts would have no peace until they got right with the Lord." She brought Mr. Chow to the Lord daily, and others of us who knew of his conviction prayed with her for him.

In November a year later, Mr. Larson was back in Laiyang to lead the annual workers' conference when all the preachers and Bible women from the surrounding villages gathered for a week of planning, inspiration, and Bible teaching. Mr. Larson longed for his co-workers and himself to be filled with the Holy Spirit; that was the theme of his devotional at each session.

As the days went by, that hunger increased. When the meeting closed on Wednesday night, he announced that he would remain in the church for prayer and invited others to join him. A few remained but most went to their rooms and retired.

Brother Li, pastor of the church, stayed for prayer. He could not sing at any time and for several days had been suffering with laryngitis, unable to speak above a whisper. About midnight he arose from his knees and began singing in a clear, beautiful voice. With that, Mr. Larson jumped up and exclaimed, "The Holy Spirit has come!" Suddenly both men were knocked to the floor as though struck by an electric bolt.

In a few minutes they were loudly praising the Lord while others were crying to Him for mercy. The sleeping ones were aroused and rushed to the church, falling upon their knees in confession of their sins, coldness, and lack of power of the Holy Spirit in their lives. Loud hallelujahs and cries for mercy rang out through the rest of the night.

Some were convinced of not having been saved, but by daylight they had entered into the joy of the Lord. Among these was Mr. Chow, the evangelist, for whom many had been praying. He refused to take a salary for further preaching, saying that he had already accepted too much for preaching without having known the Lord or the power of the Spirit. Now and then after that he had to sell a few acres of land to get money to support his family.

Mr. Larson went back to his home in Laichowfu just in time for the workers' conference of that section. His burning testimony so moved the people that they continued in meetings through Christmas. Chinese leaders as well as missionaries so died to themselves that the Holy Spirit gloriously filled them.

In January during the Chinese New Year's vacation time, a small group of church workers and missionaries in Hwanghsien invited Mr. Larson to lead a week's prayer meeting. One by one, those attending were brought low before the Lord as the Spirit revealed what He wanted to prune from their hearts and lives. He could not fill them until they were emptied of self, and that act had to be performed by each one.

What joy the filling of the Holy Spirit brought! Martha Li, wife of one of the evangelists, walked up on the platform to give a testimony. She stood there for about two hours with the light of heaven on her face, pouring out praise to the Lord, using the words of the Psalms.

It was a humbling experience when missionaries had to confess to Chinese their lack of love and patience. When missionary and Chinese were brought low together, there was no longer any East or West.

Dr. Glass, Dr. Culpepper, Dr. Life, and Dr. Abernathy were set on fire by the Holy Spirit. They, with Mr. Larson, were invited to church after church in Shantung, where the Lord worked mightily. They then moved into Honan Province, where a great reviving began in the churches.

Every church in Shantung felt the effects of the revival. Before it came, the attendance at our North China seminary had gotten down to three and a half students. Not that we had half a man, but one student was only half-time. The next year after the revival swept over the province, the junior college building had to be taken over for the seminary. Every year afterwards, as long as missionaries remained, there were 150 students—all that the building could accommodate—with a waiting list in every church.

While it was hard on some leaders to hear their converts declare that they had not been saved when they had previously joined the church, all rejoiced together that the Lord had done the exceeding abundant, beyond anything that we had known to ask or think. How we thrilled over seeing Christians come for an associational meeting and sit all night praising the Lord together!

Little Nina Lide ran upstairs one day and said to her mother, "Daddy is down in his study just a 'Halleluin!'"

We came to know something of what Isaac Watts meant when he prayed, "O for a thousand tongues to sing my great Redeemer's praise."

But it was not just the song of praise which thrilled everyone. When a testimony would be taken to the heart of the lost by the Holy Spirit, causing that one to break down and weep over his or her sin, we knew that we were in the midst of a mighty work of God.

Many opium fiends were saved and delivered from the binding habit. Quarreling women were transformed into loving, motherly saints, and many sick were healed and demons cast out.

Perhaps most important of all was the transformation of our Chinese preachers. When the Holy Spirit had filled them, it was amazing how the Word of God was revealed to them. Seminary teachers marveled at the riches which the poorly educated brought forth.

Many farmers became preachers. During the winter months, when unable to work because of frozen ground, they went two by two throughout sections where there were no churches, just telling what they knew of the living Lord. So many people professed to be saved that Dr. Glass, president of the seminary, and Pastor Kwan, president of the North China Baptist Convention, made a tour through a number of villages to see about forming churches of the believers and sending some full-time preachers to them. The two men were sometimes kept up all night just reading the Word of God to the new converts.

One Chinese woman who did not know one Chinese character (word) from another, lived in such close fellowship with the Lord that she would know when He wanted to speak to her. She would go into her bedroom and sit quietly and ask, "What is it, Lord?" The Holy Spirit would then give her a chorus of praise with a tune. When she had been given three hundred of these, a preacher visited her village and wrote them down—both words and tune—from hearing her sing them. They were printed and sung all over North China.

A Great Surprise

Marvel not that I said unto thee, Ye must be born again
(John 3:7).

After Lucy Wright had been a faithful, hard-working missionary nurse for nine years, I received, on an October day, a most surprising letter from her. She was so filled with the joy of the Lord that she had to share the good news with me. The day before, she had been born into the family of God!

Lucy was a most lovable, charming person, guarded in her remarks about others, easy to live with, and in every respect delightful. However, something which I had not been able to understand was that I had not had the oneness of spirit with her that I did with other missionaries. There seemed a barrier between us.

Of course, I rejoiced that Lucy was happy in the Lord but did not agree with her that she had just been saved. I surmised that her new uplift from the Lord was so wonderful that she was underestimating all of her former experiences with Him. In my reply to her letter I avoided the terms, "born again" and "saved," only expressing my joy that she had been so blessed and was rejoicing in the Lord.

Our mission stations were sixty miles apart, which meant that I saw Lucy only once a year at our mission meeting. At that time all of the single women got kissed! The following summer when I arrived in Chefoo for mission meeting and all the ladies came out to meet me with that annual greeting, Lucy among them, that "wall" between Lucy and me was gone. I felt the same spiritual kinship with her that I did with the others.

At five o'clock the first afternoon of mission meeting, I asked Lucy Wright to go with me for a walk. My first sentence to her was, "Lucy, tell me why you thought that you had not been saved until last October?" She told me the following experience.

The autumn before, when Miss Monsen was in Lucy's station leading meetings, Miss Monsen had requested all of the missionaries to ask each person whom they met whether or not he or she had been born again. If they got an answer in the affirmative, they were to ask what evidence they had of the second birth. Lucy, wanting to cooperate, tried to ask that question of one woman after the morning meeting.

To her amazement, as she asked this question she had a strangling feeling and the suggestion, "You are not born again yourself. How dare you ask that question of another?" Although she tried again and again through the day, that question stuck in her throat before each person.

In utter amazement she asked herself, "What does this mean? Can it be that I myself have not been born of the Spirit?" So uneasy did she become that for two days she sought assurance in her former works of churchgoing, Bible study, tithing, singing, Sunday observance, and so on. But all to no avail. Then the third night she got on her knees alone before the Lord and prayed, "Lord, show me my condition before Thee!" The faithful Lord, knowing the sincerity of her soul, brought before her the sins of a lifetime and revealed something of the exceeding sinfulness of her own heart.

For the first time, Lucy saw the meaning of Calvary. When she had taken refuge in the death of Christ, she became conscious of a cleansing and was filled with the joy of the Lord. For the first time, she came into personal relationship with God.

As Lucy shared with me some of the attitudes of her past, I knew that she could not formerly have been a child of God. When she was twelve years old, the other girls of her Sunday school class joined the church. They and the teacher wanted

Lucy to join. She did so, partly to please them and partly because she thought that being baptized would make her a Christian.

When I asked why she went to the mission field, she stated that it was a result of having felt that service was what God expected of Christians. Since her father and younger brother were physicians and surgeons, her choice of nursing as a profession seemed the natural thing to do.

In church and college she heard of the need for missionaries in China. Through her nurses' graduation sermon, she felt God was leading her to go there as a nurse. The subject was "China's Need for Christian Nurses"; the text: "Who knoweth whether thou art come to the kingdom for such a time as this?" The leading was clear, and after more than a year's resisting it, she gave in at a student volunteer meeting.

What a soul-winner Lucy Wright became after having been born of the Spirit!

CHAPTER THREE

Continuing Revival

Revival fires continued to burn. Earnest prayer and witnessing, with daily confession of sin, kept missionaries and Chinese Christians aglow. The Lord sent other co-workers whom He used to fan the fires of holy zeal into a mighty flame.

Dr. John Sung

If ye shall ask . . . I will do
(John 14:14).

Dr. Sung, who became known as the Billy Sunday of China, was the oldest of twelve children. His father was a preacher and his mother was a woman of prayer, both products of old-time Methodist mission work.

When John Sung finished high school he was sent to the United States to a state university to study. His father hoped that John would prepare to teach and later help send the other brothers and sisters to the United States to study.

During his first year in America John was faithful in church attendance and was very interested in the YMCA work on the campus. In his second year he was made president of the college YMCA and was active in all forms of Christian work. But in his third year he lost interest in his church and even refused to serve when again elected president of the YMCA.

In his fourth year John seldom went to the YMCA meetings and never attended church on Sunday. After he had studied three more years under "American heathens," he did not believe anything that his parents had taught him.

In the meantime, the brother next to John came to the same university. In true "big brother" style, John made him black his shoes, do his laundry, and act as servant in general.

When John received the Doctor of Philosophy degree and became "Dr. Sung," he was ready to return to teach in the University of Peking. Then he became disturbed indeed over having departed from all that his godly parents believed. How could he face them? The nearer the time came to go back, the more miserable he became. Finally he decided to remain in the United States a year longer and attend a seminary. From his own study of the Bible he would decide whether his parents and the missionaries were right, or his university professors.

Dr. Sung chose what he supposed to be the best theological seminary in America, but to his amazement he soon found that his professors, though brilliant men and delightful teachers, did not accept the Bible as the Word of God and a true record of God's dealings with man. In spite of this shock, he continued his study with deep interest, and evidently his teachers delighted in the brilliant student. One of them assigned him a seat in the choir of the church which he pastored (even though Dr. Sung could not sing), so he would be able to hear the sermon without waiting in a long line to get only standing room.

That trained scientific mind had not been studying the Bible many months until he saw that Jesus Christ was either God come in the flesh to die for man's sin, or He was the greatest impostor that the world had ever known.

The more clearly he saw the truth, the more miserable he became over his own sin and failure in the sight of a holy God. One day when he could stand the burden no longer, he got on his knees in his room and prayed, "Lord, I believe that you are God come in the flesh, and You came to die for my sins! I put my sins and my sinful self upon you! Come into my heart and be my Lord!" The Lord did just what he had asked Him to do, and Dr. Sung jumped up and went running down the hall, praising the Lord and telling the fellows that he had been saved.

When he went to class praising the Lord, teachers were as amazed as fellow students had been. Dr. Sung became so heartbroken over both students and faculty that he could only plead with them to turn to the Savior. They thought that he had lost his mind and had him sent to an insane asylum!

He would say to the psychiatrist, "I am not crazy! I have just been reborn. My soul which has been in misery is filled with the joy of the Lord and I cannot but praise Him!" But since the faculty of the seminary had sent Dr. Sung there, the psychiatrist did not release him, although they found no reason for his being kept.

He spent 193 days in the institution, just reading the Bible all day long. He was soon convinced that what China most needed was not science teachers but preachers of the gospel, and that he must give his life to telling people about his Savior.

Some furloughed missionaries from Korea heard of Dr. Sung and requested his release, promising to return him to the institution upon any sign of insanity.

Finally he was on his way back to China. Fearing that his family would overpersuade him to teach, he got out his diplomas and threw them into the Pacific Ocean. He would have no evidence that he had passed his examinations and was qualified to be a teacher.

Upon reaching his country, he first went home to praise the Lord with his parents, and then arranged to marry the girl to whom he had been engaged since childhood. He allied himself with the Bethel Bible School of Shanghai and became the school's field evangelist. He was joined by six of the Bible School graduates, who formed the "Bethel Band," which went all over China preaching and singing the gospel.

The Chinese high regard for education led the best-educated people to hear Dr. Sung. The fact that his Ph.D. was in science especially attracted the educated, for they had been under the impression that science and the Bible did not agree. They not only came, but, due to the fascinating way that sin and the Savior were presented in the power of the Holy Spirit, they came forward confessing their sin and their desire for Christ. All the space at the front of the building and down the aisles was filled with the kneeling, whose tears of repentance left wet spots on the floor.

With Dr. Sung, following Christ was not made easy. Wrongs must be made right insofar as possible. After a two-week campaign in Peking, twenty thousand dollars were paid back on old debts or wrongfully gained money.

In our Shantung churches so many debts were so old that the person to whom the money was due was either not living or could not be located. When the "conscience money" was brought to the churches, the brethren announced that the Lord did not want that kind of money in His treasury. It was used to create a fund for beggars.

One day Dr. Glass was kneeling near the long-time treasurer of the large city church at a prayer meeting. Suddenly the treasurer cried out, "Lord, have mercy on me! I've stolen! I'm a thief! I have stolen from God!"

In astonishment Dr. Glass said to himself, "Not you, Brother Wang; surely not you! All these years you have been such a trustworthy, devoted deacon, faithful trustee of the seminary, and upright Christian gentleman. You just could not have taken money from the church treasury!"

After a while Brother Wang got control of himself enough to say, "I have not paid my tithe to the Lord! According to His Word, I have stolen it from Him!"

No doubt Brother Wang had thought himself a liberal giver. He was not content to turn over a new leaf and begin tithing. He had an old debt which he wanted paid. He would pay any price in order to be altogether right with God.

Fortunately, Chinese keep accurate household and personal accounts. Brother Wang counted up his tithe from the time he became a Christian, more than twenty years before, subtracted from it the total amount contributed to the church, and had left such a debt that he had to sell some land in order to pay it. What a flame he became for the Lord after getting altogether right with Him!

Dr. C. W. Pruitt said of Dr. Sung, "No living man has given up more for the gospel!"

With him, every moment besides that necessary for personal care was spent preaching, praying, preparing his messages, or engaging in personal interviews. Little interest was shown in any subject except as it related to his Lord. Then he was all attention.

Before Dr. Sung's meetings in Tsining, the missionaries had been praying for Dr. Hou, who had been educated in a mission school. He not only had quit going to church, but also had been ridiculing those who did go.

From the first service, Dr. Hou was there to hear the scientist. We missionaries watched his face day by day, as first he showed interest, then concern, and, after a few more days, misery. Imagine our thrill as we saw him go down the aisle and get on his knees, acknowledging himself a lost sinner in need of the Savior.

At the close of the meetings, he volunteered to be the leader of one of the twenty-four evangelistic bands which had been organized. He became concerned about a church six miles from the city. Not having a leader, the members had grown so cold that not only would no one lead services, but they had quit meeting together. They had even stored their harvested crops in the little church building.

Dr. Hou left his drugstore and clinic and, with the pastor of the city church and a Spirit-filled church member, went out to the little church to stay a few days. The people came to hear them.

Dr. Hou led the first service, giving his personal testimony to the change the Lord had wrought in his heart. For three days the three men testified, prayed, and preached until late at night, longing for the Holy Spirit to come in transforming power. By the last day people had become so heart-hungry for the gospel that they were willing to come by way of repentance and confession of sin, and more people who were dead in sin were brought to life.

That new group formed a witnessing band of fifteen members. Without a preacher, church services were started again and a Bible class was held each evening where twenty met to study.

Another interesting convert during Dr. Sung's meeting in my church was a young teacher who was the twenty-seventh child of his mother. She said that she would have had a real family, had not her husband died when number twenty-seven was a baby. I supposed that it was just as well that the first twenty-five did not live, since the boy and girl who were left, came near starving.

The boy was sent to a mission school and one day, while standing to recite, fainted. Upon investigation, the teacher found that he had not had a bite to eat in three days. He was such a bright and promising student that a missionary paid his expenses through high school and university. While at the university, he gave up his belief in Christianity.

When we saw him go forward and kneel in response to Dr. Sung's message, we knew that another miracle was taking place.

When prayer centered on another doctor, we expected something to happen again, even though he was a slave to a bad disposition, cigarettes, and opium. After a few days of hearing the gospel he was saved and instantly delivered from every unholy habit. His testimony and his daily presence at the evening Bible class thrilled us for months, and when he became a deacon and one of our strongest leaders, we were filled with praise to our God.

Recognizing Dr. Sung to be a man of power in prayer, Christians with physical ills began coming to him for prayer for healing. He gave the Word of God and prayed for their healing, only after he was convinced that they wanted health in order to serve the Lord more effectively. The Lord honored the prayer of faith and many were thus healed.

Joseph, son of Deacon Chiang, developed tuberculosis of the bone in a lower limb, when six or seven years old. He spent years in the children's ward of the mission hospital in Laichowfu, where he was loved and tenderly cared for by Dr. Jeannette Beall and Alda Grayson, superintendent of nurses, and their staff.

When Joseph was about fourteen, Dr. Sung was leading meetings in Pingtu. Sinners were turning to the Lord, and saints were seeing the Lord work wonders.

Mr. Chiang, Joseph's father, wrote a letter to Dr. Sung describing Joseph's condition and asking prayer for his healing. Dr. Sung read the letter to that congregation, who were in tune with the Lord. Then, laying the letter on the lectern, he put his hand on it and said, "We will all now pray in unison for the Lord to heal Joseph."

A volume of sincere prayer went up to the throne from cleansed hearts. Joseph began improving immediately; little pieces of bone worked their way out through the flesh and skin. Within another year he was working on the farm.

During the Pingtu meetings, a number of people wanting to be healed went, or were carried, to the home of the missionaries, Mr. and Mrs. Earl Parker, where Dr. Sung was staying. Among these was Mrs. Loh Kin T'ang, who had not walked since the birth of her son eighteen years previously. She was carried into the home by two men and seated on the floor. Dr. Sung kneeled down and, after praying, anointed her with olive oil. Then he commanded her in the name of Jesus Christ to rise up and walk!

Mrs. Loh got up immediately, stood for a moment, and then walked out of the home, down two sets of stone steps to the street, and upgrade for a distance of a hundred yards to the church. The song and praise portion of the service had begun.

Mrs. Loh walked up on the platform and praised the Lord for having healed her.

Her husband was an English teacher in a mission school in Chefoo. When their son wrote his father of the mother's healing, every sentence of the letter included "Praise the Lord!" or "Hallelujah!"

The father was disturbed indeed. He reasoned, "This just cannot be true. My wife has spent months in the mission hospital in Pingtu, and Dr. Yocum has told me that she will never walk! My son is going off on a religious tangent!"

After another day or two, he became so concerned that he asked for a leave of absence for a week to go home and straighten out the family. The donkey-back travel would require four days to go and return, and he would need two days at home.

Chinese homes have a brick or mud wall around their yards for privacy and for protection of what they have inside. The double doors for the gate are closed from the inside with two wooden bars.

When Mr. Loh reached his gate he heard someone sweeping the yard. He called out, and the bars were slipped aside and the two doors pulled open. There stood his wife. Mr. Loh rushed inside, closed the gates behind him, and fell down on his face, confessing his sin of unbelief and coldness toward the Lord. He got up saying, "Praise the Lord! Hallelujah!" in every other sentence.

Father, mother, and son—what evangels they became, going from house to house and village to village, just bragging on Jesus! Mr. Loh gave up teaching and did full-time village evangelistic work with Pearl Caldwell and Bonnie Ray.

Soon after the healing of Mrs. Loh, Mr. Parker and Miss Caldwell were leading meetings in her home village. Mrs. Loh walked a mile to witness to Mrs. K'iao, who had not walked for twenty-eight years. After hearing what the living Lord had done for Mrs. Loh, Mrs. K'iao wanted to go to church. Expecting to go home walking, she had a pair of shoes made.

Her son carried her on his back and put her on a chair in the aisle of the crowded women's wing of the church. Men and women did not sit in the same room. The women from their wing had a side view of the preacher, without being seen by the men who sat in the main part of the church facing the speaker.

The opening part of the service took plenty of time, and Brother Parker had prepared a good message and was revived in his soul. Mrs. K'iao, having gone there to be prayed for, became impatient and kept asking, "Why doesn't he hush and let them pray for me?" Finally some of the women just knelt around her and prayed in an undertone. Since non-Christian women often talk at church, Brother Parker, accustomed to the noise, just faced the men and went on with his sermon.

When the Lord touched Mrs. K'iao's body, she got up and started home, with the shouting women following her. Some of the brethren went out to quiet them down, only to join in the loud "Hallelujahs," and before the good sermon was finished, the whole congregation—including the preacher—were in the yard and street shouting praises to God.

Mrs. K'iao walked down the main street of her village a quarter of a mile to her home, and anywhere else afterwards that she wanted to go. She was seventy-two at that time.

As in the days when Lazarus came back to life, people—including missionaries—traveled long distances just to see "Mother K'iao." Only the Lord knows how many unsaved were convinced of the truth of our living Lord and turned to Him as a result of that miracle.

After a few more years Dr. Sung began in each of his campaigns to have a healing service for all who wanted to attend. Hundreds of people at these services either went or were carried down the aisle and passed by him for his prayer for healing. Without a chance to learn their spiritual state, he prayed for each to be physically healed.

Alas, the weakness of human nature! Some enlarged their infirmity in every testimony, until minor ills had become incurable diseases. Others loudly praised Dr. Sung for his power to heal. While Dr. Sung himself would have been the last to have stolen the Lord's glory, others in their enthusiasm talked of the instrument instead of the Lord Himself, and our Lord would not stand for that. He will not give His glory to another.

While Dr. Sung was in his prime, he developed intestinal tuberculosis. In spite of his own prayers and those of his many friends, he suffered agony for a number of years and died when only forty-three.

Could Dr. Sung's closing years explain why we do not now see more people definitely healed in answer to prayer?

The New Secretary Came

Which doeth great things . . . and wonders without number
(Job 9:10).

When revival fires had been burning in North China long enough to stir the devil into a rage, the new secretary of the Foreign Mission Board, Dr. Charles E. Maddry, came for a visit. He was accompanied by Dr. J. B. Weatherspoon, then professor of homiletics at Southern Baptist Theological Seminary. Dr. J. T. Williams, of Shanghai, went with them over China as interpreter.

Tsining was the first city in North China to be visited. They were met at the railway station twenty miles away, by Frank Connely in his car. A few hours' association with Dr. Connely would convince anyone that he was no religious fanatic.

At the supper table Dr. Maddry remarked in jest, "I hear that Katie Murray is casting out demons in the name of the Lord over in Honan Province!" I calmly replied, "Yes, we often come in contact with demon-possessed people among the Chinese. The Lord used Dr. Connely to cast out one here last Sunday!"

All eyes were on the man at the head of the table, who in a humble manner related the following:

Brother Chang, a church member from a village a few miles away, and Brother Liu, a new convert, had come to church bringing a stranger who could not speak. Brother Chang asked the pastor to request the brethren to remain after the services and pray the dumb devil out of the neighbor whom he had brought. Some of the loudest testifiers picked up their hats and went grinning toward the door as if to say, "That is too much for me."

The pastor, one old church member, and Dr. Connely went to the prayer room with the three men and got on their knees.

After each had prayed, they asked the dumb man to say, "Praise the Lord." Though trying his best, he could not get his lips open. For a week he had been in that condition, having been seized suddenly.

After having prayed for some time with the same result, Dr. Connely turned to the man and, with the voice of authority, said, "In the name of the Lord Jesus Christ, I command you dumb devil to come out of this man!" Immediately the man opened his mouth and started talking.

I then told our American visitors of how Mr. Liu, the new Christian of the group, had a few weeks previously been brought to the city by Brother Chang with the report that he was possessed by a demon that had absolute control over him. Sometimes it threw him into the water and sometimes into the fire, or anywhere else.

I was the only missionary there at the time. The Chinese pastor came asking me to go with him to lay hands on Mr. Liu and pray the devil out. I told him that I would go and pray, but that I would not lay hands on him since Jesus never put His hands on demon-possessed people. As a result of the praying, Mr. Liu was completely delivered, which led to his becoming a Christian.

Mrs. Connely told the guests of numbers of sick people who had been healed in answer to prayer.

The visitors heard similar experiences related at each mission station and listened to glowing testimonies of those who had been delivered from bondage to opium, cigarettes, wine, adultery, hatred, covetousness, selfishness, and fear of evil spirits. They saw crowds packing the churches to hear the gospel; they heard the footsteps of people making their way to the churches long before daylight, assembling for the six o'clock Bible study and prayer together; and they were told how the gospel was being carried to outlying sections of the province by "hot-hearted" laymen.

After Dr. Maddry had completed his visit of all the mission work, he held a conference in Shanghai of representatives from all the mission groups. At that conference he stated that, when traveling through Shantung and Honan provinces, he had felt that he was reliving the Acts of the Apostles.

CHAPTER FOUR

Alone upon the Promise

During the Depression of 1932, the executive secretary of the Foreign Mission Board, Dr. T. B. Ray, wrote a similar letter to each of thirty-five missionaries on furlough, requesting each to look for other work until times got better. Dr. Ray stated that the Board was receiving only enough money to keep on the field those missionaries who were still there. What a blow!

A New Leading

There is no want to them that fear him
(Ps. 34:9).

When I received Dr. Ray's letter, I realized that I did not have to return to China just because I had been there for fourteen years. Neither did the fact that the Board could not support me determine that I should *not* go back. Recalling how Judah's good king, Hezekiah, took his unpleasant letter to the Temple and spread it before the Lord, I decided to do likewise.

Five minutes' walk from my home was a little Methodist church. It was kept open at night for men to go in and sleep when traveling to and fro looking for work. One morning as soon as it was light enough for the men to be gone, I arrived at the church. Choosing a suitable prayer place, I began to seek the Lord's will. After two months of daily meeting the Lord there, I knew in my heart that He wanted me to return to China.

Then came the question: How would I be able to go? In my Old Testament daily reading I had reached Isaiah. While turning the pages, I saw unfamiliar words, even though they were not underscored:

> I will go before thee, and make the crooked places straight: I will break in pieces the gates of brass, and cut in sunder the bars of iron: and I will give thee the treasures of darkness, and hidden riches of secret places, that thou mayest know that I, the LORD, which call thee by thy name, am the God of Israel" (45:2–3).

"Thank you, Lord!" my heart responded. "The 'how' is the Lord's concern. The riches are in secret. Since He knows, that is sufficient."

I had to be willing to give up the privilege of working under our Board with a group of missionaries who, to me, were the Lord's choicest. They had their tried-and-proven mission policy, and, while advising, they left each to respect the Holy Spirit as final guide.

I had friends who had gone out as independent missionaries because of failure to come up to our Board's regulations in either health or educational requirements. While I appreciated the contribution which they were making to the cause of Christ in China, I would never have chosen to be one of them. But I had to get willing to go that way, or even under some other board.

I wrote a letter to the secretary of the Foreign Mission Board, asking for the privilege of returning to China to work with the same relationship to the Board, to the missionaries on the field, and to the Chinese Baptist Convention as I had formerly. The only difference now would be that I would not receive funds from the Board for any purpose whatever. I assured Dr. Ray that I would make no appeal to any church for funds. I asked for the privilege of working without Board support until it could take me on again. And if I could never again be supported by the Board, I would in no way hold the Board responsible. With this request I began to pray earnestly indeed! If the Lord wanted me to remain with the Board, He would move Dr. Ray's heart to agree to that.

The afternoon after my letter was mailed to Dr. Ray, a friend from Augusta Road Baptist Church, Greenville, South Carolina, Mrs. C. E. Hatch, drove over to my home. She came to tell me that the Lord had revealed to her that I was to return to China. She said that at a prayer service the night before, she had been given the engagement ring of a widow, and other gifts to help send me back. She wanted to be my secretary, receiving and forwarding any funds that came in.

Dr. Ray agreed to my returning on the terms I suggested. He also offered to secure second-class passage on an American steamer across the Pacific at a missionary discount, for about $300. When I had that amount and enough to cross the continent in a day coach, with sufficient funds for a railroad ticket from Shanghai to North China, I praised the Lord indeed. By the time to purchase my ticket, the Sunday school of one of the churches in Spartanburg, South Carolina, had sent the amount needed for a Pullman. A retired missionary in Los Angeles secured passage for me on a Danish freighter to Shanghai for $112, thus effecting a saving of nearly $200 over the original estimate for ocean travel.

Earlier in the summer I had been notified that the girls' school in East Shantung, where I had formerly worked, had been reduced, for lack of funds, to an eight-grade school. The mission decided to transfer me to the western part of the province to work with Martha Franks and Dr. and Mrs. Frank Connely. The only question in my mind concerning the transfer was what Frank Connely might think of my arriving to work on his field with no money for living or for my work. However, that, too, could be committed to the Lord.

Martha Franks wrote, "We need you. If you can secure passage money, come on back and live with me; and we will get along the best we can on my salary, going fifty-fifty with it."

Frank and Mary Connely, not knowing that Martha had written, wrote the following: "Come on back and live and eat with us. We will stretch two salaries to do for three and manage some way. You shall have everything that we do." In addition to this, Frank sent a check for one hundred dollars to help on my passage.

These factors enabled me to set sail with a light heart, knowing that a warm welcome awaited me, whether or not I had any visible funds. My traveling companion was Miss Alice Huey, whose passage and support was being provided by the Woman's Missionary Union of her home state, Alabama.

A group of praying friends accompanied us to the steamer in Los Angeles Harbor and, gathering in our stateroom, commended us to God and pled that we might be made a blessing to those on board. In response, the joy of heaven filled our souls. I usually suffer from seasickness, but I knew that on that voyage the Lord would either control the Pacific Ocean or me, for they had asked in faith that I be saved from seasickness.

Five nationalities made up the passenger list of twenty-seven. The ship, being Danish, had officers and crew from that country. I had not before seen such courtesy shown passengers.

For three months I had been asking the Lord to choose the steamer on which I was to return to China, and when I found myself among that number I knew that those were the people with whom my heavenly Father had placed me. Miss Huey and I began to pray for all on board and to look for opportunities to speak about our Savior.

The Lord especially laid on our hearts a lovely young Russian woman who was married to an American marine stationed in San Francisco. She was returning to Manchuria to visit her parents.

She was so full of life and fun and personal charm that it was only a few days until she was the center of interest and all aboard were calling her by her first name, Lueba. How I wanted her to know the Lord!

One cool evening as I sat alone, reveling in the beauty of a gorgeous sunset, Lueba came and nestled down beside me to keep warm. Slipping my arms into hers, I asked if she had been born from above. In quick response came one question after another, until she knew what I meant, and something new began to fill her mind.

The next day we had another long talk which revealed her heart need and, after a few days, another which showed a genuine desire to be saved. However, she was rooming with a Jewess. The roommate and another Jewess, with the latter's husband, soon had Lueba so under their influence that she feared their ridicule too much to turn to Jesus as Savior.

The Lord's Storm

O my God . . . make them afraid with thy storm
(Ps. 83:13, 15).

A few days more of prayer and trust, and our God stretched forth His mighty hand in a terrific storm. It began early on December 31. During the morning, I stood in a sheltered place in the center of the back deck and, holding to the railing with both hands, looked out on both sides at what we were passing through. Never could I have imagined anything like it! My heart thrilled with the thought of the God of such power being my own loving heavenly Father and actually living inside me!

More and more terrible the storm grew. About noon a portion of a tremendous wave struck the ship. Dishes on the dining tables went smashing to the floor. The two sideboards fell, face forward, emptying their contents of silverware and other table service. Dishes of food ready to be served slid from the galley tables and broke. Men turned white with fear, and women screamed as they were hurled across the lounge. No sooner was one such shock over than a similar one followed. Lunch was cooked three times that day. When the few who wanted to eat were finally seated in the dining saloon, another lunge caused everything to slide off the tables, while people and chairs went under the tables.

All day long and through the night, the captain remained on the bridge at the helm and the chief engineer also on duty the twenty-four hours, responding to the captain's signals for power to be turned on or off. The first officer had the responsibility of the passengers. Poor man! He looked like death itself as he went from one to another administering what today we would call tranquilizers. He saw that Miss Huey and I did not need any.

We traveled only ninety-three miles in the twenty-four hours, and that not in the direction of Shanghai.

When the first lunge of the storm came, I rushed to the lounge where most of the passengers were to see if I could help anyone. Our dear Lueba was wringing her hands and begging for someone to pray. The Jews sat helplessly around her, unable to pray or comfort. They were as frightened as she and others who were crying and praying. Well might they have been, for if one of those mountains of water, containing tens of thousands of tons, had struck the ship full force, it would have been destroyed.

I went to Lueba and, putting my arms around her, responded to her call for prayer. I was calm in the assurance that we would come to Shanghai in safety. In the name of King Jesus I lifted my voice to the God who holds the sea in His hand, and besought His comforting presence and protecting care. I assured her that we would have it until our journey's end. I was able to tell her of my own assurance that Jesus had come aboard that ship in Los Angeles, for He was living in my heart. The ship on which He traveled could not go down, not unless He willed it. She became quiet but held on to me, begging that I not leave her.

Clinging with one hand to the stationary sofa on which she lay, and holding my Bible with the other, I read to her, but loud enough so others in the lounge could also hear. I read a number of passages from God's Word, and sang one hymn after another of His peace and watchful care, until she was asleep.

Words cannot describe the feeling of my heart! It was more than assurance and rest of mind. It was joy unspeakable bubbling up and filling my soul! God the all-terrible, God the Creator and Controller of all the forces of nature, was in tenderest love surrounding me, His child. In fact, from His Word I knew that I was with Christ, so hidden in God that I was just as safe from the power of the angry billows as if I had been in heaven itself! All that I could do was to rejoice in it and praise Him.

The three Jews and other passengers sat quietly and listened while I told them of what Jesus, God's Son and our sacrifice, came to mean to me when I laid my sins on Him at the age of sixteen, and how at that very moment He was filling my heart with Himself. I told them of His promise to come a second time, and that many believed it would be soon. God spoke to those Jews, Russians, Chinese, Scots, Americans, and to the Danish first officer through my words. Afterwards, we marveled and praised the Lord when a number of people told us that the expression on Miss Huey's face and mine confirmed our testimony of peace and calmness.

My lunch was sent up to the lounge. In the presence of those "good sailors" who could not eat, I praised God, who was working a miracle in me, and ate and enjoyed it all.

By midafternoon, when Lueba had rested and had time to think things through, she asked me to go to her cabin with her and teach her how to pray. I explained how we come to God through Christ's death, and suggested that she pray in her own way. She so poured out her heart to God that if I had understood Russian, I would have learned something about praying from her.

A greater storm was raging in her heart than that outside. Her sins were separating her from the God whom she longed to know, and in anguish of soul she confessed and pled for deliverance. When she opened the door to her heart at which Christ had been knocking for several days, she was filled with His own peace. In the days that followed she quietly witnessed to passengers and officers, as occasions offered.

The remainder of the journey was made on calm seas under smiling skies. The first officer admitted only to Miss Huey and me that he had expected the whole deck floor to blow off, which would have meant death for us all.

When we arrived in Shanghai, I calmly walked into the American Oriental Bank and deposited the two hundred dollars which I had saved by taking the Danish freighter instead of an American passenger steamer. When I reached Tsining, which was my ultimate destination, I handed Frank Connely the check which he had sent to help on my passage. I was entering upon a new phase of my mission career (without Board support), but had money in the bank to live on for a few months.

I had a bedroom at the Connelys' home, and I fixed a little study out in their backyard. I took my meals with Martha Franks. Each month without fail I was able to pay my share of the expenses.

Upon my decision to return to China that time, I had told the Lord that my food would be left with Him, whether good or bad. Just about that time this verse from King Solomon's prayer leaped from the page into my heart, "Feed me with food convenient for me" (Prov. 30:8). I did not need the food of a king, neither would I be properly nourished on that of a Chinese coolie, so my food would be the right kind for me. Praise His name!

I had also told the Lord that I would not take my prayer time to beg Him to supply my needs. I would go on as formerly, praying for the Chinese for whom I was responsible and leaving my bread and butter to Him. Only once during the two years did I backslide in this matter.

In the second autumn when funds were getting low, I prayed for money. How ashamed I was later when I learned that gifts to our mission board had so increased that they were ready to appoint some new missionaries and would not do so without resuming support of the one on the field. The two Christmases before, many friends had sent money, but that Christmas only a little came. The Lord knew, even though I did not, that my salary would begin with January. The first year I had received the exact amount for living as the other missionaries, and the second year I had a little bonus of thirty dollars extra sent. The Lord knew that they were not having enough.

Friends spoke of my returning to China that time by faith. To me, it was not by faith but by the living Lord. The two years without support from a mission board were no more by faith than my former years had been, when a group of men by faith had definitely planned work for the year on the basis of what the churches had given the year before.

The difference was that the gifts went to a committee or board, who would wisely divide them according to the need of each missionary, without respect to the ability of any individual to sway an American audience with his appeal. Not only was the money divided justly, according to system, but the fact that our Board was able to get ninety-three cents of every dollar to the field, meant that more actually reached the missionary than if individuals had sent their gifts directly, with all the involvements with foreign postage and exchange.

Bank Failure

My God shall supply all your need according to
his riches in glory (Phil. 4:19).

During the following spring I saved up a little money for a few new summer dresses. I arrived in Chefoo for our annual mission meeting a few days early, and went to town the very next morning. I selected two pretty patterns of blue silk for dresses, wrote checks for them, then took them to a tailor.

The next day I went to town to buy other things, but when I started to write a check the clerk said, "We cannot accept that check."

Holding up my checkbook for him to see, I said, "This is a perfectly good American bank in Shanghai!"

He answered, "You just go round to the bank and exchange your check and bring us the cash."

Leaving my package, I confidently arrived at the bank, only to be informed that the American Oriental Bank in Shanghai had closed the day before. I not only had no money for that package, but had to make good the checks of the previous day.

However, I was not disturbed. I knew the Lord would straighten the matter out. Of course He did, and here is how. Dr. Williams, our mission treasurer in Shanghai, was ready on the appointed day of the month to leave his office for the bank to deposit a month's salary for each of the Baptist missionaries in China, when a "chance" caller came in and detained him until after banking hours. The next morning the bank did not open. So Dr. Williams arrived for our mission meeting with a briefcase full of Chinese money, a month's salary for each of the North China group.

I was able to pay up my shopping bills and get back home. The two years without a salary had so completely delivered me from money that I just committed the situation to the Lord, knowing that I would get along some way until the next month.

The next day as I started with a Bible woman to visit some of the sick Christians in a hospital two miles away, I found that I did not have a dime for ricksha fare. I had to tell her why I had changed my mind about going. It was soon noised abroad that the missionary had no money.

The next morning I found only one egg on my breakfast plate. Not having American cereals or bacon, I was accustomed to eating two. When I asked the cook the reason for such economy, he replied, "Don't you know that American bank in Shanghai has failed? You can't afford to eat two eggs!"

Brother Hoh, a wheelbarrow man who had food only when he had a load to push, and who could not even afford a wife, came in to say, "I have heard that the American bank has failed, leaving you without money, not even enough for ricksha fare. I have a friend who has a ricksha, and when you want to go anywhere just let me know and I will borrow it and take you without charge." And then, looking at me with eyes full of Christian love, he added, "And I have a dollar, and if you need it you may have it!"

One of the Presbyterian missionaries had fifteen dollars which she was saving for a new afternoon dress when she would go to the port the following summer. She sent the money to me and I "ate the dress."

At Christmastime my sister sent some dress goods in her usual gift box. Among the pieces was a beautiful pea-green all-over lace. Now that Presbyterian missionary was a blonde, and what could be prettier on her than pea-green! I gave her the material, and it made for her a dress more beautiful than anything she could have secured in Tsingtau. After using it one summer, she went on furlough and sent the dress to me. I passed it on to a redheaded missionary, for whom it must have been dyed in the beginning!

So no one had been denied in order to share with me, and I had eaten two eggs.

CHAPTER FIVE

Grace for the New Work

When I began traveling from Tsining over a five-county area, I knew that I had been promoted. My method was first to spend a week in Bible study with the organized church in the county seat. Christians would come from all directions— one or two from a village—bringing their bedding roll on their shoulders and, in their hands, a few steamed rolls and a little jar of turnips pickled in brine. To go with this food, the church would add a drink of hot millet broth. At night the men's "beds" were spread on the brick floor of the church, while the women were "bedded down" with the pastor's wife next door.

In Country Churches

As thy days, so shall thy strength be
(Deut. 33:25).

It was most satisfying to have a part in building up the country churches. We usually took a short New Testament book for study for the week, though sometimes I taught by subjects. In the evenings all attending classes went out on the streets, visiting from house to house, inviting the unsaved for an evangelistic message.

After the county-seat church meetings I went to the villages which had little chapels. Occasionally I was able to spend a week in a village not previously visited by a missionary. There, meetings were held on the threshing floor.

Sometimes I spent a month at a time out on these trips, never hearing a word of English except what I spoke to the Lord. Neither did I see a fire, though it might be December. The thirty pounds of clothes that I wore kept me warm during the day, and my warm bedding and hot water bottle were sufficient at night. But, oh, the transfer time from warm bed to cold room in the morning! I had to get up in time to have my own quiet hour with the Lord before the neighbors began to stir, since I was always on exhibition.

What an ordeal getting into those three suits of "long handles" down under the covers in the dark! Of course, the foot usually went a few times where the arm should go! And those eight stockings, how they twisted!

After breaking the ice to wash my face, I was awake quite enough to pray, so down the street I would go to the haystack—my prayer place.

I always let my Bible woman have the room for her praying, since my clothes were warmer than hers. My inner clothes were English wool, and my Chinese garments were wadded with silk floss, which was warmer than her cotton wadding. She didn't have a fur garment either.

Raking aside the frosted part of the hay, I would kneel down. Being the only one awake for miles around, I knew I would not be disturbed. As I looked up to the stars and worshiped and interceded, what "flavor," as my Chinese friends would say!

It was on one of these country trips that I met Mr. Pi (pronounced Be). He was the most highly educated man in his county. He had heard the preacher at the county-seat chapel preach a few times but was not impressed. One day when he took a journey of several miles by wheelbarrow, the pusher, Brother Ho, who did not know one Chinese character, told him about the Lord. Brother Ho had enough sense to memorize only one Bible verse, but he had been born of the Spirit, and he told his passenger what the Lord meant to him. The elegant gentleman scholar was definitely impressed and, upon reaching home, went several miles to the church at the county seat and purchased a New Testament. He read it and, in so doing, passed from death unto life. He said that others had talked to him about Jesus Christ, but the wheelbarrow man showed a personal acquaintance with Christ.

Just before the Japanese army entered Shantung, I was at Mr. Pi's church. Fearing that suffering might be in store for the Christians, I was trying to prepare them for it through a study of the First Epistle of Peter. One day during the study, Mr. Pi said in a prayer, "Lord, you know that I have read everything that Confucius and the other sages of China ever wrote, but never have I read anything that has the flavor of what that fisherman Peter wrote!"

Sometime afterwards, Mr. Pi was going by train to the capital of the province, Tsinan. He saw a fellow passenger in the coatroom whom he thought must be a Christian. He was not smoking, not restless because the train was slow and late, but was sitting in peaceful contentment. Mr. Pi thought, "If that is a Christian brother, I surely want to meet him!" But the man was handsomely dressed, and Mr. Pi was only in cotton, so he hesitated to speak. Finally, afraid that he would miss the opportunity of coming to know a brother in the Lord, Mr. Pi thought of a plan. "Hallelujah!" he exclaimed.

The gentleman turned around, extended his hand, and said, "Oh, you are a Christian! I am, too." Together they traveled, talking of the Lord, and parted to meet again.

Village Joys

Blessed be the LORD *God, . . . who only doeth wondrous things (Ps. 72:18).*

On an autumn day a man walked twenty-five miles to the city of Tsining to ask for someone to go to his village and tell his family and neighbors of the God whom we proclaimed. No one could go. After a few months he came again, but still no one was free. When he came the third time, I said, "I am going to that village."

Our camping outfit and food supplies were packed on a wheelbarrow, and Mrs. Han, a young Bible woman, and I went in rickshas. Most of the village were in the receiving line! The little boys were dressed in keeping with the weather, in their skins! Our enthusiasm for the greeting cooled a bit when we entered the living quarters provided for us by our host who had done the urging, and saw an ox tied at one end of the room.

I looked at Mrs. Han, and she looked at me and said, "If the King of glory could come down to this earth and be born in a stable for us, we can endure this room for ten days." I agreed with her that we most certainly could. We praised Christ that He had been born in our hearts and would enable us to endure the smell.

The room was eight feet wide, the regular width of a Chinese village home, and about ten feet long. To the right of the door, along the wall, was a narrow wooden bedframe, with Kaffir corn stalks laced across with string. Mrs. Han put her bedding on it. The other bed ran across the end of the room. I had my camp cot but no room to put it up, except on top of that bed.

By the wall opposite Mrs. Han's bed was a little table where we were to do our cooking and eating, and beyond that stood "Mr. Ox." He could have swished his tail in the soup. If we had had soup, it certainly would have been oxtail soup!

The dear women, never having seen an American woman, just had to linger and look at this one with white skin and blue eyes. One of them said, "She is just as pretty as an eggshell! What made her white?" Perhaps that was the time when someone said, "I know. She drinks cow's milk!"

It was eleven o'clock by the time they had all looked enough and left, and we were in bed. I was just too tired to follow my good habit of being asleep in two minutes. Too, I soon found more living creatures than just the ox in that room. What my fellow missionary Dr. Jeannette Beall calls "China's millions," were crawling from the bed below, all over me, biting as they crawled. What could I do about that number one enemy of China's poor?

For a moment I was tempted to be upset; then I prayed, "Lord, I am not here on a pleasure trip; I am here to tell these people about You. I cannot see them tomorrow unless I rest. Down in Egypt You sent the very small animals scampering at Your rebuke. Now just turn the heads of these lice in another direction and let me sleep." In a moment I was fast asleep and never saw another one in my bedding.

Never did people or ox receive such attention! At the break of dawn the feeding began. First a daughter-in-law came with a basket of finely cut wheat straw, a bowl of wheat bran, and a pan of water, and stirred with a stick which rubbed against the stone trough. When she had gone, another came to stir, and call to the former to bring what was lacking in the proper proportion, the real motive of her visit being to look at the American while she slept.

The first morning I forgave all, knowing that farmers like to get an early start to work. But when the lazy old ox stood leisurely chewing his cud all day long, I asked if he could not be fed a little later. The lady of the house replied, "An ox must be fed at the same time every day if he keep fat!" Only a day or two was he led out to plow.

With crowds following us everywhere we went, it was difficult to get a place to pray. Mrs. Han and I would put the women and children out of the room and close the crippled door, appointing someone to stand guard. We could then claim the promise of the two agreed, and pray for the Holy Spirit to use the Word we were giving, to work in the people's hearts.

That prayer time, however, did not take the place of my being alone with the Lord, where I could talk to Him out loud and depend upon the promise to the One calling upon Him in the secret place. Trying the shade of a big tree out in the field, I was surprised to be let alone. Upon returning, I found women distressed over my having ventured to a tree that "had a god in it." While pained over their superstition, I rejoiced to learn that one quiet spot was mine. Before the week was over, the Lord sent along a farmer and some little boys, who, from hearing the gospel, had lost all fear except the consequences of their own sin.

During the day Mrs. Han and I went from one courtyard to another. Usually the women were sitting on straw mats, taking apart quilts and winter clothes for washing. Where sheets are not used, this task must be done once a year. Each member of the family has his own quilt which he folds as an envelope and slides into from one end. He then takes off his wadded clothes and carefully spreads them on top of the quilt.

The poor people must take their winter clothes apart, not only for washing, but also because the top and lining are used separately and two summer garments are made from one winter one. Before cold weather the cotton will be cleaned and fluffed up and put in again. Alas, winter always catches some families before they get all the winter garments put back together.

Sitting on the mats beside the women, we explained to them their sinful state, their failure to glorify God and worship Him, and what the loving Lord had done about their sins. We told them that God's Son, also being God, had taken their sins upon Himself and taken their punishment.

Some replied to us, "I can't read; I am just a pan of starch, too stupid to understand anything new."

They could understand other things. We were amazed at their ability in running the home. The women would buy the exact amount of cloth for each child's new garment—so many feet and inches—and not half an inch would be left after the cutting. They also had sense for the most intricate gambling games.

In the evenings the group met on a big threshing floor. My kerosene lantern was hung on the mud wall, and my Bible verses, written on strips of paper with pictures and posters to illustrate them, were held in place by thorns from nearby bushes. One hour of sitting on the ground and listening was such a good start that all wanted two.

The men worked in the fields as long as they could see, and the supper had to be cooked after they got home, lest an extra wheat root would have to be burnt to keep it hot. So it was nine o'clock before we could begin our service. This late beginning, of course, made bedtime very late.

One day Mrs. Han asked our hostess if she could keep the family a little quiet in the early mornings so the missionary could get the sleep she needed. The next morning our hostess woke me up to tell me that she would keep the daughters-in-law and children quiet, "So you just go right on sleeping," she said.

The vegetable and millet market came to a village every fifth day. When it came our turn, it was Sunday and we would not buy. The next market day was in a village too far away, so we found ourselves with no food. We could buy eggs in the village, but no hens. Hens were laying, and no Chinese woman would make such a poor business deal as to sell a laying hen. We had to buy a rooster, which we could not boil tender. Mrs. Han, the Bible woman, put a piece of saltpeter in the pot, and the rooster got tender; but she got to eat him—I couldn't.

When we began to cook and eat, the flies always arrived. When it rained, more and more of them came. What better shelter for a fly than an ox stall! Big ones and little ones, black ones and green ones flew in! Not being able to sit under my tree, the only way I could get alone was to walk the little paths through the fields in the mud, where I could cry to the Lord, the God of Israel.

I said, "I am one of your spoiled children. All my life I have been accustomed to screened houses and clean food. Now, I just can't eat with those flies all over my food. Down in Egypt you had flies come and go at Your word. You are the same today and You are ready to work in the same way if my situation demands it. Now please do one of two things for me: either take the flies away, or enable me just to go ahead and eat and not mind them. You then take care of any disease germs which they may put into my body. Just whichever You wish to do will be good enough for me!"

Certainly He would grant one of the two requests. I was His child and there in obedience to His command to tell people about Him. Which do you think He did? Not a fly flew into that ox stall the remaining five days that I was there witnessing and teaching!

You will agree that was a miracle. I can tell you one bigger than that!

When we came to the last night of the meeting, it had rained so no one could sit on the ground. Kaffir corn stalks were brought and put on the side for the women to sit on, but the children and the men just squatted in front of me. The children, after their choruses, memory verses, and Bible story, soon tired of their squatting position and scampered off home to bed, leaving a vacant space between me and the group of men.

Feeling that some with whom Mrs. Han and I had no opportunity for personal talks might be ready to come to the Savior, I invited such to come forward. I would have been thrilled had one come. To my joy, the whole group of men just came squatting up.

We missionaries did not teach the Chinese to pray. We just told them that anyone could approach the holy God if he came to Him through His Son, the only mediator. I urged those men to open their mouths as well as their hearts, in confession of sin and in thanksgiving for Christ's death for them.

What a volume of prayer in that undertone! I could only distinguish the words of the one at my feet as he thanked the Lord for taking the punishment for his wine drinking, opium smoking, gambling, and bad disposition. Eight or ten had previously come to our room one by one and knelt at the foot of the cross in humble confession and faith and gone away rejoicing.

If those people were born of the Spirit, that was the greatest miracle of all earth's wonders. "Cooties" and flies have no enmity against God in their nature; but when a human being realizes that he is deserving of hell, admits his guilt, and willingly turns away from sin and chooses Christ as his Lord, that is a miracle!

Journeying Mercies

Thanks be unto God, which always causeth us to triumph in Christ (2 Cor. 2:14).

I had not been in Tsining many months when, on account of Mrs. Connely's illness, Dr. Connely asked me to take an engagement for him. It was at a Bible conference for Chinese preachers and Bible women of the Pochow and Kweiteh fields of Anhui Province. Knowing only twenty-four hours before starting that I was to go, I was tempted to tremble over the thought of giving two messages a day to the Christian workers, including missionaries. However, I had learned that one cannot tremble and trust at the same time, and I dared not go without trusting.

I had remarked to Mr. Tai, the young preacher who was to be the other speaker, that perhaps my dread in going to the meeting was due to the fear that my Chinese language would not be as good as that of the older missionaries who would be present. He exclaimed, "mercy on us! May the Lord save us from going over there with the sin of pride in our hearts!" We went down on our knees to get rid of it.

At the first railway junction we went to a little inn to await the next train. We were on our knees praying for the conference when the "bellboy" appeared in the open door and asked, "Are you ready for cigarettes?" Seeing that we were not quite ready, he left us alone!

After five hours' travel to Hsuchow railway center, just over the border of Kiangsu Province, and as many hours west into Honan Province, we were at the city of Kweiteh. The remaining forty miles were covered in the mission's Model T Ford. Upon arrival, we had touched four provinces, been enroute thirty hours (not counting the Sunday spent at Kweitch), and spent only $2.50 each in U.S. money! We had traveled third-class, there being no fourth, and had saved three-fourths of the first-class fare! On two of the trains our coaches were like freight box-cars with long benches running along the sides.

A big snow fell the first day of the conference, and the coldest wind of the winter blew in at every door and window of the unheated church building. Like Nehemiah, those in attendance were doing a great work and could not be disturbed, not even by the weather. Of course it took more time to get ready for the day, when all the winter clothing had to be put on. But I had learned that enough of the right kind of clothes would keep one comfortable in the coldest weather—well, warm, if not comfortable, for the burden of the clothes prevents the use of that word "comfortable."

The Lord was with us during the meeting—hearing all our prayers and using the Word that was being proclaimed—so nothing else mattered. Some were saved during the time. Others were revived and brought their besetting sins and weights to the foot of the cross. A number of the Chinese co-workers seemed to get a new vision of their opportunity to serve the Lord. When the ten days were over, our hearts were overflowing with praise to God.

Although our getting back to the railway over the forty miles of snow-covered road had been committed to the heavenly Father, the Model T refused to run. And no owner of mules would send his precious animals out on a two-day-and-return trip to Kweiteh over such roads. The only other possibility for transportation was what people called "the bus." The agent claimed that by leaving at five in the morning, the trip could be made while the ground was still frozen. Warmer weather during the middle of the day would turn the road to mud.

Even though we had not been able to retire early the night before, we were up at three o'clock the morning we were to leave and at the station on time, with tickets in hand. When the bus, a five-passenger car, rolled out, seven men—fat from their winter "quilts" (clothes)—scrambled into it with their arms full of bundles. The outside of the car was piled high with their bedding rolls, bicycles, baskets, and suitcases. The agent kept telling us to get in if we wanted to go!

Eight passengers were left standing. That many would justify the cost of sending another car. But gasoline had been provided for only one car, and more gas could be secured only inside the city after the gates would open at six o'clock.

About seven o'clock, ten gallons of gas were finally obtained and put into a small truck the size of a jeep. The truck had no springs, no self-starter, and no disposition to be cranked. After a time of pushing, the engine started. There being no step, I climbed in at the back, as gracefully as my heavy costume permitted.

Two little wooden benches about six inches wide, and too high for any Chinese, ran lengthwise in the truck bed. They were not stationary until we all were packed on them. But only three or four hours, I thought, and the forty miles would be ended. Humpty-dump we went over the frozen ridges, thinking that we would be shaken into nerves and aches and pains of all sorts.

Oh, if that bumpy traveling could have lasted! The snow on the road began to melt into a slush which made pulling so difficult the engine boiled every few minutes. A "footman" with a five-gallon tin of water hung on to a fender. When the driver didn't have to stop to let the engine cool, he had to stop at a well for the footman to refill the tin. Usually with the halting, the engine went "dead" and all had to climb out and push!

Then a tire went flat! We had to wait an hour in the mud and slush, which got deeper all the time. The passengers who wanted to get home for the Chinese New Year reviled the driver and complained in true human fashion. Mr. Tai and I were able, by the Lord's abundant grace, to keep a patient, Christian spirit. And, gradually, we saw a change in the attitude of others.

Mr. Tai loaned his gloves to the driver and was the first one to help push and the last to give up. I pushed once, but seeing the engine unable to appreciate my assistance, I just saved my energy to endure the ride.

That day we went twenty miles and used seven and one-half gallons of the gas. In the evening, we stopped at an inn. As the passengers and the footman sat around in the courtyard, they heard why and how they must be born again. A high official who had sat by the driver and who had been able to help push the truck because of the weight of the silver dollars in his military belt was inside smoking his opium.

Two Mohammedan women seemed to be hearing of the Savior for the first time. Their roll of bedding, which had been tied on the outside of the car, was wet and muddy. But I bought a bowl of fire-coals and dried two quilts a bit, one for Mr. Tai and the other for the women and myself. The board-bed was too narrow for three people, but another wide board like the two original ones was laid on two stools beside them, and the bed was complete! With my fur coat spread over me, I slept warmer than I did "soft"!

The poor footman had to sit up for lack of bedding, so that night seemed long to him. He called us at midnight, at 2:00 A.M, and again at 4:00, asking us to get up. He wanted to tie on the baggage so it would be ready by the driver's starting time.

However, we need not have rushed, for the kerosene added to the gas did not improve the starting ability of the engine. It was eight o'clock before our souls were delighted with the engine's first "hiss."

We were flying along, making nearly fifteen miles an hour, when the young officer who was packed in just back of the driver's seat suddenly exclaimed, "My nose must be blown!" Now that was a problem for a handkerchief is no part of a Chinese soldier's equipment. The only opening of the bus was at the rear. He reached it by stretching himself full length over the crowded knees of all, while we had a refreshing laugh.

The next excitement was another flat tire, and all of us jumped out. I had become a near-athlete by that time.

The silver-dollar-burdened official marched up and down the roadside to keep warm. I saw in the old tire-burst an opportunity to speak to this official. While not knowing what to say, I trusted the Lord to put the right words into my mouth. Politely greeting him, I said, "You do not have to be bound by sin! The Lord Jesus Christ can set you free," and walked away.

The official called Mr. Tai to know what I had meant, and after a few minutes Mr. Tai went away, leaving the man with something to think about. Soon he called Mr. Tai again, and after the two had gone aside for thirty minutes, the official came to tell me that he had become a Christian. He confessed to being burdened with more weights than silver, and bound by more sins than opium.

A family nearby were kind enough to warm us by burning some of their grass fuel on the floor (ground) of their reception room. That visit gave me an opportunity to tell them about my Savior. The donkey tied at one side went on with his breakfast, undisturbed by the smoke and ashes, or by the message of sin and the Savior.

When the truck finally was pushed off by the villagers, Mr. Tai and I praised God for the stop, even though during the delay the ground had thawed and the mud-sticking had begun. The car proved more difficult to start than the day before. However, having committed that day's travel to the Lord, who calls things that are not as though they were (Rom. 4:7), I did not fear an explosion of the kerosene in the engine.

Finally we reached the station. We had time before the train arrived to go to an inn and buy some food and to get the first layer of mud brushed off. At the inn we met a Christian army officer and his wife who were away from home, church, and all Christian acquaintances. While they were keeping up their family worship, they said, it had "no flavor" because they were living defeated lives. Mr. Tai was able to encourage them and give spiritual food.

The cold train traveled with the speed and smoothness of a freight, and the hard benches were too high. But what a relief not to have to get out and push! About midnight we were at Hsuchow again, where we were to catch a north-bound train for home at 7:00 A.M. Mr. Tai didn't think it worth the money to go to an inn, but, to me, the shorter the time the more precious the rest. We chose the best inn advertised, thirty cents a room with iron beds and springs. But the beds had no mattress, and quilts were ten cents apiece extra! However, those beds brought "beauty rest," compared with the beds of the night before.

The next evening at six o'clock we reached our homes, too tired to hold up our heads any longer. But we were grateful, beyond words to express, for all the ways in which the dear Lord had smiled upon us.

My Ears

What is man, that thou art mindful of him?
(Ps. 8:4).

In 1933 I began having a buzz in one of my ears. The ear specialist of Peking Union Medical College Hospital diagnosed the trouble as the eardrums becoming concave. He told me that I would gradually lose my hearing, for no medical science could prevent a convex eardrum from becoming concave. I *thought* that I turned the matter over to the Lord immediately. I returned home and told the Connelys that when I could no longer hear, I would not annoy my friends pretending that I could, but would admit deafness and use a hearing aid.

When I told a visitor from America about the diagnosis, she replied, "If I were you, I would not accept deafness like that! If I were a missionary called to do the work that you are, I would take my ears to the Lord and ask Him to heal them now!" After that, I began daily adding to my prayers, "Lord, heal my ears if it be Thy will." However, nothing was made definite, and no doubt I would have been surprised had my ears been healed.

Two years later I was working alone in Tsining. Our church had no pastor and I had heard no preaching for more than a year, except my own and that which a few laymen could do, which was even poorer than mine! I became hungry to hear good preaching. Our church invited Pastor Fan Wei Ming, pastor of the big city church over in Hwanghsien and vice president of our North China seminary, to come and preach for a week.

When he arrived, my ears were buzzing, first one and then the other. This was most annoying, and I imagined that I was not hearing well.

Knowing that Pastor Fan had been used to praying for the sick, I asked him the first day to pray for my ears to be healed. He put me off in an indefinite manner and went on majoring on his main theme, "Christians should live holy lives." Using the feasts of the Old Testament, he reminded us that the Feast of Unleavened Bread, when all leaven must be put out, preceded the Feast of Pentecost. He urged us to search the heart for any leaven, which he made typical of sin.

Waiting to cooperate in the meetings and be blessed, I began praying for the Lord to show me the leaven in my heart and life. He showed me a few things. One of these was the fact that I had formerly considered that one-tenth of my possessions was the Lord's and nine-tenths my own to use as I liked. I was convinced that in the future I must seek the Lord's will in advance for the way every cent of the nine-tenths should be spent.

Twice daily we went to church, and each time the power of the Lord was upon the speaker. He showed us from the Word how holy we must live in order to have fellowship with the Lord and see His power flow through us to others.

One day at the table I burst out crying and exclaimed, "I have said that if the Lord will for me to be deaf, I was willing, but I did not know what I was saying! I do not have to hear conversation that belongs to this world, but if I cannot go to the house of God and hear His Word preached, I cannot live! I just cannot be deaf!"

Pastor Fan only admonished me to turn my ears over to the Lord. At the church, he went on with the kind of preaching that kept us searching our hearts. After a few more days, I was made to realize something of the exceeding sinfulness of my own heart. "Take out leaven? I am nothing *but* leaven! I cannot take out my very self! The poison of the devil is in my nature!" What a black sight! I could neither eat nor sleep and tears streamed down. Just the thought of what I was by nature gave me the physical backache.

At three services I was the first to respond to the altar call. No marvel that the King of glory had to come down to this sinful world and take a human body. Someone had to take the punishment for all that I was, which was unlike holy God, and only God in the flesh could do that. How I had used my ears to sin! All my life I had reveled in compliments. The pride of life! Those ears were presented to the Lord for His cleansing, like Isaiah's lips of old, which only could be cleansed by coals from off the altar.

The last Sunday afternoon of the meeting a few gathered in my living room, so heart-hungry that they could not let the meetings come to a close without a new uplift from the Lord. Heaven opened and God began to pour joy into our souls. I could only kneel by the chair and laugh, as one wave of joy after another came. Those who could put their praise into words prayed, but I just let them speak for me. Later Pastor Fan asked me if I still wanted prayer for my ears. A number of Scripture passages were suggested, among them Exodus 4:11, "Who maketh the dumb, or deaf . . . "Have not I the Lord?"

While I was reading the various passages, there was a physical sensation on each side of my face as if tight tendons were loosening up. Pastor Fan then read from James 5 and prayed.

I had previously felt keenly the burden of the work in the five counties. But absolute relaxation now came. I did not have a responsibility in the world! All that I had to do was just to stand there and let the Lord do what He wanted to do through me.

But while I was so joyous in my soul, my ears were still buzzing, and after a few days, they began to ache. They had never hurt before that time. Now, one would buzz and the other ache, then both would buzz and both ache. Thinking that it was the devil trying to make me doubt that the ears were healed, I held on to the Lord's will for my ears and endured the discomfort.

After about a month, when the pain was almost unbearable, I said, "Lord, you know that these ears are not mine! They were definitely given over to You, and since they are Yours, they cannot hurt unless You let them hurt. Now if You do, it will be for some purpose and You will enable me to stand it, I know."

After another week or two the pain and buzzing completely stopped.

Two years later, after having gone through the Japanese War alone, I came on furlough. While it is the Board's policy for furloughing missionaries to go for a checkup, the Board's secretary, supposing that I was a nervous wreck, suggested I go immediately to my state Baptist hospital, stay as long as necessary, and get all the treatment needed.

When the ear specialist had completed his examination, I asked, "Are my eardrums growing in?"

"Why did you ever think that?" he replied.

When I told him what the ear specialist of the hospital in Peking had said a few years before, he said, "I cannot understand such a diagnosis! Your eardrums are in perfect condition!"

I then added, "Something happened after that. We prayed for them to be healed, and if they are all right now, it is because the Lord worked in them."

"Faith can do great things, if you have it!" he quietly answered me.

To me, it was not our faith, but just the loving Lord making it possible for me to continue to go to the house of God and hear His Word preached! When the doctor had pronounced my ear drums in perfect condition, I realized that the buzzing and aching which followed the prayer for healing had been caused by the necessary physical readjustment of the drums.

The Lily of the Valley

I am made all things to all men, that I might by all means save some (1 Cor. 9:22).

Soon after being transferred to Tsining in 1933, I met Mr. Huang, the city councilman for our section, called in Chinese "the street elder." He came several times a year to collect the quarterly taxes, or to inform us of some new regulation which the city council had passed, such as every household cooperating with the fire department by keeping a barrel of water by the front gate.

I always took advantage of the contacts with Mr. Huang to tell him something about the Savior. Being of the old school and too polite to look at a woman, he would sit with his eyes on the corner of the room and completely exasperate me by saying, "All religions are good! Buddhism is good; Taoism is good; Confucianism is good; Mohammedanism is good; and Christianity is also good!" My Lord and Savior was not even to be mentioned the same day with these man-made religions!

A few years later Mr. Huang came sauntering through my yard, dressed in a rich tan satin brocade toga that just cleared the ground. He had an air of possessing the universe.

A Presbyterian friend leaving on furlough had sent some of his tulip bulbs to me. Never were flowers watched with more eagerness or enjoyed with more delight than those red, yellow, and purple blooms. When the Christians admired them, I told them that when they multiplied, I would share them.

Seeing my tulips, Mr. Huang began to exclaim and ask all about them. Of course I could not tell the proud Mr. Huang that I would give him some bulbs when they had multiplied. But when he had gone, I put three of the prettiest tulips in a pot and sent them over to his home with my card.

Another time I had a lily of the valley in my garden. The sprigs had been given to Mary Connely, who gave the plant to me when she left for the United States. I watched over it with the same tender care she had. Imagine my joy when the early days of May brought up those first three dainty, fragrant blooms.

The next day, over came Mr. Huang, profusely repeating his thanks for the tulips and strutting through the yard in peacock fashion to see what else had bloomed. Lo! he spied the lily of the valley! He even humbled himself enough to smell it, and asked many questions about it.

When he had gone, I said, "I am after Mr. Huang's soul, and if it is going to take Mary Connely's lily of the valley to win him, it will have to go!" I put the blooming portion in a pretty little pot and sent it over.

Mr. Huang came over immediately, exuberant in his thanks, and acting so much like an old friend that I invited him in. He sat and looked at me while I told him of the mighty God having become flesh in order to die, and doing so in order to take the punishment for my sins and his. After listening attentively, he went home with a copy of one of the Gospels and some tracts.

The following Sunday evening Mr. Huang was sitting on the back seat at church, looking amazed at himself for being there. The next Sunday he was a few benches down the aisle, and by the third Sunday he was halfway to the front of the church.

By the end of the summer Mr. Huang had gotten to the second bench from the front. In the meantime, he had been to my home many times, each time hearing more about the Lord and taking home more and more gospel tracts.

Since our church had no pastor or preacher at that time, I had to lead many of the church services. One Sunday evening in September Mr. Huang sat drinking in the message of Amos 4:12, "Prepare to meet thy God." At the close, I asked anyone who wanted to get ready to meet God to get on his knees where he was. I expected so many that there would not be room for them at the front. Imagine my joy at seeing that proud Mr. Huang go down on his knees before the Lord!

The next week, Mr. Huang started attending the early morning Bible class and prayer meeting at six o'clock. After a few months of daily searching the Scriptures, he was sure enough of his salvation to make a public confession and ask for baptism. He sent his children to the mission school and one by one they turned to the Lord. The two oldest, a son and a daughter who were in high school, volunteered for Christian work. His wife and other near relatives were saved. Hurrah for the lily of the valley!

Tyranny

The wicked plotteth against the just, and gnasheth upon him with his teeth (Ps. 37:12).

The happy Christian Huang family prayed and longed for deliverance from the Japanese, little dreaming that a greater enemy would soon arise from within their own land. Their treatment when the Communists occupied their city is an illustration of the tyranny of the so-called People's Government of China.

Mr. Huang had supported his family for years on rent from a number of residences which he owned in the city of Tsining.

When the Japanese took the city, they commandeered the houses and used them during the eight years in which they occupied East China.

Upon the withdrawal of the Japanese, Mr. Huang resumed control of his houses and again rented them.

When the Communists came, needing living quarters, they accused Mr. Huang of having taken property which did not belong to him. Officials put the occupants out and moved into the residences themselves.

Because Mr. Huang protested, his wife was arrested and kept in prison for several weeks. She was then tried by the new court of the city, which was composed of street urchins and "down-and-outers."

Mrs. Huang was still in prison during the trial and was not permitted to have a lawyer or anyone to speak in her behalf.

A Communist official who was presiding at "court" asked of what the woman was accused. A little boy arose and stated that, during the previous summer, in the rainy season when he was wading in the street in front of the Huang home, Mrs. Huang came out and slapped him on the face. Two other urchins made accusations which were just as absurd.

The official went into a rage and asked what punishment the People's court would suggest for such a terrible woman.

One of the little boys who had accused her, having forgotten what he had been primed to say, arose and shouted, "I move that we fine her five thousand dollars!" At this, the chairman yelled out, "You mean *fifty* thousand dollars!" The boy assented, "Yes! Yes! Fifty thousand dollars!"

The city officials then confiscated everything that the Huangs possessed, even their clothes, and sold all, leaving the family paupers.

CHAPTER SIX
The Japanese Come

In 1934 Martha Franks was transferred to Hwanghsien to work in our North China Baptist Seminary. In the spring of 1936 the Connelys went to America on furlough, where for health reasons they were kept for two and a half years. I was the only Baptist missionary left at Tsining.

The Lord's Guidance

In all thy ways acknowledge him, and he shall direct thy paths (Prov. 3:6).

The latter part of July, 1937, I went up to Taishan, fifty miles away, for a few weeks' rest. While there a call came from the United States consulate, asking me to proceed to the coast.

However, on the morning of August 1 there was an earthquake that made even the greatest mountain in East China, Taishan, jerk and quiver. Since no small damage was done in Tsining, it was necessary for me to return there to see about property repairs.

Upon reaching Tsining, I found a city alarmed indeed. Before plans for repairs of our property were completed, more urgent calls came from the consulate advising me to proceed to the coast at once before railway lines were broken, making escape impossible.

With no pastor at the Tsining city church, how could I leave the sheep without a shepherd at such a time! I was burdened also for inexperienced Chinese co-workers in surrounding counties on the Tsining field who would have no one to consult about the work. However, there seemed no alternative except to go, so I packed to be gone indefinitely.

The Christians gathered in the yard while I stood on the steps of the Connely residence and read to them Psalm 46. The more mature understood that I was leaving in order to cooperate with my government. To others, it meant that I was pointing them to the Lord for protection, while going to a safer place myself.

On the way to port I met one freight train after another with loads of people inside, between the coaches, and on top of the boxcars, all fleeing to the interior. And upon arrival in Tsingtau I found a city that seemed to be dying fast. Most shops were closed, and foodstuffs were soaring in prices.

No sooner had Alda Grayson, Mary Crawford, and I rented rooms, set up housekeeping, and made out a program of work in Tsingtau, when the consulate advised us to leave for the United States. The daily paper announced that President Roosevelt urged all Americans, without exception, to leave China. The government would not be responsible for protection of any who chose to remain.

How would we answer? The President had not sent us to China. Twelve years previously I had asked our Foreign Mission Board secretary to accept a statement from me requesting that nothing should be said if I should lose my life or any amount of earthly goods in China. The Lord had carried me to China. During the coming months and years, China would need missionaries as never before.

Those who chose to remain had to accept the fact that one place was about as safe as another, except, of course, the actual battle front. Of the nearly one thousand people who already had been killed by one bomb explosion in Shanghai, nearly all had been Chinese who had fled there for safety.

Hospital workers were not only permitted, but expected, to remain at their posts, and I was reminded that in "Christian wars," chaplains also are permitted to remain in war zones. While chaplains are men, women on the mission field often have to do the work which men do not go to do.

For two and a half months I remained in Tsingtau, where I had a good vacation and helped with the mission work. One day, I knew in my heart that the Lord wanted me to return to Tsining and stand by those people in their suffering. I went to the American consulate and reported that I was returning, as I always wanted the government to know exactly where I would be.

Trains were running only at night to avoid being bombed. The eleven hours' travel from Tsingtau to the capital of the province, Tsinan, was a long night of joyful praise to the Lord for the privilege of returning to the Chinese Christians, to stand with them in their dark hour and take what they would have to take.

After spending a day in Tsinan, I took another train that night. It may have been well that I could not see the bombed trains along the way.

What had been fear in the hearts of people before I went away, had become panic, as men and women rushed from one place to another to find shelter. Women were actually losing their minds, and children were screaming in their helplessness.

Never did one receive such a welcome! The Christians said to me, "Since you are not afraid and can trust the Lord and come back, we will trust Him and quit being afraid."

We opened our church for service every evening. People who had not formerly been interested in the gospel came. The city was filled with refugees from northern cities which had already fallen to the Japanese, and many of them came. Sometimes the church could not hold the crowd and some had to go away.

Two teachers were able to take turns with me in leading services. We always gave an opportunity for any who wanted to be saved to come forward and wait for an after-meeting. Knowing that many of the people soon would be moving on west to keep ahead of the incoming army, I wanted to get those who were being saved clearly established in the Lord before they left. One evening I suggested that any wanting personal help come to my house at the noon hours. To my surprise, thirty-five came. I put them into a class which met daily at the church.

We were having, as usual, our early morning Bible class and prayer meeting which had been going for ten years.

So many wounded were being sent back from the front that the one hospital was soon filled; the high school was closed to make room; large private homes were commandeered; and some stores were ordered to pack up their goods and turn their buildings into places for the wounded. I gave my afternoons to the hospital, where I had been especially invited. It was two miles away, but I never took a ricksha because I would have passed hundreds of people who were there that day but might be dead the next. Walking both ways, I could hand out a gospel tract to everyone I passed.

Thus I lived for eight busy weeks, trying to make every moment count for eternity. Most of the morning time was spent seeing callers who came for various reasons, then preparing for Bible classes and evening meetings. But I did guard the time for my own prayer and devotional Bible study. I knew that no matter how busy I might be for the Lord, I would soon become useless unless I took time for my personal fellowship with Him day by day.

One Saturday after I had gone at that speed for a month, a man who had attended some of the night meetings waited after the noon class, saying that he wanted to be saved. We got on our knees before the open Bible and started reading verse after verse on sin and its consequences, comparing man with God's holy standard for him.

Just to be sure that he knew what sin was, I asked, "Mr. Wang, what is the greatest sin you ever committed?" To my astonishment, he replied, "Murder." In a family feud he had killed a man, and because all in the village were related, the murderer was protected.

What a glorious message I had for a murderer! I showed him that while, according to God's holy law, he deserved to forfeit his own life for such a sin, the Lord Jesus Christ had done just that in his stead. It took two hours to lead that man to where he was rejoicing in the Savior. What a change came over his face!

That one trophy would have been sufficient reward for all that I endured during the war, had I been looking for rewards. Day after day the expression on the man's face changed, as peace and joy took the place of fear and distress. At that time the Chinese government of the city had gone west. It was not necessary for him to confess and surrender to a Japanese government when they assumed control.

When I reached home after that "new birth," it was three o'clock, too late to go to the hospital. I dropped on my knees and asked the Lord what to do with these two hours before supper and the evening meeting. Immediately, I thought of a young couple who, some months before, had shown interest in the Lord. I had not heard of them since returning to the city. I supposed that the Lord wanted me to visit them. But that was not according to reason. They lived as far away as was the hospital.

I began to feel myself to see if I were not too tired. For the last month I had not sat down even five minutes a day to rest. And anyway, who from South Carolina would not want Saturday afternoon off!

Some weeks before, I had put L. L. Legter's little book on the fullness of the Holy Spirit on the arm of my comfortable chair to read, but, not having sat in the chair, I had not opened it. With myself I reasoned, "I just know that it would please the Lord for me to sit down and relax and read this little book." But the few paragraphs which I read had no "flavor," and my heart was uncomfortable.

Taking my tract-bag, I started; but on reaching the end of the first block, where I should have turned north, I felt drawn to go south. Without arguing with the Lord, I just turned south. In the middle of the block I met a man in civil service uniform, to whom I handed a tract. He was surprised indeed at seeing an American woman in that part of China at such a time. I told him of the evening meetings at the church around the corner and invited him to come.

Reaching the next corner, I felt no leading to continue south, so I turned north and went on and outside the east city gate to make the call. Returning, walking faster than anyone on the street, I handed everyone a tract and invited each to the evening meetings.

As I passed another man in the same kind of civil service uniform, he said as he took the leaflet, "I approve of this! My wife's people in Tsiensin are Christians." When I reached the church, the first man whom I had met on the street was on the front seat, and a little later the second man came. They waited for the after-meeting and in a few days both were clearly saved.

The Lord's Reward

The LORD *directeth his steps*
(Prov. 16:9).

On my visits to the hospital I was never able to get around even one time to all the men in one ward. And every day some died without hearing of the Savior.

One day when I stopped outside the big ward on the second floor where I, humanly speaking, should have gone, I asked the Lord where to spend the next three hours. I felt led to go to the third-floor ward. Without debating that I had been there the day before, I went.

By the side of a bed was a fifteen-year-old soldier boy who had come to visit his wounded friend. Upon finding that the boy knew nothing whatever of the gospel, I invited him to attend the night meeting at our church. When he told me that his company was just passing through the city and would be there only one night, I suggested that he attend the one night. City gates were closed at dark and he did not know whether his company would be billeted outside or inside the city walls, but, if inside, he promised to attend. I told him there what I could about the Lord in the few minutes that I could give to one person, being aided by the patient who had heard a little the day before.

At the evening service I looked everywhere for the lad but did not see him. However, he had been lost in the crowd and, at the close of the service, came forward wanting to be saved. He was led to the Lord by a young teacher who left him rejoicing with a New Testament. After a few weeks I received a letter from the boy, written from a western province. He thanked us for having led him to the living Lord and added that if he had to give his life for his country, he would not be afraid, since he knew that he would go to his Savior.

One Sunday night at church I noticed on the back seat a fine-looking young man in an army aviator's uniform. The next evening he was a few benches forward, and the third evening he was near enough to the front for me to reach him with tracts before he got out. The fifth night, he came forward and remained for the after-meeting. I suggested that he come to my house the next afternoon so that some of the young men in the church could help him.

He arrived at 2:00 P.M. Mr. Tai, a local young man who had finished at our North China seminary and had been preaching in the eastern part of the province, had just come home to preach in Tsining. He was a good personal worker as well as a splendid preacher. He was there to help me. With Bible and posters we began teaching. The aviator was especially impressed by a poster portraying the broad and narrow ways. The gate to the narrow way represented Christ, and the way was only wide enough for the person himself to enter without his bundle of sin.

While we were talking, praying, and yearning for the aviator to have the truth revealed to his heart by the Holy Spirit, Mr. Ma and Mr. Yen arrived. In July, Ma Ying Tang, superintendent of education for the county, had been saved. Afterwards, he brought his friend, Mr. Yen, with him to church. As was my custom when a new face appeared at church, I had set my prayers upon him.

Upon returning from Tsingtau, I had learned that Mr. Yen was an official in a county seat a few hours by train to the south of Tsining. I wrote him a letter urging him to turn to the Lord. He said that he had been interested in becoming a Christian since Mr. Ma was saved. Upon receiving my letter, he became so eager that he got excused from the office for the day to come to Tsining!

What an opportunity! We read and explained and illustrated, trying to enable both Mr. Yen and the aviator to see that God had already done His best when Jesus became His Lamb to die, that their sinful selves and all of their sins might be put on Him. Afterwhile, seeing that they understood with their minds, I stated that it was now a matter of their wills. They must choose to make Christ Lord, as He would not come into their hearts otherwise.

When I asked for their decision, Mr. Teng, the aviator, replied, "I want to enter the narrow gate." Mr. Yen expressed the same desire, so we got on our knees before the Lord. Mr. Tai prayed, I prayed, and then Mr. Ma prayed most fervently for them.

I asked if either Mr. Yen or the aviator had anything they wanted to say to the Lord. Mr. Yen began pouring out his heart in confession of sin, then of faith in Christ's death. When he had finished, Mr. Teng followed. By supper time they were rejoicing in release from sin and the indwelling presence of the Lord. What a glorious afternoon it had been!

Mr. Yen returned to his work and I never saw him again. But I rejoiced in the few letters written, as long as he could get them through.

Mr. Teng not only continued coming to the evening meetings but was able to arrange his daily schedule so he could attend our noon Bible class where he "devoured" the Word. An evening or two after his conversion, he brought another member of the air force, Mr. Chang, of whom he whispered on the side, "Prayer brought him." Within a few days Mr. Chang professed to be saved.

While Mr. Tai had been away in the eastern province, his wife suddenly lost her mind. Since I was the only one to whom she would listen, and that only occasionally, I had the responsibility of the crazy woman added to my other work. Instead of getting better when Mr. Tai arrived, as we had expected, she continually grew worse.

At midnight on the twenty-third of December, I was awakened by the sister of Mr. Tai, calling that her sister-in-law had cut herself to death. Grabbing my fur garment, and some bed linen from the hall cabinet for bandages, I went running, in the hope that she had not died. But there lay that lovely young mother with her blood poured out. Her non-Christian mother was screaming in true heathen style, "Who will pity me! Who will pity me!"

Both children had been awakened. The three-year-old was crying because he knew what had taken place, and the younger because he did not know. The father and his high school sister took the children over to my house, while I spent the rest of the night helping my servant prepare the body for burial.

Early the next morning we got a casket and had a little funeral service in the yard when the Christians came to the morning prayer service. We were able to get the burial over before the bombing planes came at nine o'clock.

The next night there was no sleep at my house, as the Tai baby, from change of food, cried all night.

Christmas

Let him take hold of my strength
(Isa. 27:5).

Our mission yard was full of refugees. We took in the womenfolk of any male member of the church, whether or not the women themselves were Christians. They brought their flour or millet and little mud cookstoves and pots. At night their bedding rolls became pallets all over the place.

We had several basements to which they could go during bombing raids, and each woman had her place assigned. The church basement was reserved for the men of the church during the actual siege of the city.

The victorious enemy drew nearer daily. As the cannon roar became louder and louder, our city people grew more panic-stricken. Daily more and more people left for the west. Shops were closed most of the day, and the bombers became more successful in their hits.

One afternoon when returning from my visit to the hosptial, I found even the Christians in great excitement over the bomb that had been dropped just across the narrow street from our grounds. I kept quoting to them, "God is our refuge and strength. . . . Therefore will not we fear, though the earth be removed" (Ps. 46:1–2). It meant something when I stood with them and quoted it.

My own favorite was John 14:20: "I am in my Father, and ye in me, and I in you," said Jesus. How safe! Anything touching me would have to pass by God the Father, then it would have to get by Jesus Christ the Son, before it could reach me; and if it did, there would be the Lord inside of me, so filling me with Himself that there would be no problem. What the Chinese friends called courage, boldness, strength, was Christ Himself living His life in me. Now you may be sure that I had my sins forgiven up to date at such a time! I was not only keeping clean enough inside for Him to dwell, but I was choosing His will in advance, daily and moment by moment.

Since Christ was faithful to the one who was trusting Him, every day was filled with joy, with never a thought of what might happen, or of any personal danger. I was in the place to which the Lord had brought me, and if I should die with the others, it did not matter. I was completely possessed with the desire to do all that I could, for all the people that I could, while I could, for the night would surely come. What kind of night, no one knew.

As Christmas drew near, the church members wanted to follow their usual custom and have a meal together in the church basement. But even the most well-to-do had no extra money at a time like that, to help provide the dinner for those who could not help themseves. Just when we had decided not to have the dinner, twenty-five dollars arrived from the Connelys especially for that purpose. So, all was planned for noon dinner on the twenty-fourth. It was thrilling to see the joy of those who were having their first Christmas and to hear their testimonies as to the change which had come to them.

While in Tsingtau the summer before, I got my first China disease, amoebic dysentery. I entered the good hospital built while the Germans were in control in that port, and within ten days was released as well but advised to see a doctor every two months for a checkup. Christmas Eve, just before the two months were up, my old enemy, the amoebic dysentery came back.

It had been a miracle what the Lord enabled me as a well woman to do at that time. Now I said, "Lord, I am the only one you have to use here. With what is already on, and the Japanese army only a few days from the city, I cannot afford to be sick. In the name of my Lord and Savior Jesus Christ, I command this dysentery to leave me." Not another symptom of dysentery have I had since!

A group of Presbyterian missionaries lived in the south suburb, two miles from the Baptist mission. They worked in that section and in twenty counties, while the Baptists worked inside the city and in five counties. We never overlapped. In all my visits to the county seats and villages I saw only three Presbyterians. Chinese are not disturbed by different denominations, as some people in America suppose. The Chinese are accustomed to several divisions of Buddhism, which has prepared them for the work of different Christian denominations.

The missionaries of the two denominations in Tsining enjoyed precious fellowship in a little English worship service held each week from home to home. Wedding anniversaries and birthdays were celebrated with a "company dinner," when each household provided part of the menu. On Christmas Day we had a big time when a gift was provided for the one whose name we had drawn, while each had the privilege of taking something for the children. That year we had our dinner at noon on Christmas Day at a Presbyterian home, after which we sang carols in English to our heart's content.

Christmas night many came forward at the church service, wanting to know personally the Lord of whom they had been hearing. I had not been fazed thus far by my two nights' loss of sleep with the Tai baby. But that Christmas evening, I was so tired that I wondered if I could get upstairs to my room. However, I found Mr. Teng, the aviator, Mr. Wang, a teacher, and Mr. Ma, the superintendent of education, waiting to ask if I would pray with them through the night.

When I asked what they wanted to pray about, they answered, "For the church work, for our country, and for Mr. Tai." The latter was so crushed over not being able to keep his wife from suicide that he thought he could not preach again to others.

I told them that many Christians had the custom of spending the last night of the old year in prayer, thanking God for the past and seeking guidance for the incoming year. They stated that they might receive orders to go west before New Year's Day. I then suggested, "You do not need me to pray with you. You stay here where it is warm and pray as long as you like."

They replied, "We do not know where to find the Scripture passages which we will need. When you pray, you quote the promises of God. We cannot quote them from memory nor do we know where to find them in the Bible."

I asked that they give me just two nights to catch up on sleep, after which I would gladly pray with them. Two of them answered that they might have to leave the very next day. As I turned to go up to my room, I prayed, "Lord, shall I pray with them or shall I not?" The answer came back, "Could you not watch with Me one hour?" I said, "Yes, Lord, through the strength which You will give, I can."

I began by telling them that there were some conditions for our praying together. The first was that no one but the four of us should know that we had prayed. I did not want to give the devil a chance to make them proud by having people speak of how warmhearted they were. The second condition was that we would not then decide to pray all night, as there was no virtue in the amount of time one spent on his knees. We would pray until what was on our hearts had been put on the Lord and completely entrusted to Him; then we would go to bed.

I read some Bible passages and soon we were on our knees before the Lord. I was just as refreshed as if it had been early morning after a good night's sleep.

Though all those men had sincerely trusted Christ as Savior, they knew little of what that might mean in this life, until the Holy Spirit began to show them that Christ was Lord and King as well as Savior. They began to see they must choose Christ's will in absolutely every detail of their lives and live for His glory only. This would entail their handing themselves over to Him now. They would learn later that, even though all had been given over in a bundle, as it were, each new experience in life would require a new and definite committal of all that was involved.

One by one they struggled through, until each had put himself into the hands of the Lord to live for the extension of His kingdom. It was then 2:00 A.M., but no one had prayed for the church, for the country, or for the grief-stricken Mr. Tai. Knowing that they were then prepared to pray for others, I went to bed. When I went to sleep in the room above, they were still praying, but I never asked what time they reached their last "Amen."

Three days later, both Mr. Teng and Mr. Ma had to leave. Mr. Ma had to walk two hundred miles to West Honan. He left his baggage behind, but he carried his Bible and hymnbook and a copy of Jane Lide's book in Chinese on the New Testament church.

The Lord's Protection

The LORD *shall be thy confidence*
(Prov. 3:26).

On the morning of January 10, 1937, a big silk store near us was bombed. The enemy army was only a day's march to the east. The morning of the 11th, I had callers with problems, making it about nine o'clock before I got away for my own quiet time with the Lord. While I was praying, I heard the buzzing of planes. Others on the place had heard the city signal announcing their coming and had gone to the basements and dugouts.

I had spiritual sense enough to know that the only way to be acceptable in God's holy presence was by identifying myself with Christ in His death. Because I was doing this I knew that the mighty Creator, the Sustainer of the Universe, was listening to me. I prayed, "Lord, there come those instruments of torture flying out of the pit of hell!" (I did not mean from Japan—I meant from the devil himself!) Now, for the sake of these helpless people who have no way of escape, will you take charge of those planes. Hold the hands of the bombardiers and do not let those bombs fall anywhere on this city today except where You permit them to fall."

I knew that the Lord had heard me. Leaving the planes with Him I went on praying for all who were attending the daily meetings. I called the names of those whom I knew and identified the others to the Lord, as the man with the gray scarf, the one with the red button on his black silk hat, the stooped one, or the student. One by one they were presented to the One who had power and love to reveal to their hearts the truth which they were hearing. I was so interested in getting everyone before the throne of grace, that I not only did not hear the planes again, but I even forgot about them.

About eleven o'clock I went down to my study for an hour's work with my Chinese secretary in preparation for the noon Bible class. He was writing in large Chinese characters the Bible verses which I wished to present to the group. We were both completely absorbed in what we were doing. The message from the Lord, I felt, must be just what the Lord wanted that day, for the next day we might not be living!

Suddenly our two-story brick house quivered, and window panes were crushed out. I thought the bomb had struck the top of the house and supposed that all of the second story was knocked off. I was preserved in perfect calm. Not a sound from my lips. Not one irregular heartbeat. The very second that the bomb struck, I knew that God had permitted it for some purpose and it was all right.

I went to the basement of the residence where the people were screaming and yelling. When someone tried to show me the broken windows, I said, "The house does not matter now. I only came to see if anyone is hurt." Finding no one injured, I went out by the basement door to the yard.

The air was black from the gray brick and tiles that had been blown into powder. My little Chinese home was wrecked, the little pastorium down, other buildings damaged and our big trees cut.

In the little basement of the well tower stood Mr. Tai's mother with cuts on her face, holding one of the Tai babies in her arms. Seeing that none was seriously hurt, I started up the steps to the school. Mr. Tai, who was standing by his mother with the other crying baby in his arms, said, "Miss Smith, do not go out now."

I answered, "I am going to see if anyone is hurt."

He said again, "Please do not go out now!"

I replied, "A moment's delay might mean the loss of a life!" I started on up the steps.

"For Jesus' sake, I ask you not to go out now," he begged.

Stepping back down, I answered, "It was for Jesus' sake that I was going, but since you feel that way about it, I will not go."

In a moment the pumper came and in great excitement exclaimed, "Old Mr. King is dead!" Mr. King was the extra gate-keeper we had employed for the emergency.

When assured that Mr. King was really gone, I suggested that we keep quiet about it lest we get the women on the place excited. But soon the regular gatekeeper came with the same word: "Old Mr. King is dead!"

"Sh-h-h!" I said. "There is nothing we can do about it, so just keep quiet, lest we get all the women on the place disturbed."

He yelled out, "But he is on my quilt!"

There was much more to attend to than getting the dead man off the gatekeeper's quilt, but we got him off. Someone on our place knew how to get in at the back door of a casket shop and buy a casket. We put the dead man in it, though we did not get him buried for several weeks. Fortunately, it was midwinter.

When I finally reached the school after the planes had gone, I found the girls all on their knees calling upon the Lord. No one was hurt.

While I stood in that basement, the second bomb was dropped in the yard just where I would have been, had I been a hardheaded old woman who did not take suggestions! That bomb had fallen about ten feet from our kindergarten building, which had a huge U.S. flag lying flat on the roof. The well tower had a flying flag; so did the church, twenty yards away. Since Japan at that time was trying to get the United States to approve of her so-called holy war upon China (her declared purpose being to exterminate Communism), we knew that the bombs that fell upon our property were accidental.

I was cut off from our mission secretary in Shanghai, but I got a telegram to the west to the American consul in Hankow to report the bombing. I also sent a note by messenger to the Presbyterian mission in the south suburb of our city. It did not take Dan Walter and Mr. D'Olive long to walk that two miles. They soon returned home to see if they could make a place for the dozen Chinese who were left. There was no question about me.

The women guests had packed their camping outfits and gone home. All on the place got busy moving house furnishings and school furniture, nailing straw mats over open windows, preparing to leave for an indefinite time.

As we went around busily, the Chinese co-workers would ask, "Why did God, in whom we were trusting, permit those bombs to drop here on our mission grounds?"

I had known the Lord since before they were born and could answer, "We never ask 'Why' about anything that God permits. He knew that we were here and He knew that we were trusting Him. We may not understand in this life, but this is not evil. The Lord permitted this for some purpose. He, the mighty God, does not have to explain Himself to human beings—at least not now."

In addition to getting the place in order, I had to pack away my personal things and select some to take. I did not know whether I would go west and keep ahead of the Japanese army, or land in a port city or even in America. Therefore, I had to take warm clothes and bedding and a few of my American clothes, as well as all important papers and mission account books.

Though firing a short distance away had been going on all the day before and throughout the night, we did not hear a cannon from eight till nine o'clock as we walked the two miles to the Presbyterian mission. But just as we got there, the firing began. Louder and louder it grew, until by two o'clock it was just terrific, but we were two miles away and getting only the noise. With the sudden hush at 5:00 P.M., we knew that we had passed into the hands of the Japanese.

My Chinese friends were given room for their pallets to be spread at night on the cement floor of the Presbyterian clinic waiting room, and I stayed with a missionary.

The next morning after the fall of the city, Mr. Walter and Mr. D'Olive went with me into the city to notify Dr. Rankin, our secretary in Shanghai, that I was safe. But we found that all wires had been cut by the military, who would install their own private lines.

While I was trying to find out from the Japanese soldiers in charge (whose language I did not understand) why I could not send the message, two Japanese military officials came along with one whom they thought was an interpreter. I asked them to go with me and see the damage their bombs had done two days before.

Upon reaching our gate, the three men whom I had left in charge of the mission property met me, trembling. "But for the grace of God," they said, "we would not be here!" They had spent the day before in the basement of the well tower, into which huge holes had been knocked on two sides. As I went on inside the grounds and saw the damage, my heart was singing praises to the Lord that the rest of us had not been there!

Two shells had entered my room. Kitchen, dining room, and bathroom were damaged, and the two bedrooms which had not suffered from the bombing had been ruined by the shelling.

My iron bed was apart on the floor. Round bullets the size of one's thumb were scattered all over the floors, with the partition walls full of bullet holes. We counted the parts of twenty shells which had exploded in our mission property, and others lay unexploded.

When the Japanese officers and I had gone over the place and reached the backyard of the Connely house, looking up at the wrecked roof, one of them said something to the would-be interpreter. He, taking out his little Japanese-English dictionary, turned and turned from one place to another until he found his words, which were: "I . . . ad-mit . . . it . . . is . . . a . . . des-per-ate . . . sit-u-a-tion!" While I quite agreed with him that it was a desperate situation, I was thrilled over the fact that the mighty God hears our prayers. He had guided the hands of those pilots and allowed those bombs to be dropped into our mission grounds in order to scatter us all out from there, that perhaps He might save the lives of some and protect the nerves of all.

CHAPTER SEVEN

Life Under the Conqueror

The Japanese came into our city like wild beasts. The soldiers had been granted three days' liberty as a reward for taking the city, but they came nearer having three months' leave.

The Christians asked me to return to our mission compound. Forty rooms in the block opposite the mission were made available for the church women and girls. All outside gates were closed, with passages opened through walls from one courtyard to another. The only entrance to the homes in the block was the front gate by my room, where hung my American flag.

Sufficient Grace

This was the Lord's doing, and it is marvelous in our eyes
(Mark 12:11).

It was Thursday when I went back into the city to live. The next day Bible classes for all in the block were begun. On Saturday I had paper pasted over broken windows in the assembly room of the church basement, and on Sunday we met there for worship. I used the message which I had been preparing when the bombs struck on the previous Monday. Such a testimony meeting we had following the message! What praise to the Lord for His protecting care! Half of the congregation had to wait until a later date to express their gratitude for deliverance.

During the following days I was busy going out in a U.S. flag-bedecked ricksha, escorting young women and girls to my place. Some of them had been hiding in trunks and clothes chests and others behind false partitions in rooms. I met those women who had gone with me to the Presbyterian mission and walked with them through the city gates past the Japanese guards back to our mission.

Former students who had fled to the country and found the villages unsafe would notify me that they were outside the city walls but did not dare enter the gates. All that was necessary was for the American to pass with them through the gates by the Japanese guards.

It was interesting to try to recognize neighbor girls dressed and made up like old wrinkled women. One of them cut her beautiful long braids of hair, dressed like a boy, and pulled her mother through the gates in a ricksha.

When our forty rooms were filled, additional space was given on two sides of the mission buildings. I patched up enough of the Connely residence to move back there. However, I kept my room across the street, in the hope that the Japanese would never know where I was sleeping on any particular night. A Bible school was opened for the 150 girls and young women, and other classes were kept going for older women.

During previous wars, I had boasted that I would always go to a port when the United States consul so advised, lest I get cut off and some other woman be left in anxiety while her husband came to rescue me. Two weeks after the bombing, a touring car and two truck-loads of Japanese soldiers arrived at our gate. Imagine my joy when Dr. John Abernathy, of the Baptist mission in Tsinan, stepped out of the car! I was too thrilled to be disturbed over the anxious wife left behind.

As soon as Dr. Abernathy heard over the radio from Hankow that our property was bombed, he went to the head Japanese official of the province and requested a travel permit to go to Tsining. The reply was "Certainly not! Tsining is on the front firing lines!" Dr. Abernathy told him that mission buildings had been bombed and one Baptist missionary—a woman—was there alone and he must go see about her. The official, greatly surprised, said, "I will go and take you. I must investigate the bombing of American property."

An estimate was made for the property repairs and the money handed over by the official.

Mrs. Abernathy had sent an invitation by her husband for me to return to their home with him. But I could not leave the responsibility and opportunity in Tsining.

The Lord gave me the good judgment not to accept money for board from the girls, since the city was liable to get shut up, causing a food shortage. Each family provided for its own girls. Only a man or elderly woman dared go out on the street to bring the cooked food—three meals in one—at noon each day. The courtyard gathering of those with the food, students, teachers, the preacher, and missionary was like a big reception, with all having opportunity to get acquainted. After the meal the guests were invited into the church to hear a gospel message by Mr. Tai.

We never urged anyone to accept Christ, but continued to give the Word until one knew that he was lost and without hope. The Christian girls and teachers daily prayed for the unsaved and asked the Lord to send the Holy Spirit to reveal the truth, claiming John 16:8, "When he (the Holy Spirit) is come, he will reprove the world of sin."

It was most gratifying to see those who were hearing the gospel message awake first to interest, then to consciousness of sin, followed by deep sorrow and such misery that they could not endure the burden. We gave no personal help until they confessed to the people against whom they had sinned and made restitution where necessary and possible. If, after that, they had not been delivered in private prayer, we pointed out the promises in the Word and prayed with them. What a joy to see the light come into their faces as they accepted Christ as Savior!

I saw more people born into the kingdom during that year and a half, than during my previous twenty-two years in China. The newly saved were invited to a class to study the meaning of the New Testament church, in preparation for baptism and church membership.

The Lord's Special Care

For he shall deliver the needy when he crieth
(Ps. 72:12).

In an adjoining home which had taken in twenty of our students, a six-year-old girl got sick. When home remedies failed, the parents called in a Christian doctor. His experience had been in the army only, and after a few days of failure to diagnose the case, he sent the child to the Presbyterian mission hospital. There she was put into a large ward full of children.

At that time, Dr. Scovel, of the Presbyterian hospital, was sick from a gunshot wound inflicted by a drunk Japanese soldier. When he returned to the hospital, he found the child in the final stages of diphtheria. He used his last injection, but it was too late. The child died. In the meantime, the two-year-old baby sister had taken the dread disease. The oldest sister, one of our pupils, had carried the sick child around in her arms among the students.

Before knowing the cause of the death of the child, I went to comfort the non-Christian mother. I found her making little red padded garments for the burial robes. She said, "We will get a casket and bury her, for she was a real person." Then she added, "But I do not know how we will get these clothes put on her, for no one will touch a dead body!"

The Chinese phrase for anxiety is "hang up the heart." Imagine one hanging by a hook in the heart. I urged the mother to "lay down or unhook her heart," telling her that I would dress the little girl for burial.

The father brought the corpse in his arms to my side porch. I put the clothes on the little body, while the big sister stood inside, looking through the window.

The strings of the little cap were tied under the chin, and the two elderly carpenters placed the body in the casket. They were preparing to nail it up when one came running with a message from the mother, "Wait! Don't take the casket out yet! The baby is dying, too!" A few minutes later the body of the baby sister was brought, wrapped in a quilt. We tied it on top of the casket and the two men proceeded to the cemetery.

How we called upon the Lord! Not only did we pray for our girls to be spared, but for the children who had been exposed to the dread disease in the hospital. Just then we learned that an epidemic was raging in the city. Even though we had had abundant opportunity for infection and for a widespread epidemic, not a case of diphtheria appeared thereafter on our compound or in the hospital ward where the first child had died.

Another blessing, over and above what anyone could have expected, was in a very different line—not necessary at all, but just one of the Lord's smiles. I had cool water to drink through all that hot summer. Ordinarily, the ice that was cut from the Grand Canal and stored in straw in little mud huts lasted until the end of May. That year, due to a cool summer and fewer customers, I had ice all summer. That blessing not only meant that the boiled drinking water could be cooled, but that a quart freezer of ice cream or sherbet could be enjoyed daily.

The Lord and I and Japanese Soldiers

Ye (are) in Christ Jesus, who of God is made unto us wisdom
(1 Cor. 1:30).

The first night after the Japanese entered the city, a company of soldiers took up quarters just over the yard wall from the Presbyterian mission hospital. Dr. Scovel, the only surgeon, was operating on the wounded all day and until twelve o'clock at night and had to have some rest. I was asked to sleep in the hospital to protect the nurses. A cot was put into his office for me and the announcement made that I should be called if a soldier should come over the wall during the night.

About six o'clock, while Dr. Scovel was at home for supper across the street, a frightened orderly came running breathlessly to tell me that he had seen a Japanese soldier come in at the front entrance! Grabbing my flashlight, I rushed to inquire of the gateman, but no gateman there! The soldier had taken the gateman's lantern, ordered him into his bedroom, and locked him in. The soldier then went to find women.

On the grounds, there were rooms built around a courtyard with a narrow path entrance. The rooms were filled with the women and girls who had been taken in for protection. When I reached the outside of the entrance, there the soldier stood inside the court. He had the lantern at his feet, his gun resting against the wall of a building, and he was taking off his fighting accouterments.

Shining my flashlight into my own face, I called out to him in English, "This is an American hospital! What is your business here?" I repeated the same in Chinese, neither of which he understood. But seeing my white face, he buckled up, took his gun, and came out, passing only two feet from me. I did not back one inch as he passed by, but gave him another scolding, to which he grunted.

I followed him to the gate, barred the doors behind him, unlocked the gateman, and then went back to see who were in the rooms built around the courtyard. The pretty girls and women fell on their faces, exclaiming, "You have saved our lives! You have saved our lives!"

After our group returned to the Baptist compound, soldiers came day by day on the pretense of observing the school, which was meeting in the church. Either our preacher or one of the men teachers would detain them in the yard until all of the girls could move to the church basement. The teacher or preacher would then take the soldiers to the church auditorium and explain how we worship or let them try to play our pump organ, while the girls went from the basement to the dormitory and from there, by a back gate, through my yard into the basement of the Connely residence, where I was living. Often, soldiers came but never saw a girl.

The married women across the street in our forty rooms were as frightened of the Japanese men as were the girls. Sometimes during a class, a messenger would come running to tell me that the "foreigners" had climbed up on top of the houses, and I would have to leave class to go get them down and out. One day a group of seven soldiers, marching in the order in which they went out to police duty, came in at our big gate demanding women. That time I went to headquarters and reported them, so that did not happen again.

One night after soldiers were moved into buildings adjoining our forty rooms, some of the frightened women next to them climbed up on the housetops and jumped down into the court where my flag was. They were taken up with broken bones. That same night three of the Bible school students who lived over there stayed on their knees until morning, praying for protection. Alas, for others, who had not been in the class, knew no God upon whom to call!

Christian men and their young wives were refugeeing in our boys' school buildings. By the middle of March, as soon as it was safe for even boys to be on the street, we opened our school. We knew that if we did not have a school by the time conditions were quiet enough for a city government to be organized, we would not be permitted to open.

Mr. Wang, the principal of a former government school, was song leader in our church. He and some other men teachers were willing to teach for only their food. One young woman church member agreed to teach the lower grades.

Soldiers entered the school grounds any time, day or night, paying no attention to the gatekeeper. Often, when I would be eating or taking an afternoon nap, the call would come, and I would go running half a block and around the corner to the school to get soldiers off the grounds. One day some of them climbed up on a roof by the school and seeing the woman teacher, for an hour and a half demanded, "The woman with the glasses." I was able to get her over to my house in safety, and she did not teach any more.

Some of the soldiers who were quartered in buildings next to the school often climbed up on our kitchen and jumped down into the schoolyard, frightening teachers, pupils, and refugees. They stood on the kitchen roof so much that we decided to take the kitchen down and build up the wall so high that they could not get over it.

Mud bricks were bought and masons employed, but the Japanese on the other side would not permit them to work. The workers sent for me. I had to climb up on the roof and stand there by the hour to keep the soldiers off the masons while they built up the wall.

Some of the soldiers came and talked in their "unknown tongue" at me, but I pretended I did not see or hear them. Others of higher rank came and ranted even louder, but I paid no attention. I was busy as could be talking Chinese to the workmen—as if I had to tell a Chinese mason how to lay mud bricks! When it began to rain, Mrs. Liu, a refugee living in the schoolyard, brought her warm Chinese garment and big umbrella for me. All day I stood on the roof until the wall was finished and the kitchen taken down.

Two or three weeks after Tsining fell to the Japanese, the Chinese tried to retake it and fought for a month. The firing was so terrific that for ten days the girls could not cross the grounds to the church basement for classes. At night they would come into my house and sit on the floor and sing while I played the piano to keep them from hearing the roar of the cannon.

During those days, Mr. Tai, the preacher, came over to get help from the commentaries on the Book of Revelation. For several years we had been studying the Bible book by book in our morning Bible class and had reached the last one. The only time Mr. Tai and I had for this class preparation was during that ten days of siege. As I would silently read, then put into Chinese anything that I thought would be helpful, Mr. Tai would write it down if he liked it.

We were trusting the Lord to take care of us, but I assure you that we, at the same time, were giving Him our utmost cooperation. We wanted a brick wall partition between us and the guns, which meant frequently moving from one room to another. One day the firing got so bad, coming from all directions, that we had to go to the basement. Too many frightened people, excited children, and crying babies were there for us to concentrate on the wonders of the Revelation. It seemed that we were right in the midst of some of the horrors prophesied.

One night during that ten-day siege, I went to bed in a south room; and when the firing started from the south side of the city, I moved to the north room. (The east room had been too badly damaged by the bombing to be used.) After a while the firing started from the north side and I went back to the south room. Of course, I was not sleeping for the noise. When I had changed rooms five times, I took my bedding downstairs and slept on the sofa. I was so pleased that I did not try the upstairs again for a week. But the roaring cannon, bursting shells, sputtering machine guns, crackling rifles, and whizzing bullets were not conducive to sleep.

However, one night I lay down on that sofa, went sound asleep, and did not awake until morning. I remarked to one in the basement how wonderful it had been to have a quiet night when we could sleep. He replied, "Quiet? It has been the worst night we have had! No one on the place slept a wink!"

After breakfast, when having my quiet time with the Lord, I looked at the Woman's Missionary Union prayer calendar and there saw my name. So while the war raged, people all over our Southland had been talking to the God of the universe about Bertha Smith, and He had listened and given me just what I needed: the ability to sleep like a baby.

The Lord not only kept me in mental rest, but also kept my heart in perfect peace all the days. I came to know what the Holy Spirit, speaking through Paul, meant by "the peace of God, which passeth all understanding!" No human mind can understand how one is kept in perfect calm, regardless of all that may be taking place around her. The hymn that I sang daily was:

Peace, perfect peace, in this dark world of sin?
The blood of Jesus whispers peace within.
Peace, perfect peace, by thronging duties pressed?
To do the will of Jesus, this is rest.
Peace, perfect peace, with sorrows surging round?
On Jesus' bosom naught but calm is found.
Peace, perfect peace, with loved ones far away?
In Jesus' keeping we are safe, and they.
Peace, perfect peace, our future all unknown?
Jesus we know, and He is on the throne.
Peace, perfect peace, death shadowing us and ours?
Jesus has vanquished death and all its powers.

Co-workers Return

My servants shall sing for joy of heart
(Isa. 65:14).

In March when trains were running again, we invited Dr. Abernathy to come baptize the large number who were waiting the presence of an ordained minister. What a joy it was to listen to the testimonies of those who had been born of the Spirit and had become grounded in the truths of the New Testament church!

I was fortunate in having Dr. Abernathy's help in planning for property repairs, too. No building materials were on the market, but we trusted the Lord and started getting our buildings back in shape. We found that merchants had buried glass in the ground and had hidden essential hardware. These they brought out secretly as we needed them.

From March until September the mission grounds were filled with masons, carpenters, and painters. There was a stack of good bricks here, broken ones over there, tiles to be used in one pile and those to be discarded in another, with broken doors and windows, good and bad ones separated. Only narrow paths were left between the heaps, by which we could get to the church and school to classes. We were amazed at how the Lord not only provided the materials needed but gave the necessary patience to all.

The big backyard of the Connely place was never so beautiful. The children's tennis court had been planted in grass after they went away to school. There were flowers beyond, filling corners and along the sides. I invited the girls over three days a week to enjoy the yard, and the rest of the time it was my own quiet walking and praying place. Twenty times around meant that I had walked my daily mile. Along with the walk, I sang my favorite hymns from memory and praised the Lord for His marvelous goodness to me, and for what I was daily seeing Him do in the hearts of those about me.

Another way in which the Lord showered His grace upon me was in the matter of mail from home. Having two unmarried sisters whose chief responsibility was writing long weekly letters to me, I was able to keep up with friends, family, and events back home. Every week when those two letters came, my next thought after reading them would be, "I will have to wait a whole week before hearing from them again!" If I had to wait eight or ten days, or sometimes for two weeks, even the double number of letters coming did not make up for the long delay.

However, in the autumn when the Japanese had trains cut off, I had to go six weeks without a letter, and every day was as if I had had my home mail the day before. After our city fell to the Japanese, we had no mail for ten weeks, but still the Lord so controlled my heart and mind that I was content without letters. This was the preparation for the time later when I would be interned and receive no mail for ten months.

By September the city again had an organized government. Japanese soldiers were under control to the extent that girls of grade school age could go safely on the street the half-block to our school, and others could come from their homes with escorts. Buildings were repaired, woodwork painted, debris removed, and two full schools opened. The nine months of Bible school had prepared young women, who formerly had been public school teachers, now to take responsibility in our own grade school, with a radiance that comes only from fellowship with the living Lord.

To my surprise and great joy, a letter came announcing the arrival of the Connelys in Tsingtau, after two and a half years in America. However, they expressed doubt as to their being able to secure a travel pass to come to the interior. Just one week later one of our church members came on his bicycle, too excited to talk, trying to tell me that the Connelys had gotten to the Tsining railway station. By the time he had finished, the Presbyterian mission car rolled up to our gate with them. What rejoicing! They said, "You do not look tired!" And I was not! Had not my Lord said, "As thy days, so shall thy strength be"?

CHAPTER EIGHT

Internment and Repatriation

After Dr. and Mrs. Connely returned to the field, I was free to take my year's furlough in the United States. Even knowing that I would be living under a Japanese government, I was eager to get back to work with the Chinese, whose hearts were so open to the gospel message. After four years under the new regime, we had become accustomed to minor restrictions and accepted with gratitude the opportunity of continuing church and school work.

On the morning of December 8, 1941, Japanese soldiers came to the school and asked me to take the Chinese teachers to our residence grounds. When I rushed around the corner to get Dr. Connely to come and see what the soldiers wanted and why, I found him standing in the yard with half a dozen around him, all excitedly trying to speak in Chinese. He said to me, "Go back and get your teachers. These soldiers have come to shut us up!"

Interned

The LORD shall be thy confidence
(Prov. 3:26).

The teachers were perturbed over walking away from the pupils to be enclosed in our residence yard. They needed comfort.

I had been in China for twenty-five years and during that time had learned, when anything new and unexpected came up, to get on my knees and turn it over to the Lord just as soon as possible. The problem then became His responsibility and I was saved from the worry of it.

But I did not go all the way to my place of prayer that day. Just as I reached the door of my bedroom the Lord said something to me. He always speaks to me in words of the Bible; something I know from memory comes to my mind just when I need it. That time it was not even a whole verse, but just a few words that popped into my mind: "There shall not one hair of his head fall to the ground" (1 Sam. 14:45). I said, "Thank You, Lord! That is enough; I'll not take time to pray now. I will go and see if I can comfort the teachers who are perturbed."

It was several days before we learned that Japan and the United States were at war. And not until we were released did we hear of the Pearl Harbor incident.

Fortunately, the summer before, when the Connelys and I went to the port of Tsingtau for our annual mission meeting, we had carried back into the interior all of the money that we could get our hands on. The Connelys had drawn on a family inheritance, and the Lord had performed a little miracle in order for me to have money.

My second summer in China I had bought, with funds from home, a large building lot at the summer resort, Peitaiho, hoping to have a few weeks' rest in a cottage each summer. Soon afterwards financial conditions became so strained in South

Carolina that I just waited until times got better to send for money to build the cottage. The better times did not come, and I never built, but kept the lot.

The summer of 1941, when I put the lot on sale, the manager of the resort just made fun of me in his letter for thinking that property in Peitaiho could be sold after the resort had been taken over by the Japanese. However, I am not to be laughed at if I have the Lord on my side. I turned the lot over to Him, asking Him to raise up someone to buy just at the time when He knew that I would need money most. Within a few weeks a German businessman in Shanghai bought the lot. I received a good price, considering the times, and I went back into Tsining with all of those paper bills inside my blouse. This money helped us to live when we were interned.

My first move, upon being interned, was to dismiss the cook. I would have time now for such essentially feminine pursuits as cooking and housecleaning. The Connelys and I decided to eat lunch together each day, which was our main meal. So as not to be a drain on either pantry, I, being one, ate with them two days; and they, being two, came to my house the third day. While we economized, we had the food that we needed. We never dreamed of anything but living there on what money we had for the duration of the war. We expected that to be three or four years. Mary Connely and I vied with each other in trying to make the best casserole dish with half a pound of meat.

I bought one pint of milk a day from a German woman. Out of that, I used milk in my cooking, every other day drank a not-too-full glass of milk for supper, and churned and made butter! But I did not have buttermilk. I saved the cream from the milk, and every few days when I went out for my walk around the tennis court, I took a glass fruit jar with cold boiled water and the few days' accumulation of cream. As I walked, I shook the jar until I had a little butter, which lasted for three suppers if I didn't spread it on too thick. I had a supply of margarine for breakfast and did not need butter at noon when I was having meat.

I was so afraid of wasting time, with nothing definite to do, that I made out a daily schedule. During the forenoon, after finishing my Bible study at eight o'clock, I listed nothing but prayer. I had chosen the Lord's will earlier in regard to either returning to the United States or going to West China in an effort to keep ahead of the Japanese army and continue to work with the Chinese. Not having been led to do either, I had remained in Shantung when the Lord knew that I would be interned. Surely He meant for me to mean just as much or more to the Chinese, confined to my own home and yard, as if I were out in active service.

I had time to bring to the Lord by name all with whom I was accustomed to working, then all other Chinese whom I knew, and all the missionaries. I prayed not only for people of China, but for all whom I knew in other countries. The many acquaintances over in America and all phases of the Lord's work were daily presented to Him.

When the Chinese observed the week of prayer for foreign mission work, the congregations would meet for prayer an hour or two each day. On Friday, when they prayed for the whole world, they met all day. A globe was put up and places pointed out as the group prayed. They went home thrilled, saying, "We have prayed around the world today!" Confined to my own room, I was able to pray around the world every day.

The days that it was my turn to cook the noon meal, I had to begin it at ten o'clock, for without American conveniences it took two hours to prepare a meal. Other days I could forget time, and when Mary Connely would call me to lunch, it would seem tragic to have to come down from "the heavenlies" just to care for physical needs.

In the afternoon I took my nap as usual for thirty minutes, then studied the Chinese language for an hour and a half. With the help of Chinese dictionaries I could, by that time, study without the aid of a teacher. After the study I practiced on the piano for forty-five minutes. This was an especial joy since I had not been able to practice since coming to China. I got out my old college music and had a grand time. When practice was over I went for my daily walk and did the churching. After supper I read until bedtime.

There was not one lonely moment during the entire six months that we three were cut off with each other. We had our own church service on Sunday, sitting in rocking chairs. And twice a week we had a party, which meant that we played Chinese checkers—just three games—and had "light" refreshments.

When we had been interned about three months, the head official, without asking if we had money, brought each of us the equivalent of twenty-five U. S. dollars. He said, "After the war is over we will get this back. You will pay it or your mission or government will. In some way we will be refunded."

The Shadow of a Saint

Except a corn of wheat fall into the ground and die,
it abideth alone (John 12:24).

The summer before we were interned, I was greatly blessed by one of the Lord's choice servants of whom I only heard. One of my Presbyterian missionary friends returned from Peking lifted up in soul over the simple messages and spiritual power of Miss Aletta Jacobaz, a young Dutch teacher in Andrew Murray's Bible College in Johannesburg, South Africa. Miss Jacobaz was using her sabbatical year visiting mission fields.

The one message that was reported to me was enough to put me to honest heart-searching. It was based on Philippians 1:10, "That ye may be sincere . . . till the day of Christ."

Translating from the Greek New Testament as she read, Miss Jacobaz said that "sincere" meant judged in the sunlight, absolutely clear, or without wax. It was the custom when too much wood was chipped out of a carving accidentally to fill in the blotch with wax. We Christians are to be sincere before the Lord—crystal clear as He sees us, with no fog at all; nothing covered up, no sham; having nothing in connection with us that is not absolutely genuine.

Miss Jacobaz made no proposition in her meetings such as asking those wanting a holier and richer life to go forward. However, she did give opportunity for personal interviews.

Handing out a sheet of paper and pencil, she might counsel with a missionary as follows:

Miss J.: What is your sin?

Mr. X.: I want co-workers to do their work my way, because my methods are better.

Miss J.: Read aloud Philippians 2:3 and Romans 12:10.

Mr. X.: "Let each esteem others better than themselves." "In honor preferring one another."

Miss J.: What makes you disobey God's commands and set yourself above others?

Mr. X.: It must be pride.

Miss J.: What is the source of all pride?

Mr. X.: It comes from the devil.

Miss J.: Please write on your sin list, "I am like the devil!"

Miss J.: What other sins are in your heart?

Mr. X.: Sometimes when in the presence of women I have lustful thoughts.

Miss J.: Please read Matthew 5:28.

Mr. X.: "Whosoever looketh on a woman to lust after her hath committed adultery with her already in his heart."

Miss J.: Write on your list, "I am an adulterer."

By the time half a dozen sins had been written out and faced, the missionary would be under such conviction that he would soon be alone on his face at the foot of the cross, pleading for cleansing.

What I heard of Miss Jacobaz made me want not only the walk with the Lord which she had, but also the power to enable me and others to see in ourselves all that could not be judged in the sunlight. I am sure that the witness and power of this woman, which was passed on to me, had a share in preparing me for the six months of prayer time during internment, which may have meant more to the Lord's work than any six months of my active service.

One spring day when I was in the yard seeing how many tulip bulbs had come up, Mary Connely came out with startling news. The head Japanese official of the city had sent his secretary to ask us if we would like to return to America. He said, "If you want to go, we will make a way to get you there!"

My instant response was, "Yes, I will go home to my mother! Someone else can count these tulip bulbs!"

It had been a previously unheard-of thing for private citizens of enemy countries to be exchanged during war, and I took it to be a definite work of the Lord upon the hearts of men. I wanted to go home so as to be ready to return when the war was over.

The Connelys told the officials that they would like to stay for the duration of the war, on condition that they be permitted to remain in their home. If there was danger of their being sent to a concentration camp, they would prefer to go home. The secretary replied, "I do not see why you should not be allowed to remain here in your home." The Connelys thought that their presence would be an encouragement to the Chinese Christian leaders. However, the day that I left Shanghai they were put out of their home and sent to a concentration camp.

Three months after the first announcement of repatriation, seven hundred American citizens were quartered in the country club outside of the city of Shanghai. The mosquitoes literally sucked our blood from sundown until sunup. Even after we retired under the nets, they could still help themselves to us as the cots were so narrow that it was impossible not to touch the net when asleep, and there, outside, were the swarms to pounce upon us.

After two weeks of that, on July 15, 1942, the Italian steamer, the *Conte Verde*, of the Lloyd Triestine Line, was ready for us. In order to get the use of city buses to go to the dock we were told to be ready to load at 2:00 A.M. All of us packed up and were ready for breakfast at 1:30—then what a wait, being chewed on by those pests! About five o'clock we got off and went through the silent streets of Shanghai singing, "On Christ the solid Rock I stand! All other ground is sinking sand!"

The *Asama Maru*, a large Japanese steamer, took eight hundred Americans from Korea and Japan, and at Hong Kong took on the Americans who had been interned in Stanley Prison since December 8, 1941.

At Singapore we anchored fifteen miles out while a darling little flaxen-haired Dutch girl, eight or ten years old, was brought aboard by Japanese soldiers. She lived in Java where her parents had been interned. At the time she was away from her parents in a boarding school. The Japanese were sending her to relatives in Holland by way of the United States.

Imagine our joy upon pulling into the harbor at Portuguese East Africa and seeing the *Gripsholm*, the Swedish exchange ship, awaiting us! It took a few days to get passengers booked and transferred, so we had a chance to see not only the Swiss mission work of the port city Lourenço Marques, but to go out into the bush to visit the work of a Swedish Baptist couple. On Sunday afternoon the local African preacher, in the little mud church building, warmed our hearts as he thanked the Lord in English for our protection and safety thus far. He said to us, "You need not be surprised that the kingdoms of this world are at war. This world does not want our Christ and His gospel. Our Lord plainly told us of these coming events that we might not be taken by surprise."

After Miss Jacobaz went to Korea and after visiting a number of mission stations, about a hundred missionaries were "judged in the sunlight" so that the Holy Spirit could fill them. They wrote to their home churches telling what the Lord had done for them, and pastors became eager to have Miss Jacobaz come to the United States. Following months of prayer and planning, an itinerary of churches was arranged from March until September. The Korean missionaries on the *Asama Maru*, thinking that she was in the United States, had been holding group prayer meetings for her work.

When they reached Lourenço Marques, two teachers from the Johannesburg Bible College met the steamer with the sad news that the ship upon which Miss Jacobaz sailed for New York had been torpedoed. After four days of exposure in a lifeboat off the coast of North Carolina, the charming young servant of the Lord had succumbed.

I had been invited to join the praying group of missionaries from Korea, and when that news came, how sadly disappointed and sorely grieved we were! Miss Jacobaz had known of Southern Baptists' many churches, of our young people, and something of our wealth. She had felt that a spiritual awakening within American churches would result in the lost world hearing of the Savior. She had been a citizen of the world, carrying in her heart the people of every land, because she had grasped something of the love which the Lord had for her. To her it was not death to die. She would never die, yet she had been living dead for years!

The Gripsholm

He shall give his angels charge over thee
(Ps. 91:11).

The large white *Gripsholm*, with a big red cross painted on each side, sailed around the Cape of Good Hope and across the Atlantic Ocean to Rio de Janeiro. We had aboard fifty diplomats, including office personnel from South American countries, who had to disembark. As we entered that marvelous harbor we saw in the distance what appeared to be a huge cross, high on a hill above the city. Drawing nearer, we found out that it was not a cross but a crucifix, the famous *Corcovado* statue, 125 feet high, carved out of cold, dead stone. Everywhere we went during our thirty hours in the port city, that lifeless image of Christ was towering above us. To us it was typical of only the dead Christ, known by so many of the people of that great continent.

Our joy was in the reports of those who had come to know the living Lord through the preaching of His Word, and were living to make Him known to others.

After a few days of sailing north toward New York, a tiny object was spotted one day on the eastern horizon. Soon hundreds of passengers and crew were standing by the railing, gazing into the distance. In a little while we discovered that our ship had changed its course and was making toward the object. It proved to be the remains of a man-of-war, all that was left, no doubt, after a torpedoing and burning. Our ship sailed all the way around that vessel with numbers of the crew straining every nerve of the eye through telescope, to discern whether or not there was life on the wreck. Only after being convinced that there was neither friend nor foe to be rescued did we resume our voyage north.

One could not but contrast the keeping of the "law of the sea" to save life with the way many of the Lord's people continue on their course, oblivious to those wrecked on the great "sea of life," with no one to rescue!

It was a happy fifteen hundred who looked upon the Statue of Liberty on August 27, 1942. We did not realize then how long it would take the FBI, in screening us, to telephone to all the references given them. We were taken alphabetically for questioning, and I assure you that I was ready to change my name and take any *Aaron* that could be found, before bedtime the third day when they got through with S!

Before many words with Board secretary or friends at the Prince George Hotel, I scanned enough of my mail to learn whether or not I was really coming home to my mother. I had left her two and a half years before at the age of eighty and not well and, at the time of parting, never dreamed of seeing her again in this life.

In the Lord's wonderful arrangement, I had four more years at home with her and had the privilege of witnessing the triumph of her faith when her time came to "cross over."

CHAPTER NINE

Surrounded by the Communists

The joy of getting back to China to work under a Chinese government with religious liberty was unbounded. With high hopes, missionaries and Chinese church leaders cleaned buildings, opened schools, and started a full program of preaching the gospel and developing fellow workers. While shadowed by the fact that Chinese Communists were entrenched in adjoining provinces to the west and north, and realizing that nearby sections had changed hands from Nationalists to Communists and back five times, we still hoped that the National army would eventually be victorious.

Last Days in Tsining

*Refrain . . . thine eyes from tears: for thy work
shall be rewarded (Jer. 31:16).*

In the spring of 1948, Fern Harrington and I were in Tsining alone. We knew that our time there was short, for the Communists west of us, who had been driven back three times, had returned with a force strong enough to hold what they were again taking. The city itself was so quiet that our Chinese friends thought we were safe for a few more weeks. Should the railway get cut north of us, we could go south, and if cut on the south, we could reach the coast by going north by Tsinan to Tsingtau.

We heard that Alex Herring had taken his family from Honan Province to Shanghai for safety, so we sent for him to come and preach for us until we would have to leave. It would be the last opportunity for a long time, we thought, for a missionary to render such a service to our Tsining church.

Alex accepted our invitation. In about the second church service he overstated a true incident which he was using for an illustration. At the next service, having realized what he had done, he acknowledged it, leaving the illustration partially crippled. This made such an impression upon the congregation that they entered into the meetings with all of their hearts, saying, "This is a true man of God who has come to lead us. He is willing to lose face to straighten out his wrongs in order to keep right with God."

The Lord blessed the results in such a wonderful way that we took it as God's fitting close to our work on that field.

Packing to leave was easy. When I returned to China after the Japanese war, I had left my household supplies stored in Shanghai, fearing that I would not be able to stay in North China very long. I had found a few pieces of furniture in Tsining after the Japanese occupancy of my house, and German people had carefully kept for me my piano and desk typewriter.

Days before time to leave, we sent the piano and typewriter and the few pieces of furniture, which would be difficult to take by train, on a little truck over the border to Hsuchowfu in

Kiangsu Province. Our trunks and other furnishings we could take by train by hiring a man who understood shipping and changing trains to accompany the goods.

At Yenchow

I will cause the enemy to entreat thee well in the time of evil
(Jer. 15:11).

Alex, Fern, and I planned to stop along the railway and work as we could, so we took the cook and our camping outfit. Tsining is on the Grand Canal, twenty miles from Yenchow, on the railway running from Nanking to Tientsin. Upon reaching Yenchow we found the railway broken both north and south of the city.

The inns inside of the city walls were filled with military officials. There was no room for us. We found rooms at a little inn outside the city by the railway station, and stayed there a week. The beds were wooden boards, but we had our own quilts to put over them. I longed for connection with that Beautyrest mattress in Shanghai, the gift of a friend.

After the first skirmish with the Reds, the Nationalist army moved inside the walled city. We went then, as paying guests, to the Catholic hospital operated by nuns. The hospital was part of a large plant in the southwest corner of the city, separated from the city wall only by its truck gardens. At the hospital we were given two rooms and meals, the same as the nuns ate.

The Communist army stayed in the villages around the city, where they kept out of sight during the day, only occasionally firing just to let people know that they were there. Sometimes a bullet would whiz through our room just where we had been, but never where we were!

The Catholic mission was in line of enemy guns for two reasons: first, because of its location, and, second, because the Nationalist general had closed the boys' boarding school and taken up headquarters in the buildings. The general enjoyed the bishop's home, while army personnel filled the school buildings.

At night all lights had to be kept off, for the city would be attacked. From the city wall, the Communists' fire was met with every instrument of war that the Nationalists possessed. The roaring cannon, bursting shells, cracking rifles, sputtering machine guns, jarring trench mortars, and exploding hand grenades sounded so natural that I could not realize that ten years had passed since I was in the besieged city of Tsining.

For the next six weeks we were in Yenchow, Fern worked on the Chinese language with her teacher, while I studied my English and Chinese Bibles, with plenty of time for prayer. Alex spent his time learning to read and write more of the forty thousand Chinese characters, and in prayer and sermon preparation.

When the war-thunder began each day at dark, we took our seats on the cement floor below the windowsill. While we were trusting the Lord to take care of us, at the same time we were giving Him our best cooperation! Our favorite pastime during those evening hours was singing the grand old hymns which we knew from memory. When we decided to go to bed, we sometimes felt more comfortable trying to sleep under our beds, rather than on them.

Alex was able to send a message through an army radio station to our mission headquarters in Shanghai when we got cut off in Yenchow. A reply stated that the Lutheran airplane, *St. Paul*, would come for us on June 18. That morning at nine o'clock, we were at the airport. We left our baggage so as many as possible of the Catholic missionaries could go.

We sat at the airport all day long, surely under the hottest sun that ever shone in June! At noon the Catholic friends sent out hard-boiled eggs and sour bread that had not risen. (It never did rise and always soured.) Pig lard was the sandwich filler. How tired, hot, thirsty, and disappointed we were at the close of the day, when every plane speck viewed on the horizon had proved to be a buzzard!

I had left the mission heavy-hearted that morning, for day after day I had been teaching the nineteen-year-old broker, who was to accompany our baggage, about his own sin and the loving Savior. While he had professed to "believe," we had seen no signs of his having passed from death unto life. I knew that when the Communists took the city they would force him into their army, and he might lose his life without being saved!

The comforting thought to me was that we could wait a few more days for the plane if, in that time, the young broker, Ming Kuang (meaning "Bright Light"), could be saved. The next day indeed he did become "Light," for he passed out of darkness into light, and Christ who is the Light of life took His rightful place upon the throne of that heart.

A German Protestant family of five, and their Chinese language teacher and her daughter from another city, were at the Catholic mission also. They were provided for by the priests in the boys' school buildings. On Sunday mornings we had Sunday school and church service and, on Wednesdays, prayer meeting—all out in the barnyard. The cook, broker, and teacher lived out there, looking after our things and sleeping in the hay. At the close of the next Sunday morning service after Bright Light was saved, he arose and, with a glowing face, praised the Lord for having been received into the kingdom of God.

The head of the Catholic mission was an attractive German priest, about thirty-five, who spoke English. He often came over for visits with us, and especially enjoyed talking with Alex. On his visit following Bright Light's testimony, I told him of Ming Kuang's new experience with the Lord, with all the delight that I would have related a conversion to a Baptist preacher. The priest asked one question after another, which Alex answered.

Even though our time in Yenchow stretched out to weeks, and the plane never came for us, our disappointment proved the salvation of one and gave opportunity to witness to others.

We did not go on the streets those days. They were too crowded with soldiers. We could not go in the vegetable gardens because they were surrounded by fences with locked gates to keep soldiers out. So the only place left to which we could walk for exercise and diversion was the barnyard.

Fern found some yarn and knitting needles in her trunk and taught Alex to knit for recreation. He laughed at himself as he began to learn, but he kept at it until he had finished knitting a darling little light blue sweater with white border, for his baby in Shanghai.

He made a chess board on the side of his suitcase, and, out of cheap Chinese laundry soap, carved chessmen. Fern had some paints, so she colored half of the chessmen black. They looked like the real thing. Alex taught Fern to play. I tried once but was too dumb to learn in the time that I was willing to give to it.

Fern and I had an outing once a week when we went to the "beauty parlor." The cook's big cooking pot in the barnyard full of hot water for a shampoo made us beautiful enough. There was no hot water in the hospital. While at the "beauty parlor," we enjoyed seeing the parachutes from the Nationalist planes come down. Sometimes several a day came in, bringing money, rice for the army, and vegetables for the general.

On the Fourth of July, the only American priest in the mission came to have dinner with us as a surprise. He had grown up in a German community in Minnesota, and while he was more German than American, we enjoyed having with us one who knew of our Independence Day. Was he surprised over the kind of food we were eating! He did not know that his telling the head of the hospital that he wanted to lunch with us had meant a better-than-usual meal, with a "special" can of Del Monte peaches for dessert.

I have never seen food so ruined in a kitchen! However, we were given the same fare that the sisters lived on. From the abundant gardens the only vegetable that came to us was cabbage, which had been boiled for three hours into a reddish pulp. The rice was always sweetened. We would not have eaten those awful starched puddings had we not been so hungry.

I lost fifteen pounds in the six weeks. Alex got sick and asked for rice gruel. It tasted so good that we asked for gruel every day for supper. One day the cook served the starch which had been made for the white bibs and headgear of the sisters. This was an accident, of course. What so grieved us was that this fare was the year-in-and-year-out diet of the sisters. The German family who was eating with the priests across the street reported a variety of good food plus all the vegetables from the garden.

The head priest feared for our safety because we were Americans. Since our government was an ally of Nationalist China, he thought the Communists would make it hard for us if they should take the city. When the city did fall to them, he suggested that Fern and I borrow nuns' costumes and wear them out, so as to be taken for Germans. We just thanked him with a smile. When we had gone, Fern exclaimed, "Now, what if we should dress up as nuns and something happened to us on the way, and we had to go up to greet St. Peter!"

Since the Lord had let us be born in America and enjoy all the privileges of that country, we would accept on the way what suffering that might come to us. Anyway, since we were trusting the Lord to take care of us, we thought that He could look out for an American just as easily as for a German.

Alex had come to Tsining when the weather was still cool; so had brought only winter clothes. By July the weather was *hot!* The sewing machine of the girls' school had been put in the hospital hall just outside of Fern's and my room, as a safer place to keep it. Having a piece of khaki in her trunk, Fern used the machine to make Alex two pairs of shorts. Then she found other material and made a pretty dress for herself.

Alex was so comfortable and pleased with his shorts that Fern wanted to make another pair for him. After her morning study she went over to the barn to her trunk to look for material that could be used. She had just gotten her trunk open and the trays out when the Communists let loose everything they had against our corner of the city.

Fern and the cook rushed into a haystack in the big barn and stayed there until after sundown. Alex and I were over at the hospital praying for a lull so that Fern could get back; and, needless to say, she and the cook, the teacher, and the broker were praying for the same.

There was a big recreation field between the hospital and the school building, and the barnyard was beyond that. The shelling continued unabated across the recreation ground.

Seeing that it was getting dark, Fern decided she could not wait longer to go back to the hospital. She said, "Lord, I cannot let Alex Herring, who has a wife and four children to live for, run any risk in coming over here to see about me. I've just got to go back! You know where I am going to be!"

She started out at a rapid pace through the barnyard and by the school dormitories. When she reached the open space of the recreation ground, there was suddenly a cessation of firing. She walked stately, in a ladylike, confident manner, across the grounds, out the gate, and down the street a little way and into the hospital entrance. The heavy firing immediately started up again. Alex was just starting to go out for her.

The continued firing was so terrific that Fern and I moved our beds into a little room across the hall in the opposite direction from the guns. I do not know why we were so optimistic as to think that we would need beds! In a few minutes we had them pushed across double windows that had a brick pillar between them. We then put the table and chairs on top of the beds and we sat on the floor.

Seeing that there would be no sleeping, and Alex's room being exposed, we suggested that he come and sit in our room. He sat on the floor and leaned against a white plastered wall at the foot of the beds. Fern sat at the head of the beds and leaned against that wall, and I sat about the middle and leaned against the outside bed.

All night long we sat listening to the bombardment of the city. The next morning about six o'clock, one of the hospital orderlies rushed into our open door and whispered, "They are here! They are here!" We knew he meant the Communists.

I had known the Lord since before either of my companions was born. I wanted to reassure them that the Lord was still on His throne and was with us, even though all seemed wrong with the world, and we were in the hands of the Communists. I started softly singing that grand old hymn, "How firm a Foundation." Seven verses of it had seen me through three or four wars before. I finished the first six verses, reminding ourselves that no other promises than those which we had were needed, and no matter what our condition, the water could not drown us and the fire could not burn us; and even when human strength was gone, we would have no cause for worry, for the Lord Himself would do for us all that we could need.

At that moment one of the Communists came to the end of the hall and threw a hand grenade that exploded on the cement floor just before our open door, about three feet from me. I sang the last verse under the bed!

> The soul that on Jesus hath leaned for repose
> I will not, I will not desert to His foes;
> That soul, though all hell should endeavor to shake,
> I'll never, no, never, no, never forsake!

It seemed that all hell *was* endeavoring to shake and succeeding fairly well, but our God was there, keeping our hearts in peace.

The hospital staff started for the basement, and all the patients who could, got up, took their bedding rolls, and went down. The nun in charge came by and asked if we wanted to go down, but, knowing that it would be crowded and not wanting to get in their way any more than necessary, we stayed on where we were.

The Nationalist army tried to escape by the city's east gate and down the highway. They were mowed down by the enemy soldiers who were hiding behind the city wall awaiting them.

The local militia were just not going to give up their city. They came into the hospital yard and started throwing hand grenades at the Communists who were across the street in the boys' school recreation grounds. This bombardment went on for hours, back and forth, *pop! pop! pop!*

After a while one of those grenades hit the brick pillar between the two windows in our room. The column was shattered, and bits of brick and cement flew over the room. Ceiling and walls were speckled except for one place. When Alex moved, an outline of his head and shoulders showed where he had been leaning. Not one of us had been touched! Miracle!

I can tell you one bigger than that! We then went down to the basement. The narrow hall was filled with patients sitting on the floor on their bedding rolls. All doors on the hall were closed. Along one side was a long backless bench filled with Chinese nurses who, led by a nun, were chanting their prayers to Mary in Chinese. Alex went into an inner room with Chinese doctors. Fern and I got standing room in the hall, I next to a full-length glass door and she next to me, and there we stood.

Not having slept the night before or eaten any breakfast, after a few hours I thought that I was tired. There was a camp chair just opposite the glass door which no one dared to use. I suggested to Fern I supposed it would be all right for me to rest awhile. I had no more than sat down when that full-length door shattered all over me! Had my face been scarred, I would have lost no beauty, but had my spectacles been broken, I would have been ruined. Having been born too farsighted, I had terrific headaches without my spectacles. There was not a scratch on my glasses. Miracle! The Lord was between me and that glass.

After that, I decided that I had plenty of strength to stand, whether or not I had eaten or slept. Sometime about mid-afternoon, when the local militia had run out of hand grenades, or too many men had been killed for the others to hold on, the Communists ran into the hospital grounds and took control.

A small mine was planted at the base of the double doors of the hospital basement. When the explosion destroyed the doors, one man's head was blown off, and people's blood spattered the walls. Three Communist soldiers rushed in, shooting as they came in that crowded hallway. One German nun was shot in the arm and a Chinese nurse hit in the hand. Of course it was bedlam. Women screamed, and Chinese patients jumped up from their bedding rolls on the floor, yelling out their fright. Fern and I were as calm as it was possible for two human beings to be! Miracle! The greatest of all.

The Chinese doctors rushed out from an inner room, caught hold of the three men, and held their arms and gun. They assured the men that there were no Nationalist soldiers there and that we were all law-abiding private civilians.

The smoke and powder fumes that filled the narrow hall were stifling. Fern and I worked our way through the standing crowd to the other end of the hall where the door opening into an inner courtyard was cracked a bit. There we got some fresh air and a seat on some vacated bedding rolls.

The three soldiers began to question us.

"Of what country are you citizens?" one asked.

"We are Americans," I replied in his own language.

"What are you doing here?" was his next question.

"We are missionaries," I said.

"Don't be afraid!" he said. "We are here to protect you!"

I thought "Sirs, you are going about it in a pretty way!"

Within a few minutes the Communists had moved in and taken over the hospital. The first time that I went out of my room that night and saw the place full of them, for a second I was so possessed with fear that I ran into my room. How ashamed I was of so dishonoring the Lord who had been my Protector and my Peace for thirty-one years through every ill-wind that had blown!

The majority of that incoming army seemed to be ignorant mountain boys under twenty. They would rush into our room unannounced and peer into our faces, asking, "How old are you?" Asking one's age is a common question in China. One of them asked me whether America was nearer to Shanghai or to Canton!

During the next few days all the Communist soldiers were busy robbing the city of everything that they could use. They knew they must work fast, for the Nationalist planes might come and bomb them out. But while they were enriching themselves by robbery, they were declaring their purpose to make an honest nation.

The mission was turned into a wreck. With broken windows and doors, the hospital began to swarm with flies. Garden walls and pigpens were knocked down, and hogs devastated the vegetables. The air was foul with the stench of unburied dead. In fact, all that appeared the same was a lovely blue sky with patches of fleecy clouds. We rejoiced that it was above the reach of sinful man's destructive powers.

CHAPTER TEN
Release

When the Communists entered the city, the first thought that came to my mind was, "Lazarus is dead!" We, like Lazarus' family and friends, had called upon the Lord earlier to deliver us. Reports of heavy fighting had kept the Lutheran plane, *St. Paul*, from coming for us, though it could have landed any day during the first three weeks. Since we had been left there until we were in enemy hands, the Lord would, we believed, get us out and win more glory for Himself than if we had gone earlier.

The Catholic priests and the nuns asked us if we would like to slip out with them at the opening in the city wall, by which the first Communists had entered. Alex, Fern, and I discussed the matter. We decided that since we did not belong to that city, but just got caught passing through, we should wait there until the

Communists set up a government. Then we would explain and ask for a travel permit to proceed on our way. All the Catholic group slipped out before daylight the next morning except the headman. He felt that he should stay and look after the mission property.

The third day after the Communists' arrival we heard that the government office had been opened. Alex and the Mennonite man went to call upon the official, while Fern and I spent the time upon our knees. Our expectation was from the Lord (Ps. 62:5). We thought that it would give the Communist official "face" to expect him to act like a decent human being. However, we were evermore calling upon our God to move his heart to grant the request.

The travel permit was granted, with the request that we tell our Shanghai friends that the Communists were not so bad as they had been reported. That was Tuesday. The permit would be prepared by Friday afternoon and the city gates would be opened for us to go out at six o'clock Saturday morning. We would be allowed to take only a limited amount of baggage.

Alex and Fern asked how far I could walk. I replied that thirty years previously I had walked from Peking to China's Great Wall. I had made fifteen miles in one afternoon and, after a night's sleep, walked ten the next morning. Now I was sixty years old and completely out of the habit of walking, for during the war years while I was in America I was wheeled in a car everywhere that I went.

They laughed when I told them that I could walk about fifteen miles. We had 150 to go to catch a train. I said, "But I am not to be laughed at! The Lord will not let me be a burden to you! If it is necessary for us to walk out of here, the Lord will give me supernatural strength to keep up. But I cannot imagine myself having to walk out of this city! The Lord has always taken better care of me than that!"

We began to search for some means of transportation. Every vehicle had been commandeered to haul loot out of the city. With our party of six and the German group of seven, we felt that the least that we could get along on would be two mule carts. I began to pray for two.

Because of the narrow streets and the difficulty of turning corners in the villages, wagons are not used, but, instead, two-wheeled carts with large wooden wagon wheels with an iron band around them. The body sits on the axle with no spring whatever. Four people can sit on the floor of the body of one cart.

I did not know that, since the Japanese regime, some of the carts had truck wheels with rubber tires. Everything being new to Fern, she had noticed the two kinds. Being humble in her petitions, she thought that one cart for the whole party was all that we could possibly expect. Her idea was that we would walk and ride in relays. While she was asking the Lord for one cart, she was adding, "Lord, please give us one with rubber tires." I, not counting on walking at all, continued to pray, "Two carts, please."

We came down to Friday afternoon at five o'clock with no wheel-cart, pushcart, ricksha, or wheelbarrow in sight. But I was still believing that He who calls the things that are not as though they were (Rom. 4:17) would provide two mule carts, and dear Fern was still expecting one with rubber tires, for the Lord knew how uncomfortable that three days of bumping would be!

To the amazement of all of us, the head of the mission asked Mr. Herring if he would like to hire the mission carts. We knew that the barn was filled with army mules, for we had heard them. However, we did not know that the mission had mules and carts.

Mr. Herring replied that we would appreciate being able to hire two carts. However, he felt we could not go out in them when those who were entitled to use them had gone out walking. The priest reminded Alex that his people could not have traveled the cart road and gotten by the guards without a permit. They had to follow the field paths from village to village. Also, he said that he would like to get the mules and carts across the border of Shantung Province to their mission in Hsuchowfu for protection. A price was then set for "my" two carts.

What decisions for women to make, when only one average suitcase or two small ones could be taken, and a small bedding roll! We knew that we would never see again anything left. I had been through enough wars to take the spoiling of my goods joyfully (Heb. 10:34), and Fern had spent three and a half years in concentration camp. Even though it meant losing most of her household furnishings, clothes, and many precious personal things, she showed that her affections had long ago been set on things above.

Those two carts! When they were pulled out that memorable morning, both of them had rubber tires! Moreover, one of them had springs, never before heard of in a Chinese cart. As we rode out of the city, the Chinese teacher, Mr. Kao, exclaimed, "I knew that the Lord was wonderful, but I never dreamed that He could be this wonderful!"

The three big mules, hitched with ropes to each cart, one pulling in front of the other two, started briskly down the road. But soon we were losing time in getting over rivers where bridges had been destroyed, and across trenches which had been dug by the enemy. When no shovel could be borrowed, we filled the ditches with our hands.

The first day we made only twenty miles, reaching a county seat which had been taken by the Communists a month before. Arriving at the west suburb we passed what should have been a cemetery—but what horror. The little dirt that had been scattered over the dead had blown off. The dogs! And the stench! What did those soldier boys who could not read know about sanitation? Anyway, they had been too busy killing more people to take care of those already dead.

Going two miles farther to the east side of the city, we were in another world. Enough land had been bought by the Baptist church members for a church and for the erection of a little school later on. In addition to the mud-brick church building, they had built five small rooms—three for the pastor's family, one for a Bible woman, and one for guests—and enclosed the grounds in a mud wall.

Our whole group was received most cordially, and within a few minutes the pastor disappeared on his bicycle. Pretty soon a man came bringing on his carrying pole a basket of eggs, eggplant, and ten pounds of uncooked noodles. All of us got busy, and in a little while we were all seated in the yard in the moonlight enjoying a good supper and feeling that we were in the suburbs of heaven.

The next night we spread our quilts on straw mats in the yard of a Catholic church. But what a night with the mosquitoes.

Late afternoon the third day we drew near the first city still in the hands of the Nationalists. Guards on the city wall discerned that we were foreigners and reported to their official, who sent out some petty officers to meet us. What relief!

They escorted us to the only train on the road, the one used to bring ammunition from Hsuchow and take back refugees. That two-hour ride! It was not a passenger train; and, being free, the coaches had not been cleaned nor had the train taken rest stops. However, we were out from under the Reds and within a few hours would reach our friends at the Presbyterian mission in Hsuchow.

Arriving at the Hsuchow railway station we purchased tickets to Shanghai for the morning. After a glorious night with Mr. and Mrs. Dean Walter, we were in rickshas going to the station when we were met by a passenger bringing bad news. The track between Hsuchow and Nanking had been broken by Communists the night before, so there would be no trains.

Back to the mission we went. Within a day or two Alex got taken on a Chinese military plane to Shanghai. Our telegrams had not been getting through, but when Alex reached Shanghai and reported our situation, our mission secretary secured *St. Paul* immediately to fly up for Fern and me and for the Catholics who had reached Hsuchow after we arrived.

CHAPTER ELEVEN

To Formosa

When Fern and I reached Shanghai, Dr. Cauthen, who was then the secretary for the Orient, asked me if I would go to South China. There was a need for someone to take over that field since the Manly Rankins were having to leave for health reasons. He suggested I visit there before deciding.

When I went to my room to pray about it, I knew at once that I was not to go there. I did not have to see the work. The Lord knew all about it, so the mission treasury was saved the expense and I the weariness of the travel.

Baptists believe that in the Lord's work, the Holy Spirit is to be the final guide of the individual though advice from others is appreciated. Dr. Cauthen counted out Kanchow for me when I made my report from the Lord.

Roberta Pearle Johnson and Lila Watson, of our mission in Shanghai, were just back from a visit to Formosa or Taiwan. When Formosa was discovered by fishermen from Amoy, who perhaps got blown farther out to sea than formerly, they called it "Taiwan," meaning platform in the bay. That has always been the Chinese name. When the Portuguese travelers got their first view of the island, they exclaimed, "Formosa Ilha!" which means "beautiful isle."

Pearle and Lila had been so impressed with the opportunities for mission work on the beautiful platform in the sea, that they began immediately urging me to locate there. My special qualification was that I spoke Mandarin, the official language of China which is used over nine-tenths of China. Too, Mandarin had been decreed the language of Formosa when the island was returned to China at the end of World War II.

For three years Chinese from the mainland had been going to Formosa to take the positions formerly held by the Japanese. When the Communists began to take over China, people daily left for Formosa by the thousands.

When I inquired of the Lord where He would have me go, I soon had the assurance that Formosa was to be my new field of service. Yet, the Foreign Mission Board had said, "No new work," and we had no old work on Formosa. I could wait upon the Lord. Would He change the mind of the Board? In the thirty-one years that I had been in China the Holy Spirit had never led me to go contrary to Board policy. If the Lord wanted me on Formosa, He would surely find a way to get me there.

When the executive committee (Chinese) of our All-China Baptist Convention met in Shanghai, they heard of my desire to go to Formosa. They decided to extend the home mission work of the convention to Formosa and "to take me on" as their missionary if the Foreign Mission Board would lend me to them and continue my support. Chinese workers would be sent over later.

On October 19, 1948, when the little plane on which I traveled circled over Taipei, the capital city of Formosa, the Holy Spirit whispered to my heart what He said to Paul when he was in Corinth, "I have much people in this city." I knew that He wanted me to find them and bring them to know Him.

The Taipei Guest House, out by the Tam Shui River, was the only inn in the city where I could get a private room. The Japanese-style inns assign as many persons to a room as can get sleeping space on the straw mats covering the floor. The guest house of the China Travel Agency was only for transients, and limited the time each guest could stay. But when my time expired, the manager, a Christian from the mainland, graciously assigned me a little room which ordinarily was used by Chinese who travel with their own bedding. A narrow bed without springs or mattress—only woven cane like the seat of a chair—a small wardrobe, one chair, and a little table beside the bed filled the room. There was just enough space left near the foot of the bed for me to get on my knees.

Dilapidated buses went down the main street and across the river at intervals of about forty-five minutes, but on no certain schedule. By the time they passed by again on their return to the city, the narrow benches along the sides of the buses were packed and all standing room was occupied. Often I could not get on the first bus that came by and had to wait another forty-five minutes and yet have the same scramble.

The only taxis in Taipei were one old station wagon and two five-passenger touring cars. Even when one of these could be hired, there was no assurance of arrival at the destination.

Pedicabs came only halfway out to the guest house, so I often walked a mile to make connection with one. Since the wide street was empty, I walked in the middle of it so that I could sing without disturbing the residents on either side.

At the close of the third day in Taipei I was tired from walking and walking to try to find a place to live or a center for our work. I was worn out from waiting on buses or standing in them, and from being tried by ricksha coolies clamoring for more money when the price agreed upon had already been paid them. I was feeling keenly the responsibility of securing property at once, since tens of thousands of wealthy Chinese were arriving from the mainland, causing real estate prices to soar. I was not having the proper food. And one of my two quilts was too thick for cover and the other too thin for mattress and springs!

I needed a new touch with the Lord, so down by the river I went. There the Japanese, in their love for beauty, had walled up the banks and made a narrow park between the river and the road that ran parallel to it. To the left was a modern artistic concrete bridge, over which walked Formosan women with Chinese ancestry, wearing Japanese shoes and carrying their babies on their backs in Japanese style. Across the river were a half-dozen Oriental junks in which the Japanese had installed American motors. But now their rusty steering wheels sat motionless. Down the river rose the smokestack of an industrial plant. Over the way was a lovely hill covered with evergreen shrubs similar to those of Japan, with a foreground of graceful bamboo waving in the breeze.

The "lawn mower" in the park was not only attending to the grass, but was cutting off the buds of lantana and ageratum. What did a big old "square ox" know about the beauty of a hillside! But the next day when he would pull his master's little rubber-tired wagon over the paved streets, he would appreciate the fact that his hoofs were protected with straw sandals, and that his "spare" pair were hanging from the axle.

Being two days by steamer or a thirty-dollar ticket by plane from my nearest American friends, I was tempted for a moment to think myself a stranger in a strange land! But another thought came, "I am my Father's daughter, out on His plantation where I have a right to be." Just then He threw upon the blue "screen" facing me, the most beautiful rainbow that I have ever seen— such width of stripes and gorgeous colors and tints.

However, something more than the beauty of color fascinated me. My mind went back to Noah and to all the meaning of the rainbow given to him. For more than four thousand years God had kept His promise to Noah not to destroy his descendants with another flood, and I knew that promise would be kept until time is no more.

What promise would the Lord keep to me? "My God shall supply all your need according to his riches in glory by Christ

Jesus" (Phil. 4:19). I seemed to need a good deal—not only a comfortable place to live, where I could have proper food but, more than that, a place to invite people to come and hear the Word of God. And how necessary it would be for me to meet those who would come, as Paul expressed it, "in the fulness of the blessing of the gospel of Christ" (Rom. 15:29).

God in His faithfulness would supply all of these needs, since it would be for His own glory. As I pondered the trustworthiness of God's promises, I noticed two fishermen pulling in their nets. Arising to see their catch, I caught a glimpse of color on the horizon, and turning around I beheld the glory which the Owner of the Plantation had cast over the western sky. Ascending the hill, I stood entranced by the gorgeous sunset and wondered when the "Sun of righteousness" comes, if His "beams" could be more glorious.

The next day, after having followed real estate men around for hours, I heard of a fair going on in the big five-story government building. Taking my bag of tracts, I went to see the exhibits. It was school day and all the students and teachers of the island were there. When I had taken my stand in a prominent place to hand out tracts with the gospel message in the Chinese language, I became exhibit number one!

Many of the students from over the province had never seen an American woman. When they kept coming for tracts, and I said, "*Mei yiu la,*" a young man standing near asked me where I learned to say "no more" in Chinese. Within a few minutes, we had exchanged cards and were chatting like old friends. He was a professor at Taiwan University. When I asked if he were a Christian, he replied, "I have been wanting to become one but did not know how." All that I could do then was to set my prayer upon him.

At the Bureau of Foreign Affairs the headman replied to the same question, "Not yet, but I want to go to your home and talk with you."

A secretary in the government land office, a graduate of the University of Tokyo, laughingly said, "I am a Chinese-Formosan-Japanese." He was wearing old U.S. Army clothes and trying to speak English. Wanting him to become a citizen of heaven, I asked why he was not a Christian. His reply was, "I very hope! You come my house, prayer; I very welcome."

Hundreds of thousands of Mandarin-speaking uprooted Chinese had fled to Formosa. They were torn away from their families, cut to the quick over the way their country was being taken by the Communists, and without a God on whom to call. What an opportunity to witness. Educated people of China had turned from idolatry fifty years before but most of them had nothing to take its place.

The city of Taipei is laid off like a wagon wheel, with bus terminal, railway station, and post office and other government buildings at the hub. Streets run out in every direction.

Day after day I went to the bus terminal, stood at a loading stop, and took out a tract in Chinese and started reading it. The long line of waiting passengers would look amazed, and one would ask, "Do you know what you are reading?" When I answered, "Yes, would you like to know?" he would reach for a tract and then the whole line would follow suit. When that bus loaded, I moved to the next outgoing one. Often I had a chance for enough conversation to secure a card with address, or I repeated, in my mind, the name and address given me, until the person had turned away, and I could record it in my notebook.

The wife of one of the United States vice consuls, Dr. Scott George, learned of my being in Taipei through my reporting at the consulate for registration. The next day she came with her five-year-old daughter, Lois, to take me to ride over the city. I then had an American friend. With tears on her cheeks, Mrs. George begged me to conduct a worship service in English. For a whole year she had heard only one sermon. It was by the secretary of the Canadian Presbyterian Mission.

When I secured a house I conducted a worship service in English every Sunday afternoon. I ministered to their need and they to mine. In fact as long as Dr. and Mrs. George were there, they took the place of fellow missionaries.

After praying for several days, with fasting, I went to the mayor of the city and asked him to let me rent a building for a church. A Formosan who had been educated on the mainland, he was so surprised and pleased that I could speak Mandarin that he was most gracious. He told me that all the business houses which had been vacated by the Japanese had already been assigned to merchants from the coastal cities of their mainland. They had made arrangement for moving their business to Taiwan before the Communists should reach their Chinese cities.

However, the mayor told me I would be able to get a lot on which the mission board could build. The decision of our Foreign Mission Board was not to build on the lot or to invest money in other property in Formosa, as I might be there only a short time. Instead, they would send money needed for rent. They did not realize that no buildings were available for rent. Japanese property had gone to the central government of China which at that time had headquarters in faraway West China. Individuals had occupied all of the houses and were selling to others for "key money" the right to move.

A House

Blessed be the LORD *my strength*
(Ps. 144:1).

An old Japanese residence was finally rented. It was the second one beyond the business houses on Chung Shan Road. While it was against Board policy to pay "key money," I counted rent in advance for two years. Two more years' rent had to be used to make the house over. From its dilapidated condition, it appeared to have been the first one the Japanese built after arriving there in 1895. The entire house had to be refloored since it would not support furniture, and I felt that I must have my own bed, piano, and desk.

The contract for repairs called for completion on December 20, and I promised to give up my room at the guest house on that date. While I moved in the house on that day, only my little eight-by-ten bedroom was floored, and I had to step from one floor beam to another getting to it.

The cook who had been with me in China arrived with Joseph Chang, one of our teachers of Tsining, Shantung, who had escaped to Shanghai. Joseph would be my secretary and general helper. They came by steamer, bringing my household supplies which had been left in Shanghai.

For the next three months my cooking was done on three bricks in the backyard. However, I still had better food than I had been living on during my first two months in Formosa.

By employing an extra set of workmen to begin at five each afternoon and work until twelve o'clock at night, I tried to get the house ready for two services on Christmas Day, which was Sunday, and for a party one evening during Christmas week. Invitations were sent out for both services. Had not the Lord still been holding onto my nerves I could have been buried under that proverbial tombstone on which is engraved, "Here lies the fool who tried to rush the East!"

The Formosan contractor knew only one word of Mandarin, which was *boo* (pu), meaning "no" or "not." He used it in reply to everything that I wanted done. You may be sure that I got tired of being *boo*-ed at by that man.

Since the partitions of the old house were removable paper doors, they could all be taken out easily and room made for about fifty people. That many folding wooden chairs were ready to be delivered from the carpenter's shop. But lo! the windows were not in. Fearing rain, which would mean cold weather, the English Christmas service had to be postponed for a week. I learned while in Formosa that the heat comes from the sun. Any day was warm that had sunshine. Chinese know enough to put on all the clothes they have, if it takes that many to keep warm, and go on to their services.

At the close of the day on December 24, I went to inquire about Mrs. George. She had suffered an attack of appendicitis and called off her Christmas dinner to which I had been invited. Dr. George asked if I could use a Christmas tree, as two had been given to him. The cook and Joseph helped me trim that tree after midnight. I cut strips of red paper while Joseph hung them on. Regardless of the climate in which he then was, the cook thought a Christmas tree needed snow, so found some cotton and pulled it into little dabs to put on. How thrilled he and Joseph were the next morning to find that, because friends had given me a shower of toilet articles when I was last at home, Santa Claus had come.

The cook said that he would save his soap for his baby. He did not realize that the little fellow would be tough enough to use a bar of Octagon soap before he would get in touch with him again.

I had persuaded the contractor to take his force elsewhere to work on Christmas Day. That rainy morning when I sat down by the fire with my Bible, I was too exhausted for the faintest Christmas thrill. The stack of Christmas cards from friends, which I had saved to open that morning to help make a Christmas atmosphere, did their best for me, but in my exhaustion I was saying, "A place to live is just not worth this much expenditure of physical, mental, and heart energy!"

The Lord came to me again, however, and assured me that I was preparing a house that people might be saved, whether they came to it or the missionary lived comfortably enough to keep well and go out after them. That message gave me so much courage that I did not mind eating a Christmas dinner of canned peas heated on the three bricks in the yard.

The Dentist

Bear ye one another's burdens
(Gal. 6:2).

A few days after Christmas, when Joseph Chang and I started out to lead a gospel meeting in a home across the city, a young Formosan with agony on his face met us at my front door. Since I could speak neither his Formosan language nor Japanese, all that I could do was to smile at him and urge him in English to come again. Mr. Chang, with the few sentences of Formosan which he had learned, tried to get him to understand why we had to go.

In a few days I received a letter from the young man which led me to believe that he had studied English under that Japanese who is reported to have hung up his shingle, "English taught here from A to K." I did finally decipher from the letter that the young man had been a dentist in Taipei, but in 1945 in the U.S. bombing had lost his right arm. With parents to support, and no doubt a wife, though he would not speak of her, he had often contemplated suicide. The greeting which he had received at my house led him to ask, "Can Jesus Christ do anything for me?"

A letter went to him immediately, setting a time for him to come. With gospel posters, my English, and Mr. Chang's bit of Formosan, we spent an evening trying to get him to understand that, because Jesus had settled our sin problem on His cross, He could say to every person, "Come unto me, all ye that . . . are heavy laden, and I will give you rest" (Matt. 11:28).

After a few hours the young Formosan was on his knees calling upon the Lord. For the next four months he came two or three evenings each week. After he had taken all that he could of my English, he would listen to Mr. Chang struggle in Formosan language through a chapter in Mark's Gospel. Finally, since he lived ten miles away, the young man had to stop coming for lack of bus fare. Then, the following summer he suddenly appeared one evening at the Bible class with an expression on his face which proved to all of the people who saw him that "if any man be in Christ, he is a new creature" (2 Cor. 5:17).

By the end of March the renovation of the house was completed. A bathroom had been added, and lo! it contained a built-in tub. It was made by one beam being laid upon another, over which was spread cement terrazzo. Two women had then come in and rubbed with pumice stone all day until the tub was smooth and pretty. Now, wasn't that a "built-in" bathtub?

After the kitchen was added and my coal cookstove was put up and I opened up the boxes of foodstuffs which had been showered upon me before leaving home, I just wanted to cook all day. When I sat down on that comfortable chair, I never wanted to get up. And that Beautyrest mattress—I wanted to sleep on it a week! All the trials—even the *boo*-ings—were forgotten.

The Sofa—An Altar

*Unto him that is able to do exceeding abundantly above
all that we ask or think (Eph. 3:20).*

I put my name in both English and Chinese on the bamboo
fence: "Miss Smith Baptist Mission." People began to come. In
addition to the Sunday services, we had Bible classes Tuesday
and Thursday evenings.

A few weeks after the Bible classes were started, one of the
men present asked how to be saved. Learning that he had no
Christian background and not wanting to "pick him green" by
letting him make a profession of accepting Christ without really
repenting and being born of the Spirit, I asked him to come for
personal help.

The next morning at nine o'clock he was there. Handing him
a Chinese Bible, I had him read passage after passage showing
something of the sinfulness of his own heart in contrast to the
holiness of God. After an hour or two he asked, "How can I, this
terrible sinner, ever get right enough to have fellowship with
such a holy God?" He was then prepared to hear what Christ
had done for him. When he was ready to surrender his will to
the Lord, he knelt by my sofa and started confessing his sins one
by one. Before he had half finished his sin account, there was a
knock at the door. I tiptoed out into the hall and said to the new-
comer, "You just take this chair here. The man inside wants to be
saved. When I get through with him, I will see you."

He said, "I want to be saved."

I answered, "Come inside and get on your knees."

After a little while there was another knock and I tiptoed out
again and said to another man, "The two men inside want to be
saved. Please sit here until I get through with them."

He replied, "I want to be saved."

I answered, "Come inside and get on your knees!" So three
men were seeking the Lord, instead of the one who had come by
appointment.

That was the way God's work proved to be on the island of
Formosa. There were always three opportunities to the one

which I had on the mainland. And I had thought back there that I was doing the greatest work in the world!

People came for help until I need never have left my home to put in a day's work for the Lord. My sofa was literally ruined by the tears of repentance shed on it, but to me it was only beautifully brocaded. Sometimes a new Christian who had not learned how to walk in the Lord came back and wept as much over his failure to show the Lord to others, as he had when he first saw himself a condemned sinner.

People who had been suddenly uprooted and torn from all that they held dear needed the steadying power of the Lord Jesus. The few Christians among them wanted mothering, comforting, and strengthening, and the thousands who had lost all and had no God were in bitterness indeed.

One morning about nine o'clock I answered a knock at the door. An attractive young woman asked, "What time do you have church service?" I replied, "Come in and we will have it now!"

Handing her a Chinese Bible, I started, as my custom was, to enable her to see herself as God looked at her, and how man had failed God in absolutely every respect. The young woman, Miss Wang, was a teacher from Peking. She had been reared and educated there and, after graduating from Peking Normal, had studied in Japan. Never one time had she heard the name of Jesus until on the way from Peking to Formosa to escape from the Communists. She had spent a night in Nanking near one of our little Baptist chapels. Being upset over leaving home and lonely, she went to the chapel, attracted by the singing. Seeing the word "Baptist" on my fence, she had said, "That is the same word as on the chapel in Nanking. I will go in and hear some more."

Having just arrived in Taipei, she had no work and no permanent place to live. She was sharing a small room with several others. The money which she had brought was being rapidly spent for food.

After having seen that if she received Christ she must die to herself, she was astonished when I said, "It is not the Lord that you want. You just want His blessings—a job so that you can have your own money and a better place to live." After a thoughtful pause she said, "I must have the Lord at any cost!"

Adding her tearstains to the others on my sofa, she truly repented and handed herself over to the Lord, making it possible to receive Him into her heart. When she was linked up with the mighty God of the universe, she was filled with joy unspeakable.

As I recorded the date of her second birth, I remarked that it was the date that Columbus had discovered America. She replied, "I have made a bigger discovery than Columbus! He only found a continent. I have discovered the kingdom of heaven!"

She often came back for Bible study and prayer. How refreshing are the sincere prayers of those who know no orthodox prayer language! She talked to the King of kings as freely as she did to me about everything that concerned her or her relatives and friends. She would close her prayer with, "Lord, I am just delighted to talk with you!"

First Baptist Church on the Island of Formosa

I will praise the LORD *. . . in the assembly of the upright*
(Ps. 111:1).

After I had four months alone in the work, Pastor Yang Mei Tsai from North China came over, having been appointed a missionary by the China Baptist Convention. After his arrival we soon secured an old Buddhist hall which had been vacated by Japanese Buddhist priests upon their return to Japan. Soldiers were living in the hall. We paid them to move out and let the congregation move in. The hall was ready for our opening meeting Sunday morning April 10, 1949, and the Chinese services were transferred from my house.

We had not seen the sun in twenty-four days. Day after day of clouds, if not rain, during the winter and early spring, meant that everything that could, mildewed; and all that could not mildew rusted. And that which could neither mildew nor rust molded, the leather shoes growing beards. Alas! the dreary days kept on until the human anatomy felt that it would do all three—mildew, rust, and mold!

That Sunday morning when I was in a pedicab going to the new church, suddenly the Lord's sun came out and the clouds rolled away as if He were saying, "I'm for you!" Assuredly He did prove to be for us. The building had been prepared to seat one hundred on backless benches, the only kind that we could afford. About two hundred people came to that first service, and those not seated were grateful for standing room.

After a few months we organized a church. Thirty-six members from Baptist churches on the mainland composed the charter membership. The Sunday after organization seventeen were baptized. How wonderful it was to have a building, with a regular church program and a Chinese pastor! The church grew and now has a membership of about nine hundred, with a building on a main street that seats six hundred. The congregation sponsors three missions, supports their pastor, assistant pastor, and three Bible women, and gives liberally to the work of the Formosan Baptist Convention. The old Buddhist hall is now used for a mission, with the church continuing to pay a small fee or rent to the city government.

Hopes Realized

What things soever ye desire, when ye pray, believe that ye receive them, and ye shall have them (Mark 11:24).

Nine months after I chose a lot in Taipei for a church building, I received an inquiry from the mayor asking if we were going to use it. He said that if I did not mean to use the lot, other people wanted to buy it. In order to save that wonderful lot, the Foreign Mission Board sent money for the erection of a little chapel which we named "Gospel Hall."

Within two weeks after opening the little building we had two hundred youngsters in Sunday School. Fortunately, when it rained, we had only a houseful, so did not have to hold classes in the yard. Before the building was dry we observed the Chinese New Year season in February with a two-week evangelistic campaign. About forty of the Sunday School boys and girls filled the front seats and joyfully entered into learning choruses and memorizing Scripture passages.

After a week of explaining the Word of God on sin and the Savior, I asked for any who wanted to be saved to come forward and wait for an after-meeting. The youngsters were asked to file out of the hall and leave their seats for the grownups who were coming forward. Instead, they marched up into the corner by the platform. When I suggested again that they file down the aisle and out, their spokesman said, "We all want to be saved!"

Expecting some to be saved, I had provided straw mats to be put on the cement floor for kneeling. About thirty of the boys and girls ranging in age from ten to fifteen knelt there with a number of adults and whispered their prayers of confession and thanksgiving to the Lord.

A few weeks later at a Sunday meeting five of the boys and girls came forward. One by one, they were led to the Savior. The following Wednesday one of them, a boy of fourteen, was drowned in a nearby river. His parents, who were Buddhist, came by the next Sunday to tell us of the tragedy and to ask us to pray the boy out of purgatory. How thankful to the dear Lord we were that the chapel had been built that the boy might prepare in time to meet his Lord.

With the week's program of various types of services, we were soon reaching people in the area with the news of the Savior and seeing more and more people turn to Him. We had found in the vicinity of Gospel Hall only one Baptist church member from the mainland of China. We then understood why we had not been permitted to build there earlier. The Lord knew of the thirty-six Baptists living within easy reach of the old Buddhist hall, whom He needed for the foundation of our first church.

Today there stands beside the Gospel Hall a church building that seats four hundred. The church has a membership of about seven hundred. The members have sponsored four missions, two of which have been organized into churches, and one of those now has a mission in a nearby village.

A New Family

They joy before thee according to the joy in harvest
(Isa. 9:3).

When I opened meetings in my little house, you may be sure that I invited the young university professor whom I had met at the fair. After about a year, he was saved and took the name Paul. In the summer his fiancee flew over from faraway Szechuan Province in China. Their wedding took place in the city auditorium where I met the mother and bride. There were then three for whom I knew to pray.

It was not many months until that beautiful bride was on her knees by the sofa coming to the Savior. Her given name was Lydia. She and Paul were then happy in the Lord, as well as being happy with each other. She soon felt at home in the new family, even though her own parents and brothers and sisters were so far away.

After a few months Paul came into my study one morning in great distress, asking if I could see Lydia. She was frantic over the news of her parents having been put to death by the Communists just because they were wealthy.

As Lydia came in and fell to a seat on my sofa she sobbed out, "My parents are lost! I will never see them again! They had no chance to be saved. Not one time did they hear of the Lord Jesus."

How precious the Word of God becomes at such a time of grief. While not being able to offer any hope for the parents, I knew her Lord would enable her to bear the sorrow. We read comforting passages and prayed until she was quietly leaving herself in His hands.

Olive Lawton had arrived by that time, and Lydia invited the two of us to her home for dinner that evening. Knowing that the family would welcome any whom she might invite at such a time, we accepted. She and a servant spent the whole afternoon preparing a delicious meal of Szechuan food.

The father, with a doctor's degree in science from a university in France, was a teacher at the National University of Formosa.

The mother was a teacher in the Normal University. Robin, the second son, was a university student. A younger sister was in high school and the youngest brother in the grades. All of us sat around the table together.

Paul, not being head of the house, could only bow his head with Lydia and silently thank the Lord for the food. Olive and I did likewise, making ours short. But the others respectfully waited until all heads were up before taking up chopsticks. I praised the Lord for that silent witness of the two. After dinner we all sat in the living room, where Paul took over, requesting me to tell the family about the Savior. I did my best to present the truth to their minds, while trusting the Holy Spirit to reveal it to their hearts.

A few more months went by, and one afternoon Lydia came with her mother-in-law, who wanted to be saved. Lydia left her with me, and after an hour or two returned to find the woman on her knees, helping to further spoil that sofa. Lydia went tip-toeing into the dining room and round and round the table, clapping her hands without sound and exclaiming in a whisper, "My mother-in-law is going to be saved! My mother-in-law is going to be saved!" And with what joy and praise the two went home!

The new convert entered a class at the church, studying the meaning of New Testament church membership, after which she was baptized. There were then three to join their prayers for the salvation of the others.

The daughter was the next one of the family to be saved by the sofa, then Robin. There were then five to unite in prayer for the two. All were so anxious over the father that they made an appointment to bring him on a Sunday afternoon for an interview. For two hours we talked and read the Word, but he left without humbling himself before the Lord. For an excuse he claimed that Christianity did not agree with science. After a church was built near his home he went occasionally just to please the family, but showed no interest in his own soul.

Ten years after Paul's conversion I visited the parents in another city where both were teachers in a new university. I found the father with an entirely different attitude. The mother had been having meetings for Christian students in the home, where he had repeatedly heard the truth. Her daily life of faithfulness in arising early for her quiet time with the Lord had made him see that Christ was very real to her. This example, with his appreciation for what Christ had done for his children, four of whom were in America for further study, had led him to begin reading the Bible for himself.

In fact, he was so hungry-hearted that he made no objections to my telling him of his sins. I led him to go as far as he could that day in seeing himself lost and undone before the holy God and asked that he write his sins on paper one by one, and constantly pray, "Lord, show me any other sins in my heart." I left, with the promise to return after two days to tell him what to do next.

To my joy upon returning, I found him convinced that such a sinner as he had absolutely no hope of getting right with God except through the death of Jesus Christ. He knelt in complete surrender, and after having put his sins one by one on Christ, he received the living Lord into his heart. I left him a happy man.

A few weeks later, after having studied a book on the New Testament church, he went to the nearest church, six miles away, and gave his testimony and was received for baptism.

(Note: My method in dealing with individuals was to have them list all known sin and sins by number. When no more could be recalled, to pray, "Lord, You are Light. Shine in my heart and show me all that is in my nature which is unlike holy God."

To settle the sin account, of sin number one ask, "Is that sin just between God and me?" If it involves no one else the sin can be put over on the Lord with thanks that He took the necessary punishment for it. That sin is then forever finished and can be marked from the list.

What about sin number two? That may have been against someone else. If so, after that sin has been put on Christ, confession must be made to the one sinned against before it can be marked out.

When the listed sins have been thus dealt with and marked out, the next step is to put oneself over on the Lord, accepting His death for that sinful nature which produces sin.

The next step that I advised was to choose the Lord's will in advance for the whole of life and for those related to it. Thus Christ could be enthroned in the heart and the Holy Spirit could be appropriated to fill and empower.)

The Doctor

And shall not God avenge his own elect, . . . though he bear long with them? (Luke 18:7).

A year after I reached Formosa a message came from a man in the southern part of the island, asking me to come down and spend a week to teach the new converts who were meeting in his home. I could not go, as I had all that I could do in Taipei.

After another year, the same man sent another message for me to come, saying that those converts who wanted help before had followed a lay leader into a group with unscriptural doctrines. He now had another little congregation who needed Bible teaching. By that time I was more involved in responsibilities in the capital city than when the first call came. Again, I could not go. That group, too, followed a similar leader.

I was asked to go to Tainan in the spring of 1952 to open new work. Upon arrival there a third call came from the same man asking me to come teach his third group. But still I was not free to go.

After nine months we were ready to organize a church in Tainan. We were just as busy as could be examining and listening to the testimonies of those who wished to join, along with teaching classes and planning a program. On one of those busy days, a little man with a black beard got off his bicycle at my door. Seeing me, he exclaimed, "You are Miss Ming of Laichowfu!"

My Chinese name is "Ming." I got to change my name upon going to China (even though I did not get a mother-in-law). Since "Smith" is not a proper name in the Chinese language, I was given one of their one hundred family names.

When the stranger asked, "Do you know me?" all that I could reply was, "It seems that I have looked into that face at some time." What a surprise when he said, "I am Dr. Wang who worked with Dr. Gaston in the mission hospital in Laichowfu."

So the Brother Wang who had been sending for me during those years was none other than the former young non-Christian doctor who had reached Laichowfu just at the time that I had arrived there as a new missionary! He had at once become the burden of prayer, not only of the missionaries and Christian hospital staff, but also of the Chinese church. After three or four years there, he returned to his home in Pingtu, still unsaved, and opened a private clinic.

He had heard only that there was a Baptist missionary in Taipei named Ming. Not being trained in the Bible, he wanted help in getting his converts established.

During the lunch together that day, Dr. Wang told me how he had been saved during the revival in Pingtu, North China. He saw three paralytics healed by the Lord in answer to prayer. One of them had been his patient, and he knew her case was incurable. The miracle startled him to the truth that Jesus Christ is not only alive, but approachable by human beings who could call upon Him and see Him do what they had asked. This fact brought to Dr. Wang a deep sense of his own sin in the presence of the living, all-knowing God, and led to genuine repentance and faith in Christ as his own personal Savior.

When the Japanese army entered the city, officers took over the building as their living quarters. Dr. Wang's clinic and residence had been the nicest building in Pingtu. They confiscated all of his medical equipment and supplies, leaving him with nothing.

When the Japanese withdrew after the war, Dr. Wang had no money for supplies to practice medicine again. He came over to Formosa and lived with his son, who was an American-trained pilot in the Chinese air force. Dr. Wang and his wife had nothing to do but go from house to house just talking the gospel.

The city in which Dr. Wang lived was only forty-five minutes by bus from Tainan. Having heard that Miss Ming was planning to organize a church in Tainan, he came asking that twenty-five of his group be examined for baptism and be included in the organization. As most of those to be examined were in the air corps, their only free time was Saturday afternoon and evening. We just had to go, even though we did not suppose that many of the group would be ready for baptism. It was something new in the Orient when three women took a bus to go examine a group for baptism, most of whom were men.

To our amazed delight we accepted twenty-four of the twenty-five for baptism. Their testimonies and examinations proved them so clearly saved that we went back to Tainan at bedtime as if floating on air. We were ready for Sunday.

Today there is a church in Dr. Wang's city, pastored by a university graduate who has finished at our Taipei seminary. The church sponsors a mission in a nearby community where many servicemen are encamped.

Good News

As cold waters to a thirsty soul, so is good news from
a far country (Prov. 25:25).

When I met James Taylor, grandson of Hudson Taylor, founder of the China Inland Mission, in Formosa in 1957, he asked, "Does the name Ma Ying Tang ring a bell with you?"

"Yes," I answered. "He was a Honan man who was county superintendent of education in Tsining and was saved there at my house twenty years ago. What do you know about him?"

"Come to see my wife," he said, "and she will thrill you with his story."

I heard the story a few months later when I was in a southern city of Formosa and was invited to the Taylor home for lunch. Mrs. Taylor told me of much that took place before she and Mr. Taylor had to leave interior China.

As the Japanese army entered Honan Province, the Taylors left for the west and opened a Bible school in Sian, Shensi Province, and organized churches. Brother Ma was ordained a pastor and became a teacher in the Bible school. The Lord Himself chose the pupils. They were refugees from eastern provinces as well as from Shensi.

One pupil who was especially bright did not even know her family name. Both parents had died in a cholera epidemic in Kiangsu Province, and she and her brother went to live with her mother's brother, whom she remembered was named Li. He was glad to keep the nephew permanently. But when the girl was twelve years old she was dressed up in a pretty garment, with a flower in her hair, and taken on the uncle's back through the rice field to the city, where she was sold as a "white slave." When older, she was put into the prostitution business, at first to wait on others. Everything within her revolted against such a life. Feeling that she could endure it no longer, she secured poison and stole out by the Yangtze River to take it and fall into the water.

As she lifted the poison to her mouth, she was startled by a voice calling, "Go back!" She looked around and, while there was no one there, again the voice said, "Go back!" Though grieved over returning to the brothel, she was afraid to disobey the voice.

Sometime afterwards a rich merchant from Peking went to the brothel and found her crying. She begged him to take her out of that place. Being sorry for her, he bought her and took her up into Honan Province, where he had business. (His wife and children were living in Peking.)

Still the concubine was unhappy. He asked, "How is it that nothing that I do for you makes you happy? I buy pretty clothes and jewelry for you, provide servants and good food, take you to the movies and theater, and still you are not happy. The Christians are happy; I'll send you to their church."

The Sunday that she went to the little church, the uneducated Chinese preacher stated that no concubine could go to heaven. She did not go to church again.

As the Japanese army drew near that section of Honan, the rich merchant and his concubine went to Sian and even to the same inn where the Taylors were. It was not many weeks until the miserable young woman went to Mrs. Taylor and asked if it were true that a concubine could not be saved.

Mrs. Taylor read and explained the Bible to her until she was ready to get on her knees at the foot of the cross and pour out her heart in confession. She arose, praising the Lord.

The husband sent for the wife to come from Peking and bring the children to Sian, to get out of the way of the Japanese army. The wife was a well-educated, highly-cultured woman, a teacher in the Peking Language School.

Before her arrival the husband, having been so impressed by the change in the concubine, went to Mrs. Taylor wanting to know how to be saved. After an hour or two of Bible reading he, too, was on his knees calling upon the Lord. Mrs. Taylor said that he poured out such a volume of sin in his confession to the Lord, that she felt the need of a bath for cleansing. The Lord met him. He arose with a heart full of praise to God.

The wife, having heard of the concubine, had purchased a revolver, planning to shoot her first, the husband next, then the children one by one, and lastly herself, thus ending the whole family. However, when she entered the home, the concubine was quiet and humble and kept in the background, giving the wife her rightful place. When the wife saw the change in her husband, heard his testimony, and saw a concubine such as she never dreamed could exist, she, too, went to Mrs. Taylor, wanting to know how to be saved. When she got on her knees and humbly confessed all of her sins, with simple faith in Jesus Christ as her Lord, she also arose a new creature in Christ.

The concubine whose name, "Chu-Chun," meant "Bamboo Princess," applied to enter the Bible school. Mrs. Taylor wrote a note to the husband asking him to release her and let her go to school.

He replied that he would place a sum of money to her name in the bank. She could live on the interest and go to school, while the original would be for her old age. He also said that Bamboo Princess was now free to live her own life, and in the future she would be no more to him than any other woman.

The following Sunday Mr. Taylor baptized the three of them in the nearby river and they became faithful members of the local churches.

A few years went by, and at the Easter season, Pastor Ma was off for the weekend preaching in another city. Early Easter morning he went out by a river for his quiet time with the Lord. While rejoicing in his risen, living Savior, he began thinking of those to the west who did not know the Lord. He became burdened not only for the outlying provinces of China and Tibet, but also for the lands all the way to the Holy Land.

Pastor Ma prayed earnestly for the people of these countries. Then he began to feel that the Lord wanted him to lead in forming an evangelistic band which would take the gospel all the way back to Jerusalem.

While Pastor Ma was out by the river, the Bible school faculty and students were having an early morning Easter service in the schoolyard. The Taylors had a map drawn on the ground of all the outlying provinces of West China and of Tibet. The call was given for anyone who was so led to go to either place to stand on the map in the area he felt the Lord was leading him.

One by one students walked out and stood on different map provinces. Some, however, felt called beyond the provinces of China and Tibet. One wanted to take the gospel to closed Afghanistan. Another believed that the Lord was calling him to take the knowledge of the Savior to Arabia to the city of Mecca.

After some months of prayer and study of the various countries and traveling conditions, and of enlisting prayer from the surrounding churches, the group of twelve, including Bamboo Princess, started out. They divided into two groups, one going toward the northwest and the other toward the southwest.

Their plan of work was to stop in centers, preach the gospel until some were saved, then teach them and organize them into a church. One worker would stay with the new congregation until leaders were trained, then go on to the next center which was beyond the ability of the new church group to reach, and there do the same. Eventually a line of churches would be established all the way back to the Holy Land.

As the group went west, they found along the way young people who had gone there to keep ahead of the Japanese army. Many of them were graduates of China's best universities. Some who were from Bible colleges wanted to serve the Lord through the "Back to Jerusalem Band." As members of the band led meetings in city after city, many young people were saved, some of whom volunteered for Christian work.

When Pastor Ma went to the city of Chengtu to enlist the interest of the churches in the new venture, he led meetings where a great number of college students were saved. Many of these also felt called to preach. Their need for Bible training led Pastor Ma to make plans for establishing a seminary on the border of Tibet.

The last news which the Taylors received from the group was through a China Inland missionary on the border of Tibet in 1951. At that time news came that two of the number were in Tibet. They were having severe trials indeed, having to hide in tall grass by the hour as they tried to travel.

Little did Brother Ma realize what the Lord had in mind for him, when in that all-night prayer meeting at my house he handed himself over to his Savior for whatever he might want.

Becoming of Age

They shall still bring forth fruit in old age
(Ps. 92:14).

"Becoming of age!" What pain! I never dreamed that anything in this life could ever hurt like giving up work with the Chinese and returning home. I was still doing about fifteen hours of work a day, and I never became too tired to get up rested the next morning.

Foreign missionaries are automatically retired by our mission board on the first day of the month following the month in which comes the seventieth birthday. My birthday is in November, and that year November 30 came on Sunday, my last day to work as a regular missionary.

I had been asked by the mission to give my last term of service to teaching Old Testament in the seminary and to establishing a new church in the heart of the capital city. Imagine my delight when I went to visit the building which had been secured for the new mission, to find it just half a block from a little lot I had considered for a church site soon after my arrival in Taipei. In six years' time we saw that the question had not been whether the Lord wanted a church in the center of the city or in a residential section where we had gone first. He had planned for one in each location.

With seminary students as co-workers, it was only a short time until we had a strong church. This group asked me to give my last week of work to leading special meetings in their church. A number were present that Sunday evening who wanted personal help after the service. I reached home at midnight, wondering why November could not have had thirty-one days.

I felt that I was just then qualified from experience for missionary work. The forty-one and a half years had been very short, interesting indeed, at times thrilling, and always rewarding. Every trial along the way had been forgotten as soon as the next person was saved.

However, I agreed with the Foreign Mission Board, that its retirement policy was good. Since the mind that we know with grows old, too, some of us would never be willing to retire, were it left to our discretion.

The dear Lord was so wonderful to me that during the last ten days He moved the hearts of seven people for whom I had been praying for some time (one of them for nine years) to turn to Him. They came one by one asking for personal help. What joy in my sorrow to see them at the airport when I left, praising the Lord for the gift of eternal life.

What contrast in my emotions when I flew away from Taipei to those I had when I docked in Shanghai nearly forty-two years before!

Yes! There would be much to go home and tell!

Questions for Group Discussion and Personal Reflection

Chapter One

1. What do you recall was happening in the world in 1917, the year Bertha Smith was appointed to China by the Foreign Mission Board of the Southern Baptist Convention?

2. What does Miss Bertha say about her intense loneliness while in Peking? What did loneliness and homesickness do to her? How was her loneliness resolved?

3. Why were some of the missionaries in Peking called "the devotees"?

4. What was one of Miss Bertha's "first China heartaches" and why?

5. Describe idol worship as practiced by "mothers and grandmothers."

6. What was the "No-God Society"?

7. How did Miss Bertha feel about marriage, being single, being childless? How did she resolve these feelings? What was Miss Bertha's "covenant with the Lord"?

8. What impact did Dr. R. A. Torrey's visit make upon Bertha? What about Dr. Charles G. Trumbull's visit?

9. What is the significance of Dr. Trumbull's phrase: "Let go and let God"?

10. Describe Bertha's Bible study of 2 Corinthians 9:8.

11. Bertha Smith writes: "Dr. Trumbull taught us to sing, not 'I Need Thee Every Hour,' but 'I Have Thee Every Hour.'" What is the difference between the two and why is it significant?

12. What is the author's definition of "courage"?

Chapter Two

1. What did the author find when she reached North China?

2. What happened in March 1927? How did it affect the missionaries?

3. Describe the persecution of Christians by the soldiers.

4. One by one discuss the significance of the following:

While we were weak, He wanted to be strength in us.
While we were stupid, He wanted to be wisdom in us.
While we were sinful, He wanted to be holiness in us.
While we were easily aroused and intolerant, He wanted to be patience in us.

5. Who was Miss Marie Monsen?

6. Who was Mrs. Charles Culpepper and what was her physical problem? Describe her healing.

7. After the healing of Mrs. Culpepper, why does Miss Bertha describe herself as a "joy-killer"?

8. Describe the meeting between the author and one of her Chinese teachers.

9. Discuss the work of Pearl Caldwell.

10. Contemplate the story about Miss Monsen that begins this way: "When Miss Monsen was packing to go from Tientsin over to the port of Hwanghsien, the Holy Spirit kept suggesting to her that she should buy some apples."

11. What did Miss Monsen mean by this statement: "Dead people cannot eat!"

12. Do you agree with the following advice given by the author?

    "We missionaries never gave comfort to anyone who became uneasy. We urged him to go make confession, and restitution where necessary, and keep praying for the Holy Spirit to continue to reveal sin."

13. Describe what happened to the Larson's cook. Contemplate the prayer of the cook when he prayed: "Lord, I thank You that I am no longer I."

14. What influence did the cook have upon his hometown?

15. Tell of the experience of Brother Li.

16. What happened to the North China Seminary after the Shantung revival?

17. Who was Lucy Wright and what was her "born again" experience? Why did Miss Bertha doubt her at first?

Chapter Three

1. Who was Dr. Sung? Describe his education in the United States. What happened to his faith as he progressed in obtaining degrees? How did Dr. Sung have his faith restored? What difference did his shared testimony have upon his listeners back in China? How did he die?

2. What was Brother Wang's problem? How did he resolve it?

3. Dr. C. W. Pruitt said of Dr. Sung, "No living man has given up more for the gospel!" What did Dr. Pruitt mean by his statement?

4. Who was Dr. Hou? What did he do?

5. Describe the physical healing of Joseph, son of Deacon Chiang.

6. Describe the physical healing of Mrs. Loh Kin T'ang. What was her husband's response? How did her healing change their family?

7. Who was Mrs. K'iao, and what is her story?

8. What were Miss Bertha's experiences with casting out demons as related in this chapter?

9. Why would Miss Bertha not "lay hands on" Mr. Liu?

10. Discuss the closing paragraph of this chapter. What does the author mean? "After Dr. Maddry had completed his visit of all the mission work, he held a conference in Shanghai of representatives from all the mission groups. At that conference he stated that, when traveling through Shantung and Honan provinces, he had felt that he was reliving the Acts of the Apostles."

Chapter Four

1. What happened in the Depression of 1932 that Miss Bertha described as "a blow"?

2. What was the impact of Dr. Ray's letter to Bertha Smith regarding her missionary service?

3. How did Miss Bertha confirm that the Lord wanted her to return to China?

4. Discuss Isaiah 45:2–3.

5. Why did Miss Bertha assure Dr. Ray that she would make no appeals for money from churches?

6. What was the miraculous way God provided to return Miss Bertha to China?

7. What impact did the letters from Martha Franks and Dr. and Mrs. Connely have on Bertha? What did they enable her to do?

8. Relate the story of Lueba and her conversion. What effect did the storm at sea have on Lueba? On the other passengers? On Miss Bertha and Miss Huey?

9. When did Miss Bertha's position resume with the Board? Describe her circumstances at that time.

10. What happened during the bank failure, and how was the money recovered?

11. What was the generosity of Brother Hoh?

Chapter Five

1. Who was Mr. Pi? How did he come to Christ?

2. Describe the experience Miss Bertha had when she went to the city of Tsining at the man's request. What was her primary work there? What were the results of her work there?

3. What is Bertha's definition of a miracle?

4. What was Bertha's experience while in the Pochow and Kweiteh fields of Anhui Province?

5. Through her painful experience with her ears, what lessons did Bertha Smith learn?

6. Who was Mr. Huang? How did he come to know the Lord? What vehicle did Bertha Smith use in order to talk with him about the Lord? What tragedy happened to the Huang family?

Chapter Six

1. Why, in the summer of 1937, did urgent calls come from the consulate advising Miss Bertha to proceed to the coast at once? What was happening at that time in China? In the world?

2. Why did Miss Bertha not want to leave?

3. Contemplate Psalm 46. What did the psalm mean to the people Bertha had to leave?

4. What was the message from the president of the United States regarding missionaries at that time? What was Miss Bertha's decision regarding leaving China and why?

5. What was the sin of Mr. Wang? What did Miss Bertha tell him?

6. Describe the aviator and his experience with the Lord.

7. Who were Mr. Ma and Mr. Yen? What role did they play?

8. What happened to Mr. Tai's wife?

9. When did the following Scripture become so important for Miss Bertha? What did it mean to her and why? (John 14:20): "I am in my Father, and ye in me, and I in you," said Jesus.

10. Describe Miss Bertha's "first China disease" and her healing.

11. Why are Chinese not disturbed by other Christian denominations?

12. Describe what happened on January 11, 1937.

13. How did the author answer the question of the Chinese co-workers when they asked: "Why did God, in whom we were trusting, permit those bombs to drop here on our mission grounds?"

14. Describe the fall of the city of Tsining.

Chapter Seven

1. How does Miss Bertha describe the Japanese?

2. What was the apparent danger for the girls and young women she protected?

3. Describe some of the ways in which Miss Bertha protected the girls and women.

4. How did the missionary keep the Bible classes and schools going? Why was it important to keep them open?

5. Who was Dr. John Abernathy, and how did his arrival help and encourage Miss Bertha? How was he able to secure a travel permit?

6. Describe the role of Mr. Tai during this time.

7. What is the meaning of John 16:8?

8. Recall the story of the two little sisters who became sick and died.

9. In your own words, what does the following statement mean? Could it also define anxiety today? "The Chinese phrase for anxiety is 'hang up the heart.'"

10. What experience does Miss Bertha describe as "one of the Lord's smiles"?

11. Who was Dr. Scovel?

12. What particular problem did Miss Bertha have concerning the Japanese soldiers?

13. What was the kindness of Mrs. Liu?

14. How did the Lord supply the necessary building materials?

Chapter Eight

1. What happened on December 8, 1941, that changed the lives of the missionaries? At that time, how long had Miss Bertha worked in China?

2. What did the Scripture 1 Samuel 14:45 mean to Miss Bertha during the December 8th trial? What was her response to the Lord?

3. Describe how the Lord used the land Miss Bertha owned in Peitaiho to help her financially.

4. Relate the story of Miss Bertha's internment. In what ways was the internment good for her?

5. Describe the prayer life of the missionaries during the week of prayer for foreign missions emphasis.

6. Who was Miss Aletta Jacobaz and how did her life and teaching impact Miss Bertha and others? What was Miss Jacobaz's unique style of counseling?

7. "It had been a previously unheard-of thing for private citizens of enemy countries to be exchanged during war, and I took it to be a definite work of the Lord upon the hearts of men. I wanted to go home so as to be ready to return when the war was over." Reflect on this statement and discuss Miss Bertha's return to America.

Chapter Nine

1. Describe Miss Bertha's last days in Tsining.

2. Who was Alex Herring?

3. What did the missionaries do while in Yenchow for six weeks?

4. Who was Ming Kuang? What did his name mean?

5. Describe the missionaries' Fourth of July celebration.

6. What were some of the miracles Miss Bertha describes in this chapter?

Chapter Ten

1. When the Communists entered the city, why was the first thought that came to Miss Bertha's mind, "Lazarus is dead!"?

2. Why didn't Alex, Miss Bertha, and Fern slip out of the city with the Catholic priests and nuns when invited to?

3. Read Psalm 62:5. What does this verse say to you personally?

4. What form of transportation did the missionaries take out of the city and how did it come about?

5. What bad news did they receive regarding the trains?

Chapter Eleven

1. Why didn't Miss Bertha accept the invitation to go to South China? Where did she go instead?

2. Discuss the following: "Baptists believe that in the Lord's work, the Holy Spirit is to be the final guide of the individual though advice from others is appreciated."

3. What does "Formosa" mean? What does "Taiwan" mean?

4. What was the official language of China?

5. What was happening in Formosa at the time when Miss Bertha arrived there?

6. What happened to Miss Bertha on October 19, 1948?

7. What were some of the problems Miss Bertha faced in Taipei?

8. How did the missionary distribute gospel tracts?

9. Describe the city of Taipei.

10. Who were Dr. Scott and Mrs. George? What role did they play in Bertha Smith's life and ministry?

11. Describe the beginning of the "Miss Smith Baptist Mission" and the work that Miss Bertha did there? What does she say about her sofa?

12. Who was Miss Wang? What did Miss Bertha tell her?

13. What was "Gospel Hall" and how did it minister?

14. Who were Paul and Lydia and what was their story?

15. What was Miss Bertha's method of dealing with individuals concerning their sins and salvation?

16. Describe what took place in Tainan in the spring of 1952.

17. Reflect on the meeting of Miss Bertha with the James Taylors. Who was Ma Ying Tang and what was the story Miss Bertha was told about him?

18. How does Miss Bertha describe her feelings about retirement?

PART II

Selections from
How the Spirit Filled My Life

CHAPTER TWELVE

A Filling of New Light

On a hot Sunday afternoon, June, 1907, when Mother and her eight sons and daughters sat on the front porch in our South Carolina home, my father came walking up the street carrying the suitcase of three guests. They were introduced to us as Rev. Troy and Luther Manness and Mr. McElrath, their singer.

Some days before, they had arrived in our town by train and put up at the hotel. When they asked the hotel manager to whom they should go to get help in securing a place to put their tent for the gospel meetings, they were directed to my father. After enough conversation with them to see that they were trustworthy men, Father asked the mayor to let them use the vacant town lot in the center of town across the street from Father's store.

Meetings began Friday evening, to last through three Sundays. Everybody in town went, and we all wanted to go, but Father said, "Wait until you find out what those men are preaching!" Lo! We learned that he had been going to each service—Friday and Saturday evenings and Sunday afternoon. (There was no Sunday morning service.) He had, by that time, heard enough to be convinced that the men were there, as he expressed it, "for the good of the town."

Mother, with her four daughters, old enough to help and trained to do so, soon had a good supper for the thirteen who sat around our table with the cakes and pies which had been cooked on Saturday, as was our custom. Needless to say, we did not have to ask to go to the Sunday night service, nor any others.

By the time meetings had ended on the third Sunday evening, the men had moved their tent to a Wesleyan churchyard eight miles out in the country. We were getting up and cooking a picnic basket of food for two meals to serve two buggies full of us who went daily to stay through three services. Crops were "laid by" and farmers had time to go to church all day.

Little did Father dream that his kindness to those strangers would mean that ten years later he would stand at the railway depot, fifty yards from the location of that tent, and say goodbye to one of his daughters leaving for China. When trying to ease his pain at the parting, I said, "Seven years will not be long and I will be back." He replied, "But I will not be here!"

When that first supper was over at our home, one of the preachers asked the four girls who stood together, "Are you all Christians?" "Yes," sister Jennie answered. I could never have answered in any other way after the time I had in becoming one; but what kind of Christians were we?

Home Church and Early Years

Growing up in a family where "yes" was "yes" and "no" was "no" with no arguing about it, and obedience and respect for our parents and old brothers and sisters was consistently instilled in us, I was a good girl. When children are taught properly at home, they show it in school. So, I never had a teacher whom I did not think was just wonderful, and I studied incessantly to please them. This meant that I was bragged on by the teachers, which I ate up! All who knew me referred to me as a "good girl," and I did not know any better than to believe it. I did everything possible to keep them approving of me.

The Baptist church, like most in small towns and the country in those days, had a pastor who served four churches. Our pastor lived forty miles away in the city of Greenville, and he came and went by train. When he came, it was his business to feed the saints. The deacons carried on the Wednesday evening prayer service (which was true to its name), the Sunday School, and later the Baptist Young People's Union.

When summer came, the church held a two-week revival, with two services daily. The twenty stores in town closed their doors for two hours for the forenoon service. If farmers came to shop, they could wait.

There were three classes of folk in the churches at that time: the warm-hearted Christians, the backsliders, and the class who were in those days called "the lost." Everybody went to church, the church being the social center, with nowhere else to go and nothing at home to keep one there.

The grand old man of God preacher, with tears rolling down his cheeks, pled with backsliders to confess their sins and come back into fellowship with Holy God. He pled with the lost to repent of their sins and flee from God's holy wrath to come, because it had been appointed unto man once to die, but after that the judgment! And while the man of God wept, preached the Word, and pled, saints prayed and the Holy Spirit moved.

Baptist churches did not have altar forms as the Methodists did, but for two weeks in the year, we had plenty of repenting space. Those sitting on the front rows of benches across the church moved when the invitation was given, knowing that people would come. They stood in orderly lines down the aisles next to the walls and continued their share in singing to the unsaved, such as: "Come every soul by sin oppressed, there's mercy with the Lord." As more came, more benches were vacated, and sometimes half the church would be turned into a "mourner's bench!"

Mourn they did, as the Holy Spirit used the Word to show them the exceeding sinfulness of sin, and they realized that only their life breath kept them out of an awful hell which had been made for the devil and his angels.

The backsliders were there too, like the prodigal of old, confessing to their Father their wandering away and doing as they pleased. They often wept sore as they realized what their sin had cost Holy God.

Struggles to Be Saved

I was ten years old when, one hot July night as I sat beside the second window from the front, the Word of the Lord went to my heart! For the first time I saw myself, at least a little glimpse of what I looked like, in the eyes of Holy God. While people called me a good girl, I would not do in His sight, who saw all the pride of my heart—the selfishness and the wanting to be first in everything, just to be praised by teachers. I wanted to make a hundred on all of my examinations, but I did not want anyone else to make a hundred! I had to excel! What an awful human being, a chip off the old block, Adam, after the devil entered into him.

Praise the Lord that we had a man of God for a pastor who knew that every human being was just like that, and he knew the remedy: Jesus Christ had come and died and taken in Himself the sin of the human family; and that was what he proclaimed.

I wanted to go to the altar that first night, but on the evening before, a girl my age had gone and people said that she was too small, that she did not know what she was doing. Therefore, I did not dare go, but there was no peace of heart for me during the remainder of that meeting, or any other time.

The next year when the revival meeting began, I publicly announced myself a lost sinner by going to the altar and telling the Lord about my sins. In spite of the fact that I had been silently confessing for a year, that was my first chance to let other people know that I was conscious of my being one of the Lord.

No one was trained to do personal work at the altar. Only the pastor was at the altar to help people, and there were always so many older ones there, who took first place, that he never got to me.

I had to go on another year with my burden of sin, shedding many a tear in secret. Over and over again I told the Lord about my sins and pled for His cleansing.

About the third year, I was at the altar next to a woman whom the pastor came to help. It seemed to me that he talked with her a long time. He just stuck his head over toward me and said, "Just trust the Lord and He will save you." He was right, but I did not know what he meant by trusting the Lord. So that meeting came to an end with the cry of my heart being, "The summer is ended and I am not saved" (see Jer. 8:20).

When I went fifteen miles in the country to my grandmother's in the summer and attended their Big Meeting, I would just have to go to the altar. Occasionally we went to other nearby country churches for their summer meetings, and I could not but make my distress known. I went forward so much at my home church that I was afraid people would think that I was just going for the fun of it. I could have assured them that it certainly was not fun. Sometimes I would almost hold to the bench to keep from going forward but then I went home feeling worse then than when I went; and when I did go, it did no good. Oh, the wretched girl that I was.

Deceived and Still No Peace

After our pastor had been with us for fifteen years, he resigned and pastored another church in the community. When his revival meeting came, we went. I was among those at the altar wanting to be saved from hell. I was about fourteen at that time, and I suppose the pastor felt that I was old enough to have some attention. He said, "Bertha, if you will just trust the Lord, He will save you. Are you trusting Him?"

I replied, "Yes, I am trusting the Lord."

He said, "Well, you are saved then."

(Now, what about one human being telling another that he is saved when the advisor cannot see whether or not a miracle has taken place inside?) He went back to the pulpit and asked anyone who had trusted the Lord at that service to stand. I stood, but I went home just as much in the dark as ever. I knew a good bit about the Lord, but He was away out yonder and I was here, under the burden of what I was in the sight of God, with no connection between us.

Born from Above

Two more summers passed, with a pastor who did no personal work. Then one last Sunday morning, after I had gone regularly to the altar as usual, the pastor asked if any at the front were ready to come to Jesus Christ and take Him as Savior. For the first time, I saw that we come to the cross of Christ to be saved. Formerly I had not differentiated between God the Father and God the Son, and I did not know what was meant by "trusting God." Even though my advice had been right, all of the Godhead was God to me. I had been all those years trying to approach God the Father directly, no doubt even calling Him "Father," when He is only the Father of those who believe His Son (Gal. 3:26). I learned that what the preachers meant by trusting God to save meant to trust God the Son, who settled my sin and my sinful self when He took my sins and me in His own body on the tree.

I was on the front seat, having gone forward at the first verse. I knew that I would go; there was no use to wait. It was but a step to where the pastor stood. I took it, gave him my hand to signify that I trusted in Christ's death to save me. By the time I took the second step, which was back to my seat, my years of burden of sin had rolled away, and the joy of the Lord filled my soul.

I think sometimes if the Lord could ever save anyone the wrong way, He would have saved me! He must really have been sorry for me. I praise Him that He never let go, but made that conviction stronger and stronger until someone said enough about Christ's death, or Christ being the Savior, for me to lay hold on what He had done for me. There is no direct road from the sinful heart to God the Father. I tried to make one, but it did not work. My sin was settled at the cross, and through Christ's death I at last came, which is the only way that anyone gets to Him.

I went home so thrilled, and so sorry for everyone else who was not in tune with the Lord, that I did not want any of that good Sunday dinner. My parents and two older sisters and both older brothers were church members and one brother and sister younger were old enough to be saved, so I just had to go to my place of prayer by the trunk in the walk-in closet in my room and plead with God for the family and for friends and neighbors.

But that joy wore off. Before many months I showed no more of the fruit of the Spirit in my life than the rest of my family, for whom I prayed that glorious Sunday when I passed out of death into life. I well knew to whom I belonged, even though at times I knew that I was not pleasing Him. When the visiting preacher, Brother Manness, asked, "Are you girls all Christians?" I knew that Sister Jennie answered right, but I longed for something more of the Lord whom I knew!

When the Spirit Visited My Family

We found that the well-bred Manness brothers were sons of a Methodist preacher in Greensboro, North Carolina, who had education, books, and twelve children. Even though they are "cheaper by the dozen," the two brothers could not afford to go to college. Therefore they attended Dr. Knapp's Bible School in Cincinnati, where they received good training. At breakfast, when we tried to decide which one of them was the better preacher, we usually agreed on the last one we heard.

They preached that people who are saved belong to the Lord—mind, body, and soul—that we should acknowledge that fact, confess all of our sins of failing the Lord, so as to be cleansed, and then hand over ourselves and let the Holy Spirit fill us. We would then be empowered to live to please the Lord all the time. We had never heard anything like that.

First, my second sister had her life made over by taking our copy of their new hymn book to the central office where she was working that summer. While reading the hymns, the Holy Spirit so revealed the truth of one to her heart that she came home with a testimony of having gone all the way with the Lord.

That so moved Mother that she was soon one of those at the altar seeking all that the Lord had for her. Up to that time we had family prayer only when the pastor spent the night with us and led it. When Mother was down at that altar before the Lord seeking the fullness of his Spirit, the Lord asked something of her, which was that she start family prayer. For a quiet woman of the home who had never even given a testimony in public or prayed aloud, that was a demand. She struggled that hot day until she had completely ruined her lovely lavender silk blouse. The change in her, how marvelous! Soon it was sister Jennie at the altar, and brother Lester, a third-year college student who discovered that he had been baptized at twelve years of age because he was convicted of sin but never had been saved. Down on his knees there, he cried to the Lord, a lost sinner, and when the Lord met him, he declared that he joined a Baptist church at the age of twelve because he was convicted of sin and wanted to be a better boy.

Bertha's turn came too, and time after time I went down wanting to be a better Christian.

Hungry for More

A message on Romans 12:1–2 was used of the Lord to make clear to me just what the dear Lord expected: "I beseech you therefore brethren [saved people], by the mercies of God, that ye present your bodies a living sacrifice, holy, acceptable unto God, which is your reasonable service. And be not conformed to this world: but be ye transformed by the renewing of your mind, that ye may prove what is that good, and acceptable, and perfect will of God."

I did not know then as much as I learned later about offerings presented to God, especially in the consecration of the sons of Aaron to become priests (Lev. 8). First, they had to be born of the priesthood; next, they had to be bathed, typical of cleansing;

then clothed in pure white linen, which must have represented the righteous standard which Holy God requires.

In those days Baptist churches did not have rededication meetings every few months, or call for people every Sunday to come down and rededicate. I did not have that kind of church background. However, I had learned from that sermon on dedication (Rom. 12:1–2) and from the Word that the sacrifice for dedication had to be without blemish—a perfect specimen of sheep—before it could be acceptable. I had for days been confessing all the sins that I knew about, and seeing that the altar meant handing self over to live for the Lord. I knew just what to do.

When the invitation was given, I went immediately, and there I had a business transaction with my Lord. I handed myself over to Him for anything that He might choose for me. His Word was that this was not something special, but only what was expected of me because the Lord saved me. It was "my reasonable service," not too much to ask.

I was ready to quit being conformed to the world, but by a changed mind toward the world (my environment) I would prove the will of the Lord for my life, which would be good, acceptable to me, and perfect. It did not take long for me to do this, so prepared was my heart. I handed myself over, accepting from the Lord whatever He might bring or not bring into my life. I literally put myself on the altar to live for the Lord only.

Filled with the Holy Spirit

The congregation still sang invitation hymns, but there was no use for me to kneel there longer. I had done what the Word told me to do, and I knew that the One who died for me could be trusted to do all that had been promised. I got up and returned to my seat. By the time I got there, joy unspeakable was filling my soul. I knew that the Holy Spirit, who had come into my heart when I was saved and had wanted to fill me those two years but could not unless I knew how to let Him, had taken over.

I thought that the sin principle in me had been removed, eradicated, and I would never sin any more. The Holy Spirit so magnified Christ that I did not sin for a good while. Or rather I was not convicted of sins by the Holy Spirit. Certainly He saw much in me that grieved Him, but He would rule those out as He saw me about to take it.

Results of Being Filled

I am full of power by the spirit of the Lord (Mic. 3:8).

When the Holy Spirit began to magnify Christ, all worldly pleasure lost its flavor. No longer did I want to talk like the world or look like worldly people. I took off my jewelry, my pretty clothes with the laces, ribbons, and feathered and flowered hats, and I wore the very plainest clothes. In nothing did I want to attract attention to myself. (While I am sure that the Lord was leading, I doubt now that He led me to go as far as I did go.) That was the way the Wesleyans dressed, and they were the only Spirit-filled people whom I knew for a pattern. (I learned later that modest pretty clothes not only keep me from ever thinking of how I am dressed, but has the same effect in other people who have to look at me.)

The Bible Became a New Book

I signed up for a correspondence course with Dr. Knapp's Bible School and was enjoying what I could understand until sister Jennie looked at some of the lessons and said, "This is too deep for you! It is a preacher's course."

Passages came alive that I had committed to memory when a child. I added many verses, paragraphs, and chapters to these. At school the principal came up to an unused classroom one day at recess time and found me sitting on an almost cold radiator on the floor reading my New Testament. He just turned on more heat and went out.

I Wanted Everybody to Be Saved

The Lord laid on my heart twenty unsaved young people about my age. I began to pray for them by name daily and saw eighteen of them saved that same summer. The nineteenth was saved some years later. The other one moved away and I lost contact.

Prayer Became Communion with God

Prayer became communion with God not only in private but with others of like mind. I was only in the ninth grade, because formerly our school had gone through only eight grades. I was described by the others in school as "Bertha has religion." The church seemed cold to me, but my joy was in attending a woman's prayer meeting on Wednesday afternoon where a "Spirit-filled" woman gave the meat of the Word, after which we joined our hearts in praise and intercession.

Failure, then Fullness

As time went on I began to discover that the sin principle in me was not removed. It too often exerted itself and I did not know what to do about it. Needless to say, I was grieved over every accidental sin which was a grief to the Holy Spirit within me. I constantly prayed to get back the glorious experience of the first filling. Sometimes the Lord in His marvelous mercy did restore perfect peace and a measure of joy, but it was not sustained and, needless to say, there was no power for service.

While I continually tried to lead someone to the Savior, I did not see many brought in genuine conviction to the foot of the cross become willing for Jesus Christ to reign over them. Being busy in church work did not completely satisfy.

During four years in college, though active in all forms of Christian organizations on campus, I led only one classmate to the Lord.

While teaching in public school, my heart broke over lost pupils, but I did not have power to win them, even though I most faithfully kept my quiet time with the Lord and His Word.

Sometimes after much confession of failure and prayer I received another uplift, but what to do with the old self I did not know.

I Went to China

I studied for two years at Southern Baptist Theological Seminary, under the old men of God there who were marvelous teachers of the Word. Then I went to China, but I had not discovered how to live victoriously all the time over the old self. I was wholly the Lord's and living there only that people might know my Savior, but how the Lord could get through me to a number of them I did not know. Not knowing continuous filling, I was unable to lead other missionaries into what I had experienced. They only described me as having "good religion." The crowds of lost people would have broken my heart and no doubt my health had the Lord not come to my rescue.

A saint of the Lord in California, Mr. Milton Stewart, knowing the heart-hunger of missionaries, left a sum of money in his will with which to build four summer conference centers in four sections of China, where missionaries could go for one dollar per day for ten days for spiritual refreshing. Most of the speakers were from America, being assisted by suitable missionaries on the field like Miss Ruth Paxson and Miss Marie Monsen.

Every summer I went away for a few weeks and always went to a conference. During my second summer in China, the speaker for the North China Conference was Dr. R. A. Torrey. He spoke twice daily on the Spirit-filled life. What an uplift to come back to the filling of former years. However, my old self still occasionally bobbed up.

The third summer, Dr. Charles G. Trumbull, editor of the *Sunday School Times*, and Miss Ruth Paxson were the speakers. What a team they were. Miss Paxson was an expert in showing from the Word of God the old nature: its loves, its pride, its desires for self-expression, and its ability to dedicate itself to Jehovah God and work hard, thinking it was serving the Lord.

Dr. Trumbull's message was "Christ in You, the Hope of Glory." Christ had been in me since I had been saved, but I did not know that. All that I knew was that He was along by my side. The truth that Christ was living inside of us had much more meaning than just being beside us. In fact, we were so thrilled in the thought that Christ was living inside of us that the old self did not bother us so much. Christ in us was stronger than our sinful natures, stronger than the other person's human nature and stronger than the devil himself. Therefore, life was never the same.

Needless to say, the new blessing created in our hearts a deep desire for the Chinese Christians to know that Christ was living in them.

We missionaries prayed together at every opportunity. There came a hunger—in fact, a definite burden—to pray for reviving in the churches, in our private devotions, missionary prayer meetings, and the church meetings. After a few years, the burden became so great that in consultation with the Chinese pastor in the city where I work, a day of prayer for reviving was set aside the first day of every month. All who could do so went to the church house at nine o'clock each of those mornings and prayed until twelve, then returned back at two in the afternoon until five. They had no speaking. A different leader each hour chose a hymn, read a Bible passage, and directed the praying.

Knowing that we prayed within the will of God, we expected a true new work of God in the hearts of leaders and lay members. "If my people, which are called by my name, shall humble themselves, and pray, . . . I will hear from heaven" (2 Chron. 7:14).

CHAPTER THIRTEEN
Self-Dedicated Moses

Moses no doubt had learned from his mother that God was to lead Israel back to Canaan and give the land to them. (Children in the East have a nurse until they are in school, and sometimes even afterwards.) His mother nurse had time to instill much into his heart, and she probably remained in the court as a maid. At any rate, there was something there for the Lord to use to call him to lead God's people out of Egypt.

He gave up life with all its pleasures and its luxuries and the glories of Egyptian court life, and went out to identify himself with a race of slaves.

Moses is a classic example of one dedicating old self to the Lord to do a job for Him. He gave up all this, and of course he thought that all that Israel would need was a leader. If he were willing to give up so much to become their leader, certainly they would cooperate.

One day he went out and saw an Egyptian taskmaster smite one of his brethren. He looked this way and that way, and when he was sure no one would see him, instead of looking up and asking, "Lord, is this the way You want it done?" he used his strong right arm and killed the Egyptian and hid him in the sand. Did he go home rejoicing over his victory? (One less Egyptian to oppress his people.) Did Moses go to bed that night pleased over the success of the day?

You remember that when he went out the next day he saw two Hebrews fighting. Moses went up to exhort the guilty one not to treat his brother so badly, but the guilty one resented the interference and accused Moses of killing the Egyptian the day before, even though Moses had done so for the sake of the Israelite!

Worse still, the news of Moses' consecrated effort reached Pharaoh, and Moses—with all his good intentions—had to flee for his life. He did not feel safe until he got all the way into the desert land in the vicinity of Mount Sinai.

For forty years, Moses—after all of his dedication to do a job for God—was in the desert following sheep. How his call from God must have puzzled him during those next forty years!

Stephen, in his sermon in Acts 7, describes Moses as being learned in all the wisdom of the Egyptians, and mighty in word and deed.

The result of Moses' self-consecrated working for God was that he spent forty years of solitude in the desert doing that which men can do who do not know one letter in books from another, or have ever been ten miles from home.

The result to the Israelites of Moses' blunder was that another generation had to go on being oppressed by Egyptians and thousands no doubt beaten by cruel overseers. Another generation found graves in Egypt because Moses was unusable.

Year after year Moses lived in the desert with the sheep. His employer gave him his daughter for a wife, which must have been a great comfort to Moses. What thoughts must have gone through his mind as he walked through that sandy desert sagebrush. What remorse over having tried to deliver his people! How his call must have puzzled him during those forty years!

One day when God was sure that Moses had come to the end of himself and all that he himself could do to deliver Israel, the call came again. This time the call came from the burning bush. God said to him, "I am the God of thy father, the God of Abraham, the God of Isaac, and the God of Jacob. . . . I have surely seen the affliction of my people which are in Egypt, and have heard their cry by reason of their taskmasters; for I know their sorrows; and I am come down to deliver them out of the hand of the Egyptians, and to bring them [into Canaan]" (Exod. 3:6–8a).

But God had not been able to accomplish that deliverance because the only one whose life He had spared as a baby for the purpose—the only one whom He had put in a position to be educated and prepared—had gone out on his own to use his own methods to meet the situation. Now the Lord, after forty years, had this man ready! Moses would not deliver them, but Jehovah God would.

"Come now therefore, and I will send thee unto Pharaoh, that thou mayest bring forth my people the children of Israel out of Egypt" (v. 10). Moses hid his face in fear at God's introduction of Himself. His reply was "Who am I, that I should go unto Pharaoh, and that I should bring forth the children of Israel out of Egypt?" (v. 11). As if Jehovah God did not know what He was doing.

All of the Lord's work has been turned over to His children. If they do not cooperate with Him so that He can do it through them, it must go undone. Moses had been in Jehovah God's desert school for forty years following sheep, and now God called again and Moses feared. No wonder, after his miserable failure the first time! One thing sure, he would never dedicate himself to go out to do a job for God again! He had come to the very end of Moses.

Exodus 4:2 says, "What is that in thine hand?" Moses replied, "A rod" (the sign or badge of a shepherd). "Take this rod in thine hand" (v. 17). And Moses realized he was going before Pharaoh with nothing but a rod—as if to say, I am nothing but a shepherd.

Moses had excuses, but the Lord won out in spite of them. When Moses was willing to go, having become nothing but a shepherd, the Lord's opportunity had come. The rod became the Lord's rod, and how He used it! Yes, how He used Moses and the rod to secure the release of Israel!

The mighty present-tense God would do just what He had said that He would. With the rod stretched out, the waters of the Red Sea divided. With the rod again stretched out, the waters closed on the Egyptian army. With the rod, he stretched up toward God in trust to Him for victory, and the Amalekites were defeated. Moses had taken his orders from Jehovah God!

God took them out across every hindrance, all through the forty years wandering in the wilderness, right up to the border of the land, because His leader was nothing but a shepherd.

CHAPTER FOURTEEN

Gehazi: The High Cost of Low Motives

Second Kings 5 contains some interesting and valuable history for us. Naaman, the highest military official, who stood next to the king in the court of the enemy to the north of Israel, was a leper. Through a captive from Israel who resided in his home, he heard of a man down in Israel who could cure leprosy.

His king gave him a leave of absence and sent him off with quite a military escort. Arriving at the court in Samaria, Naaman presented the letter of introduction and request from his king to the king of Israel.

The king of Israel, thinking that the Syrian king was trying to find some excuse for invading Israel, rent his garments and exclaimed, "Who can cure leprosy but God?"

God had His prophet in Israel, named Elisha. When he heard of the situation, he sent a message to the king: "Send that man to me and he will know that there is a prophet in Israel."

Naaman and his party—quite a number in their war chariots—all went down to the humble cottage of Elisha. Elisha knew the pride of that heathen captain, and he knew that Naaman would have to become humble before Holy God could meet him. The prophet helped the Lord out by not even going out to meet the great man. He just sent his servant, Gehazi, out to advise the great man that Elisha had said to go down to the river Jordan and dip seven times, with the promise that if he did so he would be healed.

Such a reception, or lack of reception, in the East was unthinkable. According to all custom, Elisha should have been outside the gate and even out in the street to start bowing when Naaman came in sight.

Naaman was angered beyond words at not being received! He was ready to go back to Damascus, and would have, had not his officials under him and his accompanying bodyguard pled with him to go do what had been suggested.

Finally, Naaman humbled himself and went down and dipped seven times and was perfectly cured.

After the way he had been treated by Elisha, he could have gone up the Jordan to the first ford, crossed over, and gone on back to Damascus. However, he was so grateful that he went up the hill, with all his company, to the home of Elisha, and had all the presents unloaded which he had brought down: ten talents of silver, six thousand pieces of gold, and ten changes of raiment. They would not have been ordinary men's suits as are worn today. No doubt the outer garments were gorgeous robes beaded with jewels.

Elisha had a seminary of one hundred students who sometimes had no food. Had Elisha lived today he would no doubt have exclaimed, "See how the Lord has provided!" His seminary would have been so endowed that never again would students have had to go out into the fields to gather a few greens to make soup!

Elisha would not accept one thing! When Naaman pled with him, Elisha's reply was, "As the Lord liveth, before whom I stand, I will receive none." Elisha ordered his life before his God, and was not going to let that heathen think that he was serving God for anything which he himself might get out of it. Hurrah for Elisha!

Verse 20 begins with, "But Gehazi." Something very different was coming. Yes, Gehazi, the servant of the man of God, stood there and *saw* all of that wealth loaded up to be carried back to Damascus.

Secondly, he *lusted* after it; then, thirdly, he decided that he was going to have some of it. Fourthly, he stepped down from that high place of being associated with the Lord's prophet and went running after some of what that heathen man had. Poor, poor Gehazi! He sinned first with his eyes, then with his heart, then with his mind and will.

He stepped down from the highest position of any man in all of Israel, that of being a co-worker of the great man of God!

It was not safe for a man to travel alone in those days, and Elisha had left what family he had when he was called to be the Lord's prophet. Gehazi had traveled with him, eaten with him, prayed with him, and had taken the place of family. They had shared the little room on top of the wall at the Shunamite's home. In fact, it had been Gehazi who had suggested that the hostess be rewarded a son for her kindness. He saw that son grow large enough to follow his father to the field where, evidently, he suffered a stroke and died. Gehazi saw that boy come back to life. He had the most blessed position of any man in Israel, that of being associated with God's great prophet. How Elisha must have loved him!

As Gehazi went running after the chariots of Damascus, he immediately found a clever ally in the devil, to put into his mind just what to say to Naaman. When Naaman knew that he was coming, he stopped his chariot, got out and called back, "Is all well?" The answer was a lie from Gehazi's lips, "All is well." How could all be well when he had sold himself to the devil? Then another lie, "My master hath sent me" (vv. 21–22). Then another, "Two new seminary students have come, just arrived since you left. They are from Ephraim, a mountainous section where people are poor and could not go away to school." And next, "they are prophets' sons and need help. Give them, I pray, a talent of silver and two changes of raiment."

Grateful Naaman would have given him all that he had if he had asked for it. He did insist that they take two talents of silver. Naaman waited there by the side of the road while he sent two soldiers back with Gehazi to carry the silver and clothes.

Gehazi's plan had worked beautifully. He had gotten more than he expected or could manage—often true of sin for a season!

As Naaman sat by the road and waited for the men to carry Gehazi's new wealth, Gehazi's mind must have soared. (The name "Gehazi" means visions.) From what follows, we see he lived up to his name.

As he saw the olive orchards he must have said, "I can have olive orchards with olive oil to sell." Passing the vineyards he said, "I can have vineyards and vine dressers, with wine and raisins for sale." At the sight of the sheep and shepherds on the hills, perhaps across the Jordan, and the herds of cattle in the meadows of the Jordan with the herdsmen, he exclaimed, "I can possess sheep, cattle, and servants!"

Eastern towns and cities at that time had towers outside the walls where watchmen looked out for the enemy in time of war. That was a time of peace and the tower was empty. Gehazi hid his loot in the house at the base of the tower and sent the two soldiers back to join Naaman.

What did that spiritually stupid Gehazi do after all of that sin? He went walking back to Elisha and reported for duty. Sin is so blinding that it makes men do unreasonable things. He did not know any better than to think that with all of the sin covered he could go on serving Elisha in the same way.

"But God . . . " How gracious was the Lord to his faithful prophet to save him from the tragedy of having a co-worker with hidden sin in his heart and life! He had revealed the whole thing to Elisha, everything that Gehazi had done and thought.

He asked, "Where did you come from, Gehazi?" Reply: "I have not been there!" (Another lie is added to all of his sins.)

(Here, I talk to the preachers and WMU leaders about sinning and going on back to church as usual, leading in prayer or preaching with sin separating them from Holy God. Sin always separates from God! I ask those present if they break the speed limit, which is breaking the law of the land and, therefore, becoming a criminal, and then go to the pulpit to preach. Who wants a criminal preaching to them? Who wants to hear a criminal leading in prayer? All kinds of so-called little sins may separate us from Holy God.)

Now look at the end of that sinning, lying hypocrite, Gehazi. Elisha must have loved Gehazi. But he could not keep such a co-worker.

Elisha had to say to him, "Was it a time to accept money and garments, olive orchards and vineyards, sheep and oxen, menservants and maidservants? Therefore the leprosy of Naaman shall cleave to you, and to your descendants forever." So Gehazi went out from the presence of Elisha a leper, as white as snow (2 Kings 5:26–27, RSV).

Poor Gehazi!

God's law forbade lepers to mingle with others. Every leper was quarantined to live outside the city or town, and it was God's law that if they saw anyone approach they had to call out, "Unclean! Unclean!" meaning, "I am a leper, do not come near me!"

Gehazi had come to that!

Oh, preacher, reader, beware of letting the devil tempt you with love of money, things, and ease! Stand straight before the Lord! You too are human, and that old self will never improve. It must be put in that position of death and kept there! The Lord is your inheritance.

CHAPTER FIFTEEN
Christ Enthroned

For to me to live is Christ (Phil. 1:21).

God's provision for holy living is Christ enthroned. Positively! The holy life is not our living, it is Christ so freely dwelling at ease in us that He actually can live His life through our personalities.

We rejoice over Colossians 1:27: "Christ in you, the hope of glory." Christ is in every believer, but that does not mean that all believers are living holy lives. Many are completely defeated. Why? Because the Christ in us does not force Himself over our wills to do anything for us. He waits for us to will that He shall control us. Holy living presupposes death to self—our constantly choosing that position for the old sinful nature. This is necessary before we enthrone Christ. Living in that position is necessary for holy living. We are never holy if we rebel against Holy God. When we permit the old self to rise up and express itself, or even want to, we grieve the One who wants to live His holiness out in us and through us.

Colossians 3:4: "When Christ, who is our life, shall appear . . . ." Philippians 1:21: "For to me to live is Christ." It is Christ enthroned in the heart and life.

Since He lived thus in Paul, He also can live enthroned in you and me, and enable us to say, "I am crucified with Christ: nevertheless I live; yet not I, but Christ liveth in me" (Gal. 2:20).

What kind of life does Christ live in us? A life that is always victorious! That is always at peace and rest! That is equal to any situation which man or the devil and his demons may create!

This is what He wants to do for us.

When experiencing the wars of North China, I learned to pray in every situation, "Now, Lord, you are equal to this!" And He always was!

The secret is not to try to follow His example in our own strength, even with His help. He has something far better for His children than that!

He means for us to "rejoice" always, and "in every thing give thanks!" (1 Thess. 5:16, 18).

Would a God of love make such heavy demands for us to carry out that they would be a constant burden? No, never. He is in us all that He demands of us. Yes, even to loving our enemies and praying for those who persecute us. (Matt. 5:44).

You may say this is not natural. Whoever thought that the Christian life is natural? The Christian life is supernatural. It is God's life in us.

Seven times Jehovah God pealed forth from Mount Sinai to Israel, "Be ye holy for I am holy," because He was to live in their midst. How else can we show our Lord to the lost world? We may tell a lot, but unless what we say is shown in our daily living, and in every emergency, our teaching will fail.

I heard a few years ago of a woman in Chicago who prayed for her sick husband thus: "Lord, I cannot stand to be left alone in the world with these two children to rear alone. I cannot be willing for You to take my husband." The husband continued to grow weaker. After a few days she prayed, "Lord, I cannot become willing for You to take him, but You are living in me. I trust You to be willingness in me!"

The husband died. The Lord was to her all that she needed as she started life over, being both mother and father to the children. However, she knew that it was not she who was getting along so well, but her Lord and Savior just expressing Himself through her.

After a time, the mother was in the hospital, deathly ill. She cried to her Lord, "Oh, my loving Lord, I cannot be willing to die, and leave my children in the world with neither father nor mother. Spare me for their sakes, if it can be Thy will!"

The next visit of the doctor brought the sad news that she had only a very short time left.

Again she prayed, "Lord, I cannot be willing to go and leave my children orphans in this sinful world, but they are Yours. I turn them over to You and I ask You to be willingness in me to leave them."

In the Lord's glorious victory, she passed on.

CHAPTER SIXTEEN

How to Let the Holy Spirit Fill

What does it mean to be filled?

When is a pitcher full of water? When there is nothing in it except water, and the water comes all the way to the top of the pitcher.

Suppose you have a pitcher of coffee and want a pitcher of water. If you empty half the coffee and fill up the pitcher with water, what do you have? A pitcher filled with coffee and water. If you leave one sip of the black liquid in the pitcher, you still have a pitcher of coffee and water. Only when you empty out all of the coffee and wash the pitcher can you have a pitcher full of clear water.

Most saved people are full of themselves and of the Holy Spirit. With some it is because they do not know that the Lord has anything better for them. Others, however, are unwilling to make the necessary break with their old selves and have only the Holy Spirit filling them. Still others are not filled because of ignorance of the teaching of the Word of God on the subject.

Since there is confusion on our relationship to Pentecost and on terminology used for the experience, it seems necessary to take a look at Jehovah God's preparation for the baptism and the fullness of the Holy Spirit.

When Jesus met His disciples in Jerusalem to be taken up from them, He quoted the words of John the Baptist (Acts 1:5), "Ye shall be baptized with the Holy Ghost [Spirit] not many days hence."

You will recall that John baptized in water when Jesus, who was to die the sinner's death, took the sinner's burial in the grave of water.

Jesus would bury them in the Holy Spirit. And Jesus was filled with the Holy Spirit from birth. He said in Luke 4:18–19, "The Spirit of the Lord is upon me, because he hath anointed me to preach the gospel to the poor; he hath sent me to heal the brokenhearted, to preach deliverance to the captives, and recovering of sight to the blind, to set at liberty them that are bruised, to preach the acceptable year of the Lord."

The disciples, believing what Jesus had said that they would be baptized with the Holy Spirit, obeyed the farewell injunction of the Lord and waited. They spent the waiting time in prayer. Their praying did not bring down the Holy Spirit. He could not have come on any other day than had been set by Jehovah God. Their praying no doubt prepared their hearts for His coming.

Suddenly, they heard the sound, rushing and mighty! It filled the room where they were sitting. When a room is filled with wind, that means from floor to ceiling and from wall to wall. The one hundred and twenty were all buried in the wind or baptized in the Holy Spirit.

The group became one body, illustrated by Paul in 1 Corinthians 12 by the human body, each individual being a finger or toe or some member of the body, of which Christ is the head. A few times in the New Testament, this body is called "the church."

God's purpose was to dwell in the Temple in Jerusalem until His Son would come, but Israel so disobeyed God that He had to forsake them and permit them to be carried to Babylon to be chastened until they were cured of idol worship.

Ezekiel, in a vision, saw God's fire come out of the Temple and be escorted back to heaven by those four living creatures and their wheels, the purpose for which they had come down (Ezek. 9–11). God has never dwelt in buildings. He set a day when He would have living temples.

At Pentecost, the fire came back, a ball of fire which divided into one hundred and twenty flames and lit upon the head of each one.

Acts 2:4, states, "They were all filled with the Holy Ghost [Spirit]." Collectively, all were baptized into one. Individually, each received his or her own flame and each was filled. Here we see them all baptized with the Holy Spirit.

All were anointed with the Holy Spirit for what the Lord wanted of each; then all were filled. Each body became a temple.

Since Pentecost, every person baptized of the Holy Spirit is joined to the Body of Christ when saved, buried into Christ as described by our Lord in John 15, as a limb is joined to the tree. At the new birth, we are buried into Him, thus we are in Him and He in us, as Jesus said we would be (John 14:20).

No one after Pentecost ever was admonished to be baptized with the Holy Spirit. No saved person in the New Testament after Pentecost is spoken of as having just been baptized with the Holy Spirit.

After Pentecost, the Word is used only in the following places, and each case refers to what took place when persons were saved. Romans 6:3: "Ye who were baptized into Christ." 1 Corinthians 12:13: "By one Spirit are we all baptized into one body." Galatians 3:27: "As many of you as have been baptized into Christ have put on Christ." Colossians 2:12-13: "Buried with him in baptism, wherein also ye are risen with him through the faith of the operation of God, who hath raised him from the dead. And you, being dead in your sins . . . hath he quickened [brought to life] together with him." Colossians 2:19–20: "Not holding the Head, from which all the body by joints and bands having nourishment ministered, and knit together. . . . Wherefore if ye be dead with Christ, . . . why . . . are ye subject to ordinances?" Colossians 3:1: "If ye then be risen with Christ, seek those things which are above."

None of the above passages refer to water baptism, and all are past tense. Water baptism is but the outward confession to the world that we have been baptized into Christ, because we have entered into His death and died in Him.

After Acts 1:5, another reference to being baptized by the Holy Spirit refers to the experience of being saved. In Acts 11:16, Peter reported to the Jerusalem Council on what God did for the household of Cornelius in Acts 10.

How may we be filled?

The Holy Spirit, remember, is holy. Anything from the devil or from our sinful natures severs communion with Him.

The first essential is to deal with sins committed since we were saved. There are just two places for our sins. They are either on us or they are on Christ. They are on us until we transfer them to Christ.

It is not enough to pray, "Lord, forgive my sins." He does not have but one way to forgive sins. His only forgiveness is transferring those sins to the cross of His Son. When does He do that? When we do!

A good plan is to sit down with paper and pen and list them. There is a reason for this. Many of those sins are against other people. Some even have been forgotten, but Holy God has not forgotten any sin which has not been covered by the blood of Christ.

While sins will not send a saved person to hell, they will break fellowship with the Lord because they come from the devil.

When all sins that can be recalled are listed, it is good to pray the following prayer: "Lord, You are light. Shine into my heart and show me anything which should not be there!" If you are sincere, He will evermore bring to mind attitudes, thoughts, words, and deeds which you may not have diagnosed as sin. Many of these may have been against others. No one can be right with God and wrong with any person in the world.

How do we settle this sin account?

Look at sin number one. Whatever it is, transfer that sin to the Lord Jesus Christ, thanking Him that He took all the punishment necessary for those sins. If that sin just involves you and the Lord, it can then be marked off, and the Lord, according to His Word, forgets that you were ever guilty of that sin (Jer. 31:34).

Sin number two may involve someone else. Place that sin on Christ and thank Him that He bore it in His own body, but you cannot mark that sin off until you have made confession and, if necessary, restitution to the person.

When you have gone through all of your list in this way, you are ready to deal with the root of sin—self.

What can you do with self? First, what has God done about it? Christ not only took your sins to the cross, He took you there! He had to put you to death before He could have anything to do with you. No one can receive a living Lord into the sinful heart until the self has been put to death.

Only God can put us to death and leave us alive at the same time. God is too holy to associate with anything that comes from the devil. Therefore, He arranged that Christ should die in our stead. When we see our sinful selves and are ready to make a break with them and enter into Christ's death, God the Father charges the death of His son to us, and sees us dead in Christ.

Dual government does not work. The "Big I" with its devil nature, when enthroned, forces the Holy Spirit into a corner of the heart.

We must dethrone it! Assign it to the place of death where the Lord has been seeing it since we were saved. When, by a definite act of your will you take a positive stand against it, refusing in the name of the Lord to let it reign over you, the Lord takes the responsibility of making self ineffective over you.

Enthroning Christ

But the Lord does not force us to live in this position in which He sees us. By just the same way we may—by definite acts of our wills and of faith—enthrone Christ to rule instead of our old selves.

Since the work of the Holy Spirit is to magnify Christ, we are then, by an act of faith, to appropriate the Holy Spirit to come out of that crowded corner and fill us! He will fill up all of the space formerly occupied by self.

If He sees that we are clean, and that He is in complete possession of us, He will fill us just as He filled the tabernacle and the Jerusalem temple when they were dedicated to Him.

First, we know by faith that this has taken place, then we know it by experience.

Some Evidences of Being Filled

Christ becomes your very life. The fruit of the Holy Spirit listed in Galatians 5:22–23 are the characteristics of Christ. If Christ is being magnified through one's personality, that ninefold fruit of the Spirit is evident.

Courage. Another fruit of the Spirit is courage. This was one of the strongest characteristics of the apostles after Pentecost. "The righteous are bold as a lion" (Prov. 28:1).

Rest. "His rest shall be glorious" (Isa. 11:10). Rest of heart, rest of mind, resulting in rest of body, with complete relaxation, is indeed glorious.

Dr. Charles G. Trumbull, in his message to missionaries at North China Bible Conference, used the expression, "Lay your deadly doing down!" He referred to the efforts of missionaries trying to please God with their good works, thinking the more they did the better. Works had to be laid down because too much of it was in the energy of the flesh.

When missionaries learned to "let go and let God" instead of depending on their own efforts, the Holy Spirit could do His work through them. They rested while the work was going on.

One of the conference speakers used an illustration of stage-coach days, when an agent sold first-, second- and third-class tickets. When all were seated, a man with the first-class ticket asked the driver, "What is the use of my buying a first-class ticket when all of the seats are the same?" The driver replied, "You will find out later on." When they reached a muddy hill the driver called out, "All second-class ticket holders get out and walk." He next announced, "All third-class ticket holders get out and push." Then, "First-class ticket holders remain seated!"

The Spirit-filled person is guided in life and service. The psalmist said, in quoting the Lord, "I will guide thee with mine eye" (Ps. 32:8). Only one near enough to see His eye can be thus guided.

One of the Lord's eternal "shalls" comes in connection with guidance: "Trust in the Lord with all thine heart; and lean not unto thine own understanding. In all thy ways acknowledge him, and he shall direct thy paths" (Prov. 3:5–6).

Guidance in Prayer

The Holy Spirit not only guides to whom to speak; He guides for whom to pray.

When in China, it was my custom to pray for Chinese in the morning, as I felt that they most needed the Lord when awake and targets for the devil. At my evening prayer time, I prayed for my family and American friends who were beginning their days and would face temptation or opportunity.

One evening, when presenting my family one by one to the Lord, I came to Broadus, my youngest brother. There was nothing that I could ask the Lord to do for him. I said, "Lord, Broadus is all right, I leave him with You."

The next morning I received a cable announcing that Broadus had passed on from pneumonia the afternoon before. The Lord would not let me pray for the dead.

All Spirit-filled people experience times when the Holy Spirit lays on their hearts people for whom they are especially to intercede.

CHAPTER SEVENTEEN

Sins Forgiven up to Date

The Holy Spirit, through Paul, urged his son in the Lord, Timothy, to follow them that call upon the Lord out of a pure heart.

Just before the Japanese invasion of China reached our section of West Shantung, I did something which I had always refused to do. I took into our mission school all of the non-Christians who wanted to come. Since one non-Christian, especially in a boarding school, could create more atmosphere than ten Christians produced, it has been my custom to take in only a small number at a time so that we might always have a Christian atmosphere.

All Chinese government schools were closed before the Japanese army reached our city, and teachers went west to keep ahead of the Japanese army.

As the Japanese took the cities, they opened schools, forcing any Chinese capable of teaching to do so. Japanese soldiers were assigned to teaching staffs to teach the Japanese language and to lead the daily ceremony of worshiping the emperor of Japan.

Needless to say, our mission school soon had all who possibly could crowd in. Young people from the finest old non-Christian families in the city came. I considered them to be our evangelistic opportunity.

We taught Bible in our school just as we did history, and we had a thirty-minute period of worship daily. All met at the school on Sunday morning and went to Sunday School and church. We did not force anyone to go to church. You see, we just had our school customs, and when students chose our school they accepted our customs.

Not being able to teach all of the Bible, I secured the finest Chinese Bible teacher in North China for that purpose, Miss Kiang Pao Shan. She was the grandchild of Christians, and as long as she could remember had been taught about the Lord, and to memorize Bible passages. She went through mission schools from first grade through junior college, then took three years' work in seminary. She had gone through that great revival in North China, where she received a special anointing of the Lord for teaching the Word.

Not only did Miss Kiang spend hours in preparation of material to be taught, but before going to each class she got on her knees with the roll of that class before her and presented those students one by one to the Lord, asking Him to take that material which would be considered that day to the heart of each pupil, whether Christian or non-Christian.

Our city, Tsining, on Grand Canal in Shantung Province, fell to the Japanese on January 11, 1937. We worked with the Chinese under a Japanese government for four years.

In the autumn of 1941, the State Department of our government, seeing Japanese attitude getting worse toward the United States, sent a cable asking women and children to return to the United States. No missionary who is well in body ever is willing to leave the work and just return to the United States.

We single women said, "This does not mean 'women and children' it means 'women with children.'" We took the matter up with our Foreign Mission Board and were informed that the Board's desire was that all women with children should return to the United States, but that they were leaving single women to make their own decisions. Any who felt led of the Lord to return home should do so; others could remain on the field.

When the cable first was received, the Bible teacher, Miss Kiang Pao Shan, asked, "Miss Smith, what are you going to do about that cable which has come from your government asking you to return to the United States?"

I answered, "I will go out into West China and keep on giving the gospel to the Chinese." I knew that I could not travel the roads where Japanese soldiers would be, but thought that I might go with a guide along the paths through the fields from village to village and eventually get across the Japanese lines and on out into West China where I hoped the Japanese would never reach. However, I never felt led to start, so just remained where I was.

Some weeks afterward, when days were short, the sun setting at four P.M., when city gates were closed and locked and not opened until sunup the next morning, the Chinese head teacher of our mission school came out to my little house and asked me to call Miss Kiang from the girl's dormitory. He wanted the two of us to get out to his home nearby and pray for his sick baby. The only doctor was outside the city wall. Sunrise next morning might be too late for a sick baby.

We took our Chinese Bibles and went out to the little home. Wanting some words from the Lord on which to base our petition, I turned to 1 John 3:22 and read, "Whatsoever we ask, we receive of him, because we keep his commandments, and do those things that are pleasing in his sight."

To my amazement, Miss Kiang said, "Teacher Ming (my Chinese name), I cannot pray for this sick baby!"

When I asked her trouble, she said, "There is a woman in our church whom I do not love. She offended me publicly more than a year ago, and from that day until this, I have had nothing to say to her. I only say good morning and pass on."

Miss Kiang knew the Lord well enough and His Word well enough to know that she could not come into the presence of Holy God and have Him perform a miracle and heal a sick child if there were anything in her heart that grieved Him.

We did not pray for that baby. We prayed for that sick Christian. We read passages from God's Word on forgiving people who sin against us, not just seventy times seven, but just as often as they sin against us, so often do we forgive them. When a Christian forgives a person, his attitude toward that person is as if that incident never had occurred.

Miss Kiang was better prepared for Christian work and more experienced than any woman in the local church. She had stood in the women's meeting and suggested some Christian work which the women might do. Miss Kiang had come from one of the oldest mission centers in Shantung Province, where the women could do much more practical mission work than the women of our new field. Mrs. Connely, in our American way of speaking straightforwardly, responded to Miss Kiang's proposition by saying, "That will not work in this section of undeveloped women." In the Chinese custom, Miss Kiang had been rebuked publicly. One's suggestion must always be accepted in public or the speaker will "lose face."

Miss Kiang's human pride had been offended and she could not take it. For a whole year she had harbored what she thought was an injustice. From God's Word, as it was read to her, she saw that it was her human pride which had been grieved when her suggestion was not accepted. It had taken an hour for her to see this, but when she did she began to weep before the Lord, and begged Him to forgive her for having held that sin of unforgiveness in her heart for a whole year. She put that sin on Christ and thanked Him for taking it in His own body to the cross. She not only thanked the Lord for His forgiveness, but told Him that she would see Mrs. Connely before she went to school the next day, and beg her forgiveness.

I then read my Bible verse again, in preparation for praying for the sick baby: "Whatsoever we ask, we receive of him, because we keep his commandments, and do those things that are pleasing in his sight." Again I was astonished by Miss Kiang saying, "Teacher Ming, I cannot pray for this sick baby."

When I asked what her other trouble was, she replied, "Do you recall that day that I asked what you were going to do about that message from your government asking you to return to the United States? You answered that you would go out to West China and just keep on giving the gospel to the Chinese. That statement has been a sword in my heart from that day until this. I am living that the Chinese people may know my Savior, but I am living in Shantung Province where my family and friends are. I have never given myself to the Lord to go away out somewhere and live among strangers that they might know my Savior."

We did not pray for that sick baby. That woman knew the Lord well enough and she knew the Word of God well enough to know that she could not come into His holy presence and call upon Him to perform a miracle and heal a sick baby unless she had placed herself unreservedly at His disposal. Since the day that she was saved, it had never been any business of hers where her human body was. All that she had to do was to find out where her Commanding Officer wanted her and put herself there. It would be no concern of hers what might happen to her.

We did not pray for that baby, but for that wonderful Christian worker with an unusual prayer life. We read passage after passage of what it cost God to save us, what it cost Him for us to be able to escape the power of sin in this life and its consequences in the next.

Away in the night, that convicted woman pled with the Lord to forgive her for not having placed herself unreservedly at His disposal. She told the Lord that He could now send her anywhere on the face of the earth that He might want her to go to tell people about Him. Then she added, "This is on one condition, I must know that You are sending me. If I know that, I will go no matter what may happen to me!"

That woman had gotten on praying ground. We united our hearts before the Lord and humbly asked Him for His own glory to touch the body of that baby and heal it. We then went home and went to bed.

The next morning the baby was all right, and so was Miss Kiang. I am sure that she went by to see Mrs. Connely and got right with her, even though she had to be at class at eight o'clock. When she went to the first class, the students remarked, "Miss Kiang, you look so happy today." She acknowledged that she had had two sins in her heart which had grieved the Holy Spirit and kept her from bearing His fruit of love and joy in her heart.

As she went to other classes, she had the same experience. She met teachers in the hallway who asked, "Miss Kiang, why so radiant today?" She gave them testimonies, and by the end of the school day all knew that Miss Kiang was like a new person.

Classes closed at 4:45. At five o'clock, here came Mr. Wang, the father of the sick child who had been healed (and six Christian boys) to my little home. He said, "Call Miss Kiang over from the girl's dormitory. We want you and her to pray for us that we may have the joy in our hearts that she has today."

We prayed with them until supper time. After supper, two men teachers and ten Christian boys came, making the same request, and adding, "We want the joy which Miss Kiang and Mr. Wang and those boys who were over here this afternoon have."

Miss Kiang and I took them one by one and brought them to the foot of the cross, to transfer every sin in their hearts and lives to the One who took them to the cross. It was ten o'clock that night when they were ready to return to their dormitory rejoicing.

The next afternoon, there was another roomful, and after supper the same. When all of the Christian boys and men teachers had gotten on praying terms with the Lord, and were bearing the fruit of the Spirit, the Christian girls and women teachers began coming. Now what do you suppose happened when they all got right with the Lord?

Those unsaved students who had been hearing the Word and studying it now saw a living Lord in the hearts and lives of their teachers and fellow students, and they wanted Him! A few had been saved during that four years, some even having led their parents to the Lord, but most of them had not dared to take a stand against their Buddhist grandparents and infidel parents.

Every afternoon until supper time, 6:30, and until ten in the evening, my little study and living room were full of students on their knees getting right with Holy God. For a whole month I did not have ten minutes to walk for exercise after school hours. I did not miss it or even think of it.

Then last, a small group still unsaved expected to come on the afternoon of December 7, 1941, but that morning when I went to school, Japanese soldiers stepped up to the school entrance and asked me to take the teachers around the corner to our residence yard, saying that they would be responsible for the school.

I had been the one to face the Japanese alone for nine months after they took our city, so after the Connelys returned, I always went for him when the Japanese appeared. When I reached our residence yard, there he stood with a half-dozen Japanese soldiers around him. He said, "Go back and call your teachers. They have come to shut us up. They say that the United States and Japan are at war."

For the next six months, no one came to my house, nor did I go out, until I walked out the gate to come to the United States on the first *Gripsholm*, a Swedish steamer bringing United States citizens in exchange for Japanese who were in the United States.

However, the few unsaved students did not need me to lead them to the Savior. Their own teachers and fellow students could do that. Not only were they saved, but a real reviving began in the church. Mr. Wang, the head teacher, was superintendent of the Sunday School and song leader, as well as a deacon. Teachers who had become flames taught grown people. Young people with testimonies taught Intermediates. And Intermediates who had gotten their sins forgiven up-to-date taught Juniors.

How did that getting right with God start? With one key woman who not only was willing to confess her sins and lay them on Christ, but who humbled herself and confessed to the one wronged, according to our Lord's instructions in Matthew 5:23–24: "If thou bring thy gift to the altar, and there rememberest that thy brother hath ought against thee; leave there thy gift before the altar, and go thy way; first be reconciled to thy brother, and then come and offer thy gift."

Miss Kiang was cleansed, first, by confessing God and transferring the sin to the cross; then she made apology to the one against whom she had sinned. She could then dedicate her cleansed personality to the Lord. She had thought before that she was dedicated, but she could not dedicate sin. So long as she had not handed her cleansed personality over to the Lord for His complete possession, she was living a rebel, with self enthroned. This so grieved the Holy Spirit that He could not produce His fruit in her.

CHAPTER EIGHTEEN

Moses' Prayer

"Therefore he said that he would destroy them, had not Moses his chosen stood before him in the breach, to turn away his wrath, lest he should destroy them" (Ps. 106:23).

Often at the beginning of a prayer retreat I use for Bible study the prayer of Moses.

Less than forty days after Israel at Sinai had trembled over the mighty voice of God pealing forth His standard of holiness for Israel, the people begged Aaron to make false gods for them. From their golden earbobs, rings, and bracelets, Aaron made a golden calf.

Moses was on the mountain receiving instructions from God. He had been fasting there for forty days when Holy God looked down and saw the idol worship. God determined to blot out the nation and make a new start with Moses' family. What an opportunity for Moses, who had given up the glories of Egypt and followed sheep in the desert for 40 years for Israel.

It had been only 40 days since Israel had heard God's rolling voice peal forth from the reeling, burning Sinai, "I am the Lord thy God, which have brought thee out of the land of Egypt. . . . Thou shalt not make unto thee any graven image . . . . Thou shalt not bow down thyself to them nor serve them" (Exod. 20:1–5).

Not only had the calf been made, but sacrifices had been offered to it. The Israelites, who were daily eating God's bread from heaven, gave God's glory to that calf. Thirty thousand of them removed their clothes and danced around the calf, stealing God's glory and giving it to a dumb idol.

When Jehovah God looked down and saw such idolatry, He knew that they deserved death. He refused to be identified with Israel any longer.

While the Israelites were down in Egypt, He constantly referred to them as "my people." To Moses, He said, "Go tell Pharaoh to let My people go!" When He saw them worshiping that idol, He refused to call them His people. (To Moses, He said, "Go, get thee down; for thy people, which thou broughtest out of the land of Egypt, have corrupted themselves" (Exod. 32:7).

Moses knew they were not his people. He never could have gotten them out of Egyptian bondage. How could he have sent the plagues to Egypt, saved the lives of oldest sons, or opened the Red Sea at the right time to save Israel and close it to destroy the Egyptian army? He cast the people back on the Lord: "Why doth thy wrath wax hot against thy people, which thou hast brought forth out of the land of Egypt with great power, and with a mighty hand?" (v. 11).

The Lord asked Moses not to pray for the people below who had corrupted themselves; just let Him alone to destroy them. He would carry out His purpose to make Israel a great nation by sending the Savior through the descendents of Moses. Moses acted as if he had not even heard God's proposition; he prayed anyway. He boldly pled for God to turn away His fierce wrath.

He faced the mighty God with his own reputation. God's honor and glory were at stake. The Egyptians would hear about it and get the wrong impression of God. They knew Him as a God of great power and wrath. If Israel should be destroyed, the Egyptians would think that He in His wrath and power destroyed them just because they did not do to please Him. Egyptians would not know that God was a God of loving mercy who forgives. God, for His own honor and reputation, must not destroy Israel (see Exod. 32).

Next, he pled God's own word to Abraham, Isaac, and Jacob, to whom He had promised to take Israel back to the land. To Jacob, Jehovah God had foretold the location in the land, of the twelve tribes, and that the Savior would come through Judah (Gen. 49:10). God could not destroy Israel and be true to His promise. Moses was of the tribe of Levi. When Moses pled God's honor and his own word, Jehovah God changed His mind about destroying Israel; but He had the leaders put to death. Moses thus, by his praying, had saved the physical lives of the people of the nation. He had stood in the gap and turned away God's holy wrath.

Moses went down and had thirty thousand of the calf worshippers put to death.

Holy God said to Moses, "Say unto the children of Israel, Ye are a stiffnecked people: I will come up into the midst of thee in a moment and consume thee."

The children of Israel removed their ornaments and mourned and wept in repentance. Moses did not excuse the people for their sins. He rebuked them by saying, "Ye have sinned a great sin: and now I will go up unto the Lord; peradventure [it may be] I shall make an atonement for your sin."

Moses returned to the Lord to seek His forgiveness. "I [Moses] fell down before the Lord, as at the first, forty days and forty nights: I did neither eat bread, nor drink water, because of all your sins . . . in doing wickedly in the sight of the Lord, to provoke him to anger. For I was afraid of the anger and hot displeasure, wherewith the Lord was wroth against you to destroy you" (see Deut. 9:18–19).

Moses did not excuse the people before Jehovah God, but said, "This people have sinned a great sin, and have made themselves gods of gold."

Here Moses won the title "the Meekest Man." What does meek mean? Not "weakness!" Meekness means selflessness. Certainly Moses deserved the title.

Next, Holy God assured Moses that Israel could go on into Canaan, but that He Himself would not go with them, lest in His anger toward their sin He might consume them. Even though He would not go, He would permit them to go and He would send an angel to accompany them.

Perhaps you and I would have said, "By sin we have lost God's presence. We do no longer deserve to have Him with us. We will have to get along the best we can with the angel." But not Moses. He knew the crowd with whom he was dealing. An angel would not do for Moses in that situation.

This shocked the people into more repentance.

Moses continued to plead the very presence of the mighty God with them. "Unless Thou go with us, take us not up hence!"

After punishing Israel with plagues, the Lord assured Moses that He would go with them and give him rest.

Moses' intercession accomplished several things:

First, because he did not let God alone, Holy God granted his request and saved their physical lives.

Second, because merciful God loves to forgive and He had a Moses to cooperate with Him in pleading with Him to do what had been His first will to do, God could forgive the terrific sin.

Third, he gained for Israel that Jehovah God might dwell in their midst, lead them into the land, drive out the seven warring nations there, give peace, and dwell among them.

Fourth, he received for himself that which he had not asked. The glory of the Lord reflected in his own countenance.

That kind of prayer cost Moses:

First, it cost his family. Moses died to himself and to his family. Moses could have been the head of a great race like Abraham.

Second, the Savior could have come through his descendants.

Third, it cost the forty days and nights of physical and heart agony as he stood in the gap.

What do you accomplish by your praying? I will answer this for you by another question. How much does your praying cost you? God needs people to stand in the gap. God needs people to cooperate with Him to accomplish His will for others.

CHAPTER NINETEEN
Resist the Devil

The devil is not just an influence, but a supernatural personality of great power, whom we are admonished to resist steadfast in the faith (1 Pet. 3:9). Because he is the archenemy of our Lord and Savior Jesus Christ, whom he aspired to supersede in the glory, and because he cannot now attack Christ, he attacks us (Luke 10:18; Isa. 14:12–18).

When working in our mission boys' school in Chefoo, an American Young Woman's Christian Association secretary with whom I had been in Peking language school called on me. When I spoke of the trouble the devil caused in the school, she said, "Bertha, you know that you do not believe in a personal devil!" I thought, My friend, you start snatching people out of his clutches and you will discover something of the powerful personality that he is. However, so long as you are satisfied to continue planting trees and seeing where women spit in hairnet factories, you never will know that he is a ferocious being with indescribable power, and living in Chefoo!

Praise the Lord. The devil is not all powerful. "Greater is he that is in you, than he that is in the world" (1 John 4:4). The Lord in us wants to be conqueror over the devil and all of his demons. He will be if we cooperate with Him. We do not have the power, but the Lord has given to us the authority to call down the Lord's power over the enemy.

How May We Be Conquerors?

First, we must give no place to the devil (Eph. 4:27). Any unconfessed, unforsaken sin or doubtful habit is a place for the devil to take hold. We must keep clean and holy all the time. What does it mean to be holy? We must not only keep all sin cleansed, but the old unholy self must be dethroned, or kept in the place of death, with Christ enthroned in his stead by a definite act of the will.

Next, we store our minds with promises of God and quote them in the face of every temptation, and continually repeat them audibly.

We Conquer by Prayer

This, too should be spoken audibly. We pray to God against the devil, to take authority over the devil and all of his demons. Command him in words loud enough for him to hear, and emphatically, to get out of the situation and stay out.

Do not refer to him and his strength and wiles too much. Keep your eyes on the Lord and His might, and keep praising Him, with no mention of the devil, unless his presence is recognized. My mother taught her children not to make too much of the devil. She said that he likes "honorable mention." Do not magnify him. Be sure continually to magnify the Lord, but do not fail to deal with the devil if his presence is felt.

We Conquer by Fasting

God's standard set for Israel at Sinai was that all males must go to the tabernacle or Temple three times a year for worship: during the Passover and Pentecost in the spring and the great day of Atonement in autumn.

Preceding the worship was a time when they fasted and afflicted their souls in repentance of sin and made the sin offering. This was followed by the peace and other offerings. Women and children went along with the men because it was a gala time, seeing all of their friends and feasting on the meat of the peace offerings.

Later in Israel's history we see people fasting in prayer when in distress. David fasted and prayed for a sick child to be spared. The psalmist called upon Israel to fast as if it were work. David humbled himself and put on sackcloth and prayed for the subjects that were sick (Ps. 35:13). The psalmist speaks of his knees being weak from fasting (109:24). In Isaiah's time, Israel was so backslidden and full of sin in the heart that even though they kept up fasting it was not acceptable to the Lord (Isa. 58:5).

The Holy Spirit, through the prophet Joel, called upon the elders, citizens, and priests to observe a fast—to gird themselves, sit all night in sackcloth, and cry to the Lord in repentance. This was making work of fasting and praying. (Orientals belted down their loose garments which would hinder their work.)

A classic example of fasting is that of Daniel. In Babylon, Daniel had a copy of the prophecy of Jeremiah, from which he learned that it was God's purpose to keep Israel in captivity for seventy years, after which He would permit them to return to Jerusalem. Knowing that the time was up, Daniel "set his face" to cooperate with the Lord and pray for His purpose to be fulfilled, by prayer and supplication, with fasting and sackcloth and ashes (Dan. 9).

In the deepest confession of the sins of their kings, princes, fathers, citizens, and including himself, he wept before the Lord, pleading for God's face again to shine on His people for God's own sake. God in His heaven heard and saw Daniel and sent

Gabriel down to reveal to him the future of Israel. Jehovah God immediately moved the heart of the new heathen Persian king, Cyrus, not only to permit Israel to return to Jerusalem, but to be exceedingly abundant in providing for the same.

Zechariah rebuked Israel for fasting with the wrong purpose in view. Even during the seventy years Israel was kept in captivity in Babylon, they observed the spring and autumn fasts, but it was not accompanied by repentance and was not acceptable to the Lord (Zech. 7:6).

In our Lord's time, fasting had become an empty form in order to appear pious. The three fast days a year had been so multiplied that the Pharisees observed two fast days each week. They were not accompanied by repentance, sackcloth, ashes, or wailing over their sins. Neither Jesus nor His disciples observed these days.

Jesus began His ministry after having been anointed with the Holy Spirit and going away into the wilderness to fast forty days unto God.

He did not say much in His teaching about it because there was too much emphasis already in empty ritual. However, He gave His disciples a strong rebuke for not fasting on the following occasion.

We learn from Luke that Jesus was taking His disciples, the twelve, up to a mountain outside of the Jewish territory to get away from the committee of detectives sent by the Jewish Sanhedrin to follow Him everywhere in an effort to find some charge for having Him put to death.

It was the purpose of Jesus to take the disciples away up to a mountain to pray (Luke 9:28), to get them ready for His coming death. He had been sorely rebuked by Peter, who was speaking for the devil, telling Him that he would not be killed in Jerusalem, when Jesus had just told the group that He would be and by Temple leaders. Jesus wanted them to get better prepared for what they would face in Jerusalem.

Peter, James, and John went on with Jesus up the mountain, and what a reward they received. Jesus took back some of His glory which He had in heaven, so that they could, without doubt, know that He was their Messiah, even though He would be put to death.

Moses came down. The Jews accused Jesus of having broken Moses's laws. He had not broken any of God's laws given through Moses, but He had broken the Jewish regulations right and left. Moses came down to let Jesus and the disciples present know that God approved of the way that Jesus had kept his laws.

Elijah, representing the prophets, came down to let the three know that Jesus was the Promised Prophet to come.

For the second time, they heard God the Father speak from heaven, "This is my beloved Son; hear Him!" (When He tells you that He is going to die, you listen!)

They heard Moses and Elijah talking with Jesus about His coming departure in Jerusalem. With what spring in their step the three must have gone down that mountain.

A poor, helpless father had brought his demon-possessed son to the nine that stayed below, to cast out the demons. In Mark 6:12-13, they went out and preached that men should repent, and they cast out many devils, and anointed with oil many that were sick and healed them.

Did they each one try to cast the demon out of the poor, afflicted boy? Did Thomas say, "Let me try, I cast out one stronger than that!" Or did Andrew say, "I am sure that I can cast him out." Did Bartholomew or Thaddaeus perhaps try in confidence; or did Judas even take his turn?

What a situation these nine caused. They not only could not help the distressed father and give release to the boy in bondage; they even gave Jesus a bad reputation.

The committee from Jerusalem who had followed Jesus that far were there with the multitude, all in confusion because the demon had not obeyed the command of the nine to leave the boy.

The father, after such an experience with them, even doubted that Jesus could cast the demon out. "If Thou canst," he implored.

Jesus could, always could, and always can. Even though that demon did his best to kill the boy, Jesus was equal to the occasion and rebuked the unclean spirit and healed the victim.

Later, when Jesus was alone with the disciples, they said, "Why could we not cast the demon out?" They should have known without asking. His reply was, "This kind goeth out only by prayer and fasting."

For twenty years, I have been fasting one meal a day when speaking. I give up the most important meal, which is dinner. It is the only sacrifice that I can make for a service, as I both enjoy fellowship with people and eating good food. This gives me a chance to go straight from the presence of the Lord to speak for Him.

From the time that I began serving on public programs, there were always two statements which I want to make to the Lord just before getting up to speak. First, "Lord I did not put myself on this program. I was invited to speak here and accepted it as being Your appointment." Second, "I have not used time for myself which I should have used in preparation. I have done the very best that I could with the time that I had; now You take over and do the rest."

About twenty years ago I learned that I was not doing all that the Bible speaks of, while through the years I had sometimes fasted when I had a burden of prayer, or in praying with other missionaries over some problem in the work and we agreed to fast.

I then began giving up a meal a day when in meetings. Since then, there are three things which I want to say to the Lord before getting up to speak—added to the two above: "Lord, I have for this service done everything that the Bible speaks of, now You take over and do the rest." And He does.

I would not give it up for anything. I do not realize that I have not eaten, unless occasionally when praying with people after service until midnight, I sometimes feel weak. If so, I take a glass of milk.

CHAPTER TWENTY

More Suggestions for Walking in the Spirit

To go forward in the Spirit-filled life there are some absolute essentials.

First: Testimony must be given. Spiritual blessings are to be shared. Cease to tell and soon there will be nothing to tell.

Second: You must constantly remind yourself that you by nature are no better than when you were saved. We have this treasure in earthen vessels. Why? That our new miraculous lives will be of God, and we will get no glory for them.

While we are no better after than before we are saved, we have a new position in God's sight. We must form new habits in the light of that position: habits of systematic Bible study and prayer; habits of keeping all sin confessed up-to-date (Confess immediately! Confess as widely as the sin is known. This is necessary for the sake of future testimony.); the habit of taking seriously the "checks"—where there is a restraint, stop and find out from the Lord what it is and take necessary steps immediately to remove the cause.

Third: It helps in going on with the Lord daily to consider our new relationship to God. The Bible illustrates in several different ways our relationship to the Triune God. We will here refer to only three:

(1) Citizens (Eph. 2:19).
(2) Child of God (1 John 3:2).
(3) Bride. "The Spirit and the bride say, Come" (Rev. 22:17).

Citizens of Heaven

Let us first consider the relationship of being citizens of the kingdom of heaven. We are citizens of heaven temporarily residing in this world.

For more than forty years, I was a citizen of the United States residing in China. On my first voyage to China in 1917, Mary Nell Lyne and I took advantage of the Japanese Railway offer to exchange steamer tickets for railways tickets through Japan from Yokohama to Kobe.

We were passing through that section of Japan. Not being citizens of that country, we did not put on Japanese kimonos and wooden clogs for shoes. We did not cover our faces in white paste or wear our hair in huge rolls over the tops of our heads, neither did we speak their language nor eat their raw fish.

We were citizens of the United States, just passing through Japan. If we always remember that we are citizens of heaven, not belonging to this world, would that not solve our problems as to manner of dress, recreation, use of money, use of time, and influence?

Children of God

Those who have been born into the family of God are called God's children. We become children of God the day that we are born into His family—born of His Spirit. He stoops to call Himself our Father.

The second way that we become children in a family is by adoption. A helpless child with no parents and no home is received into a home and legally becomes a child. He has no right there. He does not deserve that home, but because of the love and goodness of that husband and wife, that child is received as their own, with all the privileges of a born son or a daughter.

It takes both of these illustrations—a physical birth in a home and an adoption—to illustrate our relationship to the Lord in being called His children. We are not born saved. God in His love reached out and snatched us out of the hand of the Evil One and brought us into His family and then put His life into us. How holy we should live in appreciation of our positions as children of God and heirs of all of His grace.

Children are supposed to favor their parents. Parents are happy for their children to look like them.

When a child and as a young woman, I went back to my grandmother's occasionally and went to church. The dear women in the community who knew grandmother's ten daughters and three sons came to speak to me, saying, "You must be Fannie's girl." When I proudly assented, they would say, "I see the favor!" Through the years when I came home on furloughs, the neighbors who came in to greet me invariably said, to my great delight, "The older Bertha gets, the more she favors her mother." When I looked around at my beautiful mother to see how she was responding to the thought of her ugly daughter looking like her, I saw the biggest smile on her face.

In my early years in Formosa, hundreds of Chinese who had been well-to-do on the China mainland and had forsaken all to escape Communism camped in a cemetery near my home. My secretary and I led a Sunday School with them once a week, although not on Sunday. When the children saw the secretary coming, they ran to meet him and called to others, "Jesus is coming!"

Do people think of Jesus when they see you? Are you holy enough to favor Him?

Parents Have a Standard for Their Children

Godly parents do not permit their children to act and look like those from worldly homes. The daily customs of the family form a standard. For instance, they teach children instant obedience. Children are never consulted whether or not they will go to church, nor do they make them go or consult them at the table about what they would like to eat. The family custom is that all go to church and eat what is served and children live according to the standard, without a word.

I heard Mr. Charles Hartwell, one of our North China missionaries, describe his leaving home to come to the United States to attend college. Miss Anna, his old sister, who already had returned to China as a missionary after having been recently in America, knew something of the life that he would enter. For weeks before his leaving, she warned and admonished. His saintly mother did her share of exhorting. The father said not a word until he extended his hand to his son to say goodby. He then said, "Charlie, don't you forget that your name is Hartwell!" Mr. Charles said he forgot practically all that sister Anna urged and most of his mother's injunction, but when temptation came he remembered his father's word, that he was named Hartwell. He knew there was a standard for the sons of that family and he must live up to them.

Children are to grow up useful to their parents. God's purpose for His children is that they become useful to Him, become His wealth.

My father was a merchant and planter. He never took a vacation during his first twenty-one years after marriage. When he went north to buy goods for his store, he traveled at night going and coming; he just could not leave the store with hired clerks a day longer than necessary.

My oldest brother, wanting to be a merchant, majored in business and joined Father in the store. After that, Father began taking a month's vacation every August. Because he could trust his business to his son, he went all the way from South Carolina to Hot Springs, Arkansas, for complete relaxation. I heard him say that he was adding years to his life by taking a vacation.

The second son wanted to be a planter, and he attended the State Agriculture College. Lester, even before he went to college, was in the habit of taking thirty or forty day laborers to the plantation and leading them all day long at steady work. He picked 600 pounds of cotton in one day. I overheard my father say to my mother, "Lester is worth a thousand dollars a year to me on the plantation." (A thousand dollars was money in 1905.) Those two sons were Father's wealth. He could entrust his affairs to them, knowing that they would be faithful.

Just how faithful are we in our Father's affairs which have been entrusted to us? Are there people already in hell whom the Lord could not save by Himself because we were unconscious of being God's wealth?

God is helpless in showing Himself to others without us. It is only in the saints that He can live. Our hearts are the only throne that He has down here in this world. Are there folk around us living for self whom the Lord wanted to prepare to proclaim His Gospel in many lands; but the Lord could not win them because He was so very poor in their parents, or in their Sunday School teachers, in their leaders, or even in their pastors? Are you as a Christian worker trying to make a name for yourself, or are you just being God's wealth?

Some children are of no value; some are even problems. A woman in my home community had a little son who seemed all right for the first few months of life; but, when it came time for him to crawl, he didn't, and later he could not stand or walk. Year by year his body grew, until he was about twelve years old; then he stopped growing.

The only word that he ever learned to say was a call for his mother, "Ma!" He could not live without her. She looked after him as if he were a babe in arms, for no one else would do.

She loved the Lord, but for twenty-two years was unable to attend church.

He had a mother upon whom he depended for everything. He cried and called if she were out of his sight. Did that mother have a son? No! She had no son in him, only a burden. Is this like many to whom the Lord is their hope? In such, He has no son to be of use to Him.

What a contrast to those for whom Paul prayed in the church at Ephesus (Eph. 1:18): "That ye may know what is the hope of his calling, and what the riches of the glory of his inheritance in the saints."

Bride of Christ

There is no closer fellowship on earth than that of husband and wife. God calls them one. In the Old Testament, Jehovah God called Israel His wife. We hear the wail of the prophets as they pled with backslidden Israel, speaking for God: "Return unto me, for I am married unto you!"

In the New Testament we are called the Bride of Christ. I have never heard a message on this, but I did some thinking on it one day and reached some reasons for our being called the "Bride of Christ."

First, brides are chosen, and so are we. We read in Ephesians 1:4 that we were chosen in Him before the foundation of the world. The man chooses for his bride the person with whom he wants to associate for the remainder of his life. The young woman loves the man who loves her. She will leave home and go to the ends of the earth with a man if she is convinced that he loves her.

We are loved with an everlasting love that can never through time or eternity cool.

A woman proves her love by giving up for the one who loves her. She gives up other friends, not only her boyfriends, but most of her girlfriends. She gives up her home, her family, and even her name. She gives up her way of living and lives to please her husband. She gives up her home community and goes with him anywhere that he needs to go.

She and the bridegroom want to be alone together. Who ever saw a bride and groom take their friends when they go on their honeymoon! Is that why I am called the Lord's bride? Does He want me to Himself? How much do I respond to that kind of love?

When my sister had been married a year, I went to visit her. She had married the fourth of five sons, four of whom were away while he stayed at home on the plantation with his widowed mother. Sister Pearle said to me while I was her guest, "John and I never have any time to be alone." They had a big home, a kitchen and dining room on one end of the house, a family living room, and back of that the old lady's room, and then a hallway and beyond that a parlor, which was seldom used. No one but sister and her beloved used the upstairs. They had three porches and plenty of yard and big trees. It seemed to me there were plenty of places for her and John Brown to hold hands and look at the moon.

What did she mean, saying that she and John never had any time to be alone? She was so dead in love with John Brown that she wanted to sit down at the table and eat with him three times a day, and she did not want anyone else there. She couldn't get enough of being alone with the one she loved.

Now, how much do you like to be alone with the Lord? Is that a test of your love?

Did you hear of the two United States soldiers in a German prison during World War II, in adjoining cells? One said to the other, "This is hell being shut up here alone!" The other replied, "This is heaven getting away from everybody in this war, shut up with my Lord and Savior!" The happy one told the other how he was saved. He handed his New Testament through the iron bars to him, called out passages for him to read, and together they discussed them. The miserable one saw his lost condition and what God had done about his sin in Christ. He got on his knees in that cell and came as a sinner to the cross, transferring all of his sins and his sinful self to the Savior. Then, since the sins were no longer on him, he could receive the living Lord into his heart. His little cell, too, became a little heaven on earth.

The first reason for a young man to choose a bride is for fellowship. The second reason is that he wants a family and must have a bride to have children. Is that the reason I am put in the position of a bride? The Lord is not willing that any should perish, but that all should come to repentance (2 Pet. 3:9). Paul called those he had won to the Lord his sons in the Lord (1 Tim. 1:1; Titus 1:4).

Then, I am to be faithful to Him in leading people to be brought into His family. How many children do you have in the Lord?

In speaking this message, I usually begin by showing a big doll dressed in beautiful bridal attire. Then, I show another bride doll with her beautiful bridal gown just covered with black spots. (The spots, of course, represent sin.) When the great revival was in its early years in North China, one of the women missionaries dreamed one night that the Lord came to her dressed in the most beautiful white robe that she had ever seen. As He came forward, her eyes were fastened on that dazzling robe. When He was near enough to speak, He said to her, "Look down at your own robe." When she did, she saw that what had been a white robe was just covered with black spots. He said, "When you were saved, I clothed you in a pure white robe. Why did you get it all spotted and dirtied up like that?" When that young woman awoke the next morning, she jumped out of bed, got on her knees, and started doing some spot removing!

The command of the New Testament is: "Beloved . . . be diligent that ye may be found of him in peace, without spot, and blameless" (2 Pet. 3:14).

How to Go On

(1) Keep on keeping clean.
(2) Keep on testifying. Water must keep flowing.
(3) Keep feeding on the Word.
(4) Keep reading some devotional book—experiences of others who have lived gloriously.
(5) Keep in the habit of praying regularly, so as to be in the spirit of prayer all the time.
(6) Keep resisting the devil.

(7) Keep cooperating with the Lord and obeying Him (Acts 2:39).

(8) Keep people you know who need to be filled not only on your prayer list, but keep making opportunities to make them hungry and lead along those who are not.

Some Bewares

(1) Do not ever get eyes on experiences.

(2) Do not ever get eyes off the Giver and on the blessing. Charles Wesley: "I looked to Jesus and the dove of peace flew into my heart. I looked at the dove of peace and it flew away."

(3) Do not ever backslide to the extent of seeking gifts.

(4) Do not make your plans where you are to be shown off for the Lord.

PART III
Letters from
China

Christmas Letter Tsining, Shantung, China—Nov. 1933

Dear Friends,

I am sitting in a sheltered nook on the sunny side of a mountain of rocks that rises inside the city wall of the seat of one of the counties that adjoins Tsining (pronounced Gee-ning). The stone wall is built up to the top and over the mountain which extends back to the north. Another range rises a few miles distant and almost encircles the city, making a pleasing sight to one who grew up at the foot of the Blue Ridge. This is the only place in the four counties in which we Tsining missionaries have work where one can lift up the eye to the hills.

A few tens of miles from here stands a monument erected to a ruler of China who was in authority when Abraham looked up to the stars and received the promise. Looking below, I see a city that has made but little progress since that day. Inside the little flat-roofed mud huts burdened women are spinning and weaving on instruments too crude to have improved in the four thousand years. All day long they work. When the cloth is finished, it must be dyed with indigo and made into garments, shoes, stockings, hats, and bedding. Since sheets are not used, the quilts must be torn up every year or two and washed and the cotton put back in. An equal amount of labor must be spent on winter clothes since they are made the same way as quilts.

Numbers of wheelbarrows are passing through the city with their human cargo. The women who cannot walk on their bound feet, and the children sit wrapped in the family supply of bedding covered with the dust of the road, while the father and son push and pull, going they know not where. The shovel, rake, cooking pot, and a few chickens tied to the barrow show that the family is in search of a new home.

Last summer the dikes of the Yellow River were again broken by the heavy rains and tens of thousands of people lost their homes, and several hundred or thousand lost their lives. No one knows the number. Three of the counties, in which we have work, suffered but not so severely as further west. Their autumn crops were destroyed, but in these counties the danger was seen in time for the woodwork of the homes, farming implements, and the donkey, where one was owned, to be taken to higher ground. There will be suffering this winter, but many will endure it in the hope of coming out of the dug-out in the spring and returning to the land and rebuilding.

For generations this section has suffered from regular floods. Evidently the more progressive who could afford a start elsewhere have sought more permanent homes, while the poorer classes have been forced to rebuild on the same plains where there is no hope but to remain so poor that all time and thought must be spent in working "to get over the days," as they call living. If ever a people sat in darkness, it is this people. On my last country trip I was kept up half the night talking with interested people. Here, where no one wants to talk on my subject and where it is too cold to stay up or get up when the sun is out of sight, my nights are so long that I have split the canvas on my cot.

This is my birthday, but what does it matter to anyone here that I was born! Would that the fact that I was born a second time might interest them, but the news which I am spending a week here to bring seems to make no difference. No, not even the fact that the King of Glory was born. The Bible woman, Mrs. Han, and I hold services each evening here in the city and have visited all the homes where we thought we would be received. Today we have been to three county villages where we sang in the streets until a crowd gathered and then proclaimed our message. They politely listened awhile, then were ready to go about their own affairs. One man did ask me to explain the book of Genesis. He had bought a copy on a market that was printed in his own language, but he could read only a few words of it. I briefly went through the first few chapters, then skipped over to the coming of the Savior.

Last night a woman came into our little service whom I knew must have a mirror in her home. I learned that she was well-dressed because she was a member of the family of the "Tzang" who was among the four most loved pupils of Confucius. The present family is about the 75th generation and is supported by the people in the county. A big temple stands in the hills south of the city where the image of the brilliant ancestor is worshipped by the public. Worship him, but Jesus is the foreigner's great teacher; let them worship Him!

But is not Shantung the province from where the great revivals are being reported? Yes, but the revivals are in sections where there has been, in most cases, years of mission work. There must still be great sections of China where the people are as blind to the truth and as dead in sin as they are in this county, and there must first be the teaching of the truth to enlighten the mind before the Holy Spirit can use it to change the heart. From many quarters comes the news of people being ready to hear as never before, and, in a county forty miles from here where Miss Franks has gone to spend a month, the missionary's message is received in any village that one enters. But this is by no means true of all of China. This past summer, I visited East Shantung, and in the city where I formerly worked, Laichowfu, Christians came from the country churches for a month's Bible Conference. After a day of Bible classes they met in the evenings for a prayer and praise service and some evenings just sat and praised God, bubbling with laughter as the joy of the Lord filled their souls. Truly it was refreshing to see their cup running over. Will such ever be true of this county? Will there be those with the time to keep witnessing until the scattered ones who would repent if they had a chance to hear? At present we are giving only a few a slight opportunity, and it seems that we should do this though, of course, one would always prefer to go where results can be seen. However, it is for us to be led by the Holy Spirit. I beg you to pray that, since we cannot go to all, we be definitely guided to those to whom we should give our time. Pray, too, for those who do not know to listen.

There are many Mohammedans in this part of China. The Bible woman asked me how such a religion could spread from Arabia here and get such a hold. Is it because the followers of the false prophet are more zealous for him than we are for our Lord, or is it that the sinful human heart can more readily accept the false than the true? Perhaps it is both.

At our city church this autumn and winter, we are putting special emphasis on the teaching of Christians. Bible Institutes are being conducted monthly, running about two weeks with classes every night. Church members are classified according to their knowledge of the Bible. The mature Christians, who are most familiar with the Word, form one group. The average church members form another, and those who cannot read and need the fundamentals of the gospel form a third. It is a joy to see the way they come and enter into the study. Pray for this work. We believe that it is the only way to develop a strong church.

To most of you I would prefer writing a personal letter, especially to you who have written, and to the woman's and girl's missionary societies that are named for me, but for two reasons I do not. One is for lack of time, and the other is the cost of postage. I cannot add a "Hey" to you without it costing twenty cents additional since all personal messages must be sealed and a twenty-five cent Mexican stamp used instead of five. So if you do not receive a personal word, you will appreciate the fact that I am practicing economy.

May the Christmas season be filled with genuine peace of heart and all the joy of soul that Christ came to bring. "Thou shalt call His name Jesus for it is He that shall save His people from their sins." When He is crowned King in our lives, He reigns and we have a desire to sing His praises. "O, Come Let Us Adore Him"!

Yours in His Love,
Bertha Smith

A Letter to Friends Tsining, Shantung, China—June 1940

My dear friends,

Two and a half months after reaching my destination is a bit late to thank you for your prayer help in leaving home and for the long journey. I thought to come back was something I just could not do, but a still small voice kept whispering, "The gifts and callings of God are without repentance." After a few days I was enabled to say, "Dear Lord, certainly I went to China because of Your calling, and if You have not changed Your mind about that call, I must not change mine. Since Your yoke is easy and Your burden is light, there will be all the grace that I need to again pull away from my mother and the other dear ones who seem to need me." When the day came, there was grace abounding for my needs and for those left behind. Praises to Him and thanks to you who were praying.

The forty-days journey back ended with great joy, for again I was in the midst of brothers and sisters because they have been born into the family of God through faith in Christ. Some new faces were in the church congregation, and I found others for whom I had prayed among the saints. Some of you will recall my speaking of an experience in going to a home where the only Christian was the youngest of three sons, and he was working away from home. The last time I went, before furlough, no one would listen.

The old mother sat by a table in the yard and continued folding and patting the clothes, preparing them to be beaten on a stone slab—their method of ironing. Knowing that I could not return soon, I was puzzled what to do. Thought I, "What would Jesus do were He here?" A pause—"He has promised to go where I go to tell people about Him, so He is here!" It occurred to me to sit down and help with the clothes. Of course, the old lady protested and all the grandchildren and some of the daughters-in-law gathered round to see the foreigner "fold and pat" the clothes. When I picked out an old-style American shirt and folded its double cuffs properly and turned the collar as it should be and smoothed, they opened wide their eyes and said, "Well, we never have known what to do with that foreign shirt!" They were then ready to listen.

The first woman to come to see me on my arrival was this woman. Apologizing for not waiting until I could get unpacked and rested a bit, she said she had such good news to bring me that she just couldn't wait. "I am now saved!" Then with joy she told about her older son having been converted when on a visit to the younger, who is a pillar of the church in a county seat forty miles from here, and of his coming home and leading her to the Savior.

The older son had told Mr. Connely before my arrival that he was anxious to see Miss Smith's face, that he had often seen her back going into their home—at which time he escaped. I see his back now since nothing but the front seat in church satisfies him!

His wife and son have also been baptized and the son of another brother. This boy said, "Miss Smith, do you remember that time you came to our house and 'preached hell'? I did not believe then, but I do now."

The neighbor across the street, who received me into his home when our buildings were bombed and later became a Christian, passed on while I was away. A young nephew came to help care for him during his last days. When he found the uncle calmly facing death unafraid, enjoying the Bible as it was read to him, and saw him peacefully "go to sleep" holding his Bible and hymn book, he immediately wanted to know the Savior who could enable one to die unafraid.

The brother-in-law of this young man is a senior in our school. His wife was not pleased over her brother becoming a Christian. A few weeks ago the husband came to me under deep conviction of sin. After he had prayed through to assurance and joy, I urged him to begin family worship in his own room with his wife, even though he might not be able to do so with the whole non-Christian family. Although I knew of the attitude of the wife toward her brother, I suggested that she might kneel with him in prayer, to which he replied, "She did last night!" A few days ago when I asked about her, he smiling said, "Oh, she is just eager to know the Savior!"

"Some have not the knowledge of God. I speak this to your shame." "If ye love Me, feed my sheep." "Commit the word to faithful men who are able to teach others." These were the words most often in my mind during the last days in the homeland and during the journey back.

Five hundred students were ready to listen to the messages on sin and the Savior at the two chapels which I have led daily, and students in the daily Bible classes have eagerly received the Word.

The second week after my arrival, a series of meetings was led by Dr. Gillespie of Kaifeng, during which many professions were made. Then came the personal work necessary in making as sure as we can that they were really passing from death unto life before being received into the church. From then until examinations began, the evenings and all out-of-school hours were given to this work. The chair and floor opposite my flat-topped desk have been stained by many a tear as one by one they came and poured out their burden of sin to the Lord. However, I was confident that some did not go to the bottom and went away perhaps trusting in Christ as Savior, but to live a life void of the victory in testimony that is their privilege to enjoy.

The first Sunday in June, more than fifty were baptized, about thirty of whom were from our school. I saw a number of the high school boys coming along the city streets, carrying their change of clothing for the baptismal service. I realized that for those who were the first fruits of their families, it was a real test. Yet I was glad that the Lord had not made following Him easy.

We have just had commencement from kindergarten to junior high school (ninth grade). The present graduating class of the kindergarten went on a "strike" last year when they learned that they were not to receive diplomas with the "seniors." They declared that it was just "too much loss of face." Their cute and clever program this year gave them enough "face" to make up for what they "lost" last year. There being no school in this part of the province where these students can continue their Christian training above the ninth grade, we have decided to add a tenth grade for them next autumn. A number of this class are preparing for full-time Christian work, and the addition of one extra teacher can take care of them for another year. We will trust in our God to supply our needs while we train these splendid young Christians for Him.

The Lord has given us faithful men and women who do not spare themselves. Three of them worked all night long averaging the grades for graduates so that more than fifty diplomas might be delivered according to the grades made. One of these teachers did not stop work for thirty-six hours. Yet their salaries at present are not enough to provide food for a man and his wife. Our head teacher, who receives the highest salary, has a wife and three small children and faithfully works on a salary that just provides food for two people. Prices continue to soar. We have just today had rain, the first since the end of the rainy season of last summer. The snow in winter was sufficient to produce only about two-tenths of an average wheat crop. What a spring of dust we have lived through! But what is that compared with the suffering of those who will go hungry!

Pray for us, and be assured that the contact with every one of you, whom it was my privilege to see while in the homeland, brought a new appreciation of what you mean to the work over here. Praying for the dear Lord's blessings upon you, I am

Yours in Christ Jesus,
Bertha Smith

A Letter to Her Mother on Miss Bertha's Birthday Tsining, Shantung, China—Nov. 1941

My dear Mother,

So many years ago today I was born into your arms! How I thank you for giving me life and for all that you did for me until I could look after myself. How I thank you for all that you continue to do from year to year, which is far more than supplying physical needs and comforts! How grateful I am that I still have you to write to, and think of and love, and how I appreciate your loving thoughts of me day by day!

I marvel when I think of how the Lord has led me up until now. Who would have thought on my birthday that He would want me to come here and give my life to these people. An average missionary's life is ten years, yet I have already twenty-four and am strong and well enough for a good many more.

Yesterday morning while I was eating breakfast Mary Connely sent over a note asking me to have supper with them. Of course, I knew that she was having a party for me, so I washed my hair and gave myself a manicure, and by six-thirty had on my blue velvet dress and a pretty corsage of the last pink rose buds and white sweet alyssum. When I went over all the Presbyterians were there, and at my place at the table were presents. The first thing I opened was a flower pot from Frank, and later I opened the mate to it from Mary. I had seen them with Mary and wanted them but did not buy. Fred and Myra Scovel gave me a pretty tidy set for a big chair. Carrie Eames gave me a pretty hanky. We had a nice supper and a good time together.

It is a beautiful day. So warm and spring-like. On Tuesday day and night we had long-looked-for rain. The very next day grains and flour and meal stopped soaring in price. There is enough moisture now to last until snows come, and if we have good snow there ought to be spring grain crops.

I have lovely chrysanthemums. Not like I used to have at Laichowfu, but prettier than we have ever had before and we hope from these we can have even better ones next year. They are still blooming outside. We are to have Thanksgiving the old time. John Abernathy can come down then and he can't get here for the earlier date. It did not matter with us here. Dr. Eames and Mr. D'Olive will be in the country both dates, so with the rest of us it was all the same. It is to be at Mary and Frank's.

I surely hope you are feeling better, and from now on will get better and better with the cool weather. Oh, how I hope you do not have a winding snow like two years ago and a winter that freezes water pipes!

May the dear Lord bless you in your soul, in your mind, and in your body, and make your last years with us the very happiest. One of the Chinese teachers came over this morning to wish me a happy birthday. I was sitting by a wee fire with a hymn book, singing happy as I could be. We spoke of how happiness did not depend on surroundings, on having or not having other people, nor on having or not having things. If the Lord is in the heart and we trust everything to Him, our hearts are happy; and if the heart is not happy, all the joys that people and things bring is only for the time being.

Here come some girls, some new converts, saying that a new girl wants to be saved and asked if they can bring her in here to pray. They said they feared that I would be taking a nap at this time. It is just after dinner. I told them to come on. I would dispense with the nap. They rushed out joyfully to bring her.

Lots and lots of love, and a heart full of thanks to you for all that you have done for me, and taught me and meant to me.

Yours devotely,
Bertha

Index